Mediated Critical Communication Pedagogy

Critical Communication Pedagogy

Series Editors: Ahmet Atay, The College of Wooster; Deanna L. Fassett, San José State University

Critical pedagogy, as Cooks (2010), Freire (1970), and Lovaas, Baroudi and Collins (2002) argue, aims to empower individuals to achieve social change and transform oppressive and unequal social structures. This book series contributes to the discourse of critical communication pedagogy by featuring works that utilize different dimensions of critical communication pedagogy to foster dialogue, to encourage self-reflexivity, and to promote social justice by hearing marginalized voices. Even though projects that focus on dynamics between teachers and students and their issues within classroom settings are crucial, this series aims to focus on works that engage critical and cultural theories to interrogate the role of larger structures as they influence these relationships in higher education. Hence, in this series we feature works that are built on critical communication pedagogy—works that function within a critical/cultural studies framework, and works that interrogate the notion of power, agency, dialogue and "voice" within the context of higher education and beyond. We argue that the work of educators and their educational philosophies are not limited to the classroom; hence, critical communication scholars are interested in connecting classroom pedagogy with life applications beyond the classroom. Therefore, this series is interested in publishing work that captures these facets.

Recent titles in the series:

Mediated Critical Communication Pedagogy, edited by Ahmet Atay and Deanna L. Fassett
Critical Administration: Negotiating Political Commitment and Managerial Practice in Contemporary Higher Education, edited by Jay Brower and W. Benjamin Myers

Mediated Critical Communication Pedagogy

Edited by Ahmet Atay and Deanna L. Fassett

LEXINGTON BOOKS
Lanham • Boulder • New York • London

Published by Lexington Books
An imprint of The Rowman & Littlefield Publishing Group, Inc.
4501 Forbes Boulevard, Suite 200, Lanham, Maryland 20706
www.rowman.com

6 Tinworth Street, London SE11 5AL

Copyright © 2020 by The Rowman & Littlefield Publishing Group, Inc.

All rights reserved. No part of this book may be reproduced in any form or by any electronic or mechanical means, including information storage and retrieval systems, without written permission from the publisher, except by a reviewer who may quote passages in a review.

British Library Cataloguing in Publication Information Available

Library of Congress Cataloging-in-Publication Data

ISBN 978-1-4985-6870-8 (cloth : alk. paper)
ISBN 978-1-4985-6871-5 (electronic)

Table of Contents

Introduction: Defining Mediated Critical Communication Pedagogy   1
Ahmet Atay and Deanna L. Fassett

1 Questioning Dialogue, Arguing Dissemination, and Cultivating Generative Doubt   13
Marcy R. Chvasta

2 Mitigating Pedagogical Marginalization: Critically Assessing the Use of Mediated Communication with Special Populations of Students   33
David H. Kahl, Jr.

3 Learning from One Another: Con/Divergences with/in/between Online Pedagogy, Andragogy, and Critical Pedagogy   47
Julie L. G. Walker

4 New Media, New Possibilities: Engaging Diversity   61
Ahmet Atay

5 Critiquing Hegemony through Mediated Critical Communication Pedagogy: Key Questions for Critical Media Analysis   75
Yannick Kluch and Lara Martin Lengel

6 Critical Engagement or Critical Mistake?: Social Media, Ethics, and Critical Communication Pedagogy   95
E. Michele Ramsey

7 Applying Critical Communication Pedagogy through Online Discussions on Stereotypes and Prejudicial Speech   113
Tabitha Hart

8 Beyond the Classroom Walls: The Intersection of Critical
   Communication Pedagogy and Public Pedagogy as Evidenced in
   "Let's Plays"   129
   Jeremy M. Omori

9 Expanding Mediated Communication for Inclusivity   145
   Allison Brenneise

10 Building Critical Feminist Media Literacy with *Hot Girls
   Wanted*: Discussing Gender, Sexuality, and Labor in the Age of
   Internet Pornography   163
   Giuliana Sorce

11 Critical Communication Pedagogy and Film   179
   Anthony Esposito and Ronald K. Raymond

Index   195

About the Editors   199

About the Contributors   201

Introduction

Defining Mediated Critical Communication Pedagogy

Ahmet Atay and Deanna L. Fassett

We live in a highly mediated and digitalized culture where most of our everyday interactions are influenced or shaped by new media technologies. As a result of this digitalization, speed is now prized in our everyday communication. Most of our communication as educators often happens through digital platforms, software, or social media applications. We continuously exchange or archive information, record textual, auditory, and visual messages, send and receive texts, and even broadcast, post, and tweet. Our classrooms are not exempt from these cultural trends and communication technologies. This book explores the negative and positive aspects of new and legacy media technologies, and their role and usage in classroom. While authors in this collection examine the rationale for and application of these technologies in the classroom, they also critically analyze the potential for media to create alternative spaces for students to express their voices within and outside of the classroom in relation to communication curricula.

This book serves to extend and enrich an ongoing conversation about whether, when, and how critical communication educators engage media (or not) in their classrooms. In addition to opening pathways to think critically about media education and media literacy in the context of critical communication pedagogy (CCP), this collection also includes practical examples of the affordances and limitations of media in communication classrooms. We came to this project from different perspectives (rooted in our divergent training in critical theory, cultural studies, instructional communication, and communication education), wanting to better understand the potential use of media in the classroom as a pedagogical approach that would facilitate discussion, provide alternative spaces for engagement and dialogue, and also offer new opportunities for students, particularly historically marginalized students, to articulate their voices and experiences with course content. That said, we invited authors to resist the naive assumption that media use in the classroom is inherently inevitable, valuable, or liberatory. Based in Fassett and Warren's (2007) framework, we asked authors to situate their discussions of mediated pedagogies with respect to the discourse of CCP in order to ask critical questions about media technologies and mediated texts as well as their role in our classrooms.

Here we share our own stories of how we came to this project as an effort to explore mediated critical communication pedagogy (MCCP). In what follows, we will share context for how attention to mediated critical communication pedagogy is timely for our collective work as communication educators. In so doing, we will briefly summarize Fassett and Warren's (2007) articulation of critical communication pedagogy is scholarship and praxis, including the guiding commitments of CCP. Finally, we will articulate the goals of this book and provide snapshots of each chapter as constitutive of MCCP. Here we will share how the authors in this collection engage CCP to advance different questions regarding how to understand, analyze, and use media of all forms in the communication classroom.

AHMET

I spend most of my awake time looking at a computer or a smartphone screen or some type of other technological device. I send and receive numerous emails, read newspapers or novels, watch television shows, talk to friends and family on webcam-based platforms, and participate in social networking sites or geolocation-based chat rooms. I also use new media technologies, including software and education platforms, to create or display course content, communicate with students, and maintain an online gradebook. Lately, I am also experimenting with online assignment submission and online take-home exams. Therefore, I am also grading online. All of these new functions enable me to communicate with my students differently, both in and outside of class. For example, students often look at their online readings in the classroom, use their dictionaries to define or translate words, and upload assignments or share links for other sites, including their own digital work. I came to this project in order to make sense of the changing landscape of higher education and the role of new media technologies as they influence or shape our classroom experiences, and pedagogical approaches or teaching styles. We are educating members of at least two different generations, Millennials and Generation Z, students who are born into a highly digitalized culture and live their lives as digital natives. I am highly invested in examining their usage of new media technologies, providing them critical new media literacies, and also understanding both the negative and positive sides of these technologies in the classroom. Hence, I am committed to creating a mediated critical communication pedagogy to examine all of these cultural and digital layers as they intersect and overlap in our communication classrooms.

DEANNA

I am a guardedly pessimistic technophile, if that makes sense. I come to questions of new and legacy media from my vantage point as a teacher who begrudgingly makes use of learning management systems and computer-aided slides, as a department chair who works with engaged and creative colleagues to meaningfully offer more than half of each semester's course offerings in online or hybrid mode in service to our profoundly diverse student body, as a parent who frets over the amount of screen time my children enjoy (and whether that's *really* as bad as some experts would have us believe), and as an enthusiast who enjoys all manner of media, from music and film, to Facebook, YouTube, and Venmo (to name a few). While I understand that innovations in technology are inevitable, I do not believe that my use of them (and especially my use of them in the classroom with students) is inevitable. From my vantage point in the Silicon Valley, the digital divide is not virtual, but starkly real. Each innovation brings with it not only a raft of affordances and limitations, but also a hidden curriculum of its own, structuring bodies in spaces (whether physical or virtual) in power relationship to one another, including some students and not others, posing differential consequences for students and faculty, and illuminating some aspects of our individual and shared experiences and minimizing others. I came to this project as someone who is interested in how my colleagues across the United States and around the world are enacting critical, equity, and justice-oriented approaches to teaching communication. And perhaps inevitably, some of these approaches engage students in media in all manner of forms . . .

EXPLOSIVE GROWTH IN MEDIATED PEDAGOGY

As influential storytellers, media makers provide a variety of narratives about education, pedagogy, and mentoring. Moreover, new media technologies have been providing different ways of communicating with people from different parts of the world, giving rise to different pedagogical techniques and approaches to analyze and address mediated representations, making sense of digitalized cultural experiences. As critical communication pedagogy scholars, we encourage others to question the nature of these stories, or the messages they aim to deliver, or online platforms where most of our digitalized communication takes place.

The new media platforms, such as social network sites, webcams, and blogs, and new media communication devices, such as smartphones, laptop computers, and tablets, continue to reshape our daily experiences from shopping to online banking, from creating digital archives to education and to communicating with people from different parts of the world. Scholars such as Atay (2018), Fox (2000), Jenkins (2008), and DePietro (2013) argue that new media technologies have both positive and negative dimensions. It is obvious that these technologies make access to information easier. They also create space for people, including minorities, people with physical and learning disabilities, immigrants, and diasporic bodies to find alternative platforms to communicate and share their experiences with others. For example, assistive technologies are increasingly enabling people with disabilities to conduct their everyday lives differently, perhaps more freely, particularly in the context of education. Access to online platforms can open space for marginalized groups to voice their issues, challenge oppressive power structures, and communicate to create social change. However, it is also the case that these media are not inherently liberatory. Any pedagogical technology, whether a social media platform, a learning management system, or a YouTube video, may serve as handmaiden to our continued dehumanization. It is, therefore, essential that we work with our students to develop the vocabulary and skills to discern and interrupt systems of power in even the most virtual of spaces.

Technology influences the ways in which we teach and communicate with our students, and that will continue. New technologies and online platforms, such as blogs, webcams, instant messaging, social network sites, and tablet and smartphone technologies that enable media convergence, provide new ways of teaching, learning, and communicating. Khaund (2005) argues that "[t]he creation of an innovative classroom for every student is now possible" (p. 114). Likewise, DePietro (2013) argues that "[w]ith new media, a successful pedagogy is an evolutionary one" (p. 2). That means as educators we have to adapt, change, evolve, and follow current cultural and technological trends to create educational and pedagogical opportunities for all students who might come from different cultural backgrounds or learn differently or may have different abilities. Further, higher education as an industry, if you will, must adapt, change, evolve to listen and learn from our increasingly diverse educators.

The interactive aspect of new media technologies may make them ideally suitable for instructional communication. Even though verbal involvement in the classroom is necessary, in some cases it is not an achievable goal. Class participation can happen in different ways, including through the use of electronic devices. DePietro (2013) claims that "[c]lass participation happens via mobile devices, tablet computers, smartphones, and the like—in addition to and sometimes instead of verbal offerings. This is the fundamental principle of interactive learning" (p. 27). When as educators we begin to see that there can be different ways of participating just as there are different ways of learning, we can be more inclusive in our teaching. It is also important to bear in mind that even when students are "digital natives," they do not necessarily engage in these technologies in the same way as their instructors, nor do they necessarily intellectually engage or challenge the power structures embedded in such technologies.

Then, what does mediated critical communication pedagogy look like? And what does it aim to achieve? Fassett and Warren (2007) argue that critical communication pedagogy is commitment to pedagogy as praxis, where teachers and students work together to observe, understand, and solve pedagogical challenges that influence and shape their learning environments and processes. They also emphasize that critical communication educators engage in dialogue to create change; therefore, they are committed to social justice–centered educational models and pedagogies. In what ways may the use of media in the classroom be dehumanizing? In what ways may it resist dehumanization?

CRITICAL COMMUNICATION PEDAGOGY

Critical communication pedagogy (CCP) is organized around two coherent avenues of investigation and practice: (1) the study of communication as constitutive of power (and, concomitantly, privilege and oppression, as well as healing and justice) in any learning context, and (2) teaching communication as a discipline of study from social justice perspectives (including, but not limited to, feminist, postcolonial, or queer pedagogies). While critical work in communication education (i.e., the teaching and learning of communication curricula) and instructional communication (i.e., the study of communication in teaching and learning contexts, irrespective of discipline, and inclusive of all settings, formal and informal) certainly precedes the publication of *Critical Communication Pedagogy* (Fassett and Warren, 2007), communication studies as a discipline has seen a marked increase in scholarship in this vein in recent years. CCP scholarship addresses all manner of topics, including ability privilege and dis/ability (Atay & Ashlock, 2016; Fassett, 2011; Fassett & Morella, 2008), assessment (Kahl, 2013), critical race theory (Calafell, 2010; Cummins & Griffin, 2011; Endres & Gould, 2009; Rudick, 2017; Rudick & Golsan, 2016, 2018; Simpson, 2010); diversity and dialogue (Atay & Toyosaki, 2018; Atay & Trebing, 2018; De La Mare, 2013a, 2013b; Hao, 2011); difference (Allen, 2011; Rudick & Golsan, 2016; Warren & Toyosaki, 2012); neoliberalism (Jones & Calafell, 2012; Kahl, 2018); and queer identity and heterosexism (Gust & Warren, 2008; Jones & Calafell, 2012; LeMaster & Johnson, 2018; McConnell, 2012). This is by no means an exhaustive list; in addition to a variety of journal outlets that publish CCP scholarship, there are also two academic book series dedicated to investigations of communication, pedagogy, and social justice (Atay & Fassett, Lexington; Parker & Frey, University of California).

Fassett and Warren (2007) articulate CCP, as both paradigm and practice, through a series of 10 commitments, which Fassett and Rudick (2018) have productively reframed into three areas of intention and focus: (1) Communication is constitutive (rather than representative), (2) social justice is a process (rather than an end result), and (3) the classroom may be a meaningful site of activism and interpersonal justice. These shared commitments draw together scholars into discussion and collaboration around the ways communication creates our social worlds (in ways that are oppressive, but that may also open up spaces for agency and praxis). CCP as a paradigm and practice exceeds the four walls of the classroom, but also takes seriously the ways in which we learn and enact power relationships in the classroom.

MEDIATED CRITICAL COMMUNICATION PEDAGOGY

Building on the commitments of critical communication pedagogy, mediated critical communication pedagogy (MCCP) concerns issues of power and privilege, engages the relationship between dialogue and media (or mediated dialogue), and finally enacts new media technologies as alternative spaces that work toward humanization—empowering students and educators to promote civic engagement, social justice, and activism. Therefore, MCCP is committed to critically examining how instructors and students use media and technology in the communication classroom but also promoting media literacies to understand (and, as appropriate, resist) the power of media and technology. As a pedagogical approach, MCCP is committed to empowering students from marginalized and minoritized backgrounds by providing alternative ways of classroom engagement. It is also sensitive to globalization in U.S. higher education, providing different modes of engagement in learning for faculty and international students. Hence, it seeks to conceptualize and enact social justice differently through the use of new media technologies, mediated texts, social networking sites, or quick media applications as possible spaces or platforms as potential sites of intergroup dialogue, civic engagement, and activism. The authors in this collection enter into and illuminate different aspects of mediated critical communication pedagogy.

GOALS OF THIS BOOK

We summarize the purpose and function of this collection as follows:

1. To theorize mediated critical communication pedagogy (MCCP).
2. To bridge the gap between media/new media studies and communication pedagogy/communication education and instructional communication, filling the void in communication pedagogy about mediated pedagogical experiences.
3. To address the usage of new and traditional media, social media platforms, and online and mobile applications to promote social change within and outside of the classroom.
4. To suggest different mediated pedagogical techniques and approaches to enact social justice and social change.
5. To interrogate the ways in which social media and online communication platforms are changing or shifting our traditional roles as teachers and students.
6. To create a media infused critical communication pedagogy, which encourages self-reflexivity and collaboration but also questions notions of access and dialogue.

OVERVIEW

We have divided the chapters of this collection into two sections. In the first section, "Theorizing Mediated Critical Communication Pedagogy," the authors engage in discussions around the use of new media technologies and mediated texts in the classroom and at large in U.S. higher education. By blending their lived experiences with ongoing discussions on critical communication pedagogy, the authors advance a discourse of mediated critical communication pedagogy by theorizing different elements of this approach. In the second section, "Mediated Critical Communication Pedagogy," the authors share specific applications of MCCP, case studies that interrogate mediated pedagogies, whether the usage of new media technologies or mediated texts in the classroom.

Following our introductory chapter, Marcy R. Chvasta's "Questioning Dialogue, Arguing Dissemination, and Cultivating Generative Doubt" opens the first section of the book. In her essay, Chvasta focuses on one of the pillars of critical communication pedagogy, examining the role of dialogue and arguing that critical communication educators should reconsider the moral valance they have attached to concepts of dialogue and dissemination, in general, but especially in this digital age. Building on Fassett and Warren's articulation of "pedagogy of relevance," she argues for the incorporation of critical media literacy in communication classrooms.

While Chvasta's piece focuses on dialogue, David H. Kahl Jr.'s chapter, "Mitigating Pedagogical Marginalization: Critically Assessing the Use of Mediated Communication with Special Populations of Students," examines the notion of power, another pillar of CCP. Kahl Jr. explores the classroom as simultaneously a site of learning and struggle, particularly for students who represent historically marginalized or "special" populations. Hence, in his chapter, Kahl argues that the uncritical use of mediated communication can further marginalize students and suggests ways for instructors to work with students to resist hegemonic structures.

In her chapter, "Learning from One Another: Con/Divergences with/in/between Online Pedagogy, Andragogy, and Critical Pedagogy," Julie L. G. Walker critically examines pedagogical challenges that instructors often face when they teach online. In so doing, she encourages reevaluation of current online teaching practices, offering andragogy as a framework for bridging the differences and potential challenges between critical pedagogy and best practices in online pedagogy.

In "New Media, New Possibilities: Engaging Diversity," Atay focuses on the role and centrality of diversity in MCCP. In this chapter, Atay argues that educators are teaching the most diverse student population the United States has known, and, as such, educators need to understand and respond to how students come from different cultural and linguistic backgrounds, may gravitate toward different teaching styles, and may learn differently. He specifically questions the role of new media technologies in the classroom, exploring their potential to create alternative learning spaces or different pathways for student participation in class discussions or engagement with course material.

Yannick Kluch and Lara Martin Lengel's essay, "Critiquing Global Hegemony through Mediated Critical Communication Pedagogy: Key Questions for Critical Media Analysis," closes the first section of the book. In their chapter, Kluch and Lengel argue for the importance of centering learning on popular culture texts since most students are overtly situated in digital culture and continuously consume popular culture products. Hence, in this chapter, they propose a popular culture–based MCCP approach to developing critical media literacy with our students.

In the second section, the authors share cases of their own efforts at mediated critical communication pedagogy. This section begins with E. Michele Ramsey's chapter, "Critical Engagement or Critical Mistake?: Social Media, Ethics, and Critical Communication Pedagogy." In her chapter, Ramsey critically questions the role of social media in the classroom. In her analysis, she considers the ethical dimensions of students' participation in online platforms and offers internal and external ethical considerations educators must attend to in order to develop critical media literacies.

In "Applying Critical Communication Pedagogy through Online Discussions on Stereotypes and Prejudicial Speech," Tabitha Hart shares her work with students to develop their skills in sharing nuanced and authentic responses to prejudicial statements they may encounter online and in face-to-face settings. In her chapter, Hart describes an activity she uses to cultivate students' sense of agency in terms of confidence and competence to pursue interpersonal justice.

Jeremy M. Omori's chapter, "Beyond the Classroom Walls: The Intersection of Critical Communication Pedagogy and Public Pedagogy as Evidenced in 'Let's Plays'" illuminates the relationship between critical communication pedagogy and public pedagogy. The main focus of his chapter is learning that happens outside of a traditional classroom—in this case, online videos of gaming strategy. Omori explores Let's Plays as an example of mediated public pedagogy whose lessons extend beyond the game itself to issues of shared social significance.

In her chapter, "Expanding Mediated Communication for Inclusivity," Allison Brenneise's inspires awareness of the need for more inclusive pedagogies. In exploring her son's learning experiences, as well as her own efforts to accommodate students with different learning needs, Brenneise advocates for moving beyond mediated accommodations to a universal design for learning that is appropriately critical and mediated. To this end, Brenneise illustrates how new media technologies can provide alternative ways to engage students who might have different educational needs.

Giuliana Sorce, in her essay titled, "Building Critical Feminist Media Literacy with *Hot Girls Wanted:* Discussing Gender, Sexuality, and Labor in the Age of Internet Pornography," focuses on the importance of creating media literacy for students. In this chapter, Sorce shares how she works with her students to critically examine different aspects of the porn industry, calling attention to the importance of creating media literacies that engage power, sexuality, and gender. Sorce underscores the importance of creating spaces as educators where our students must interrogate the influence of mediated representations of gender, sexuality and sex in their lives, including pornography.

We close this section with Anthony Esposito and Ronald K. Raymond's chapter, "Critical Communication Pedagogy and Film." Here the authors argue that films may be a valuable path into mediated critical communication pedagogy for many students and instructors, especially as they may be particularly suited to discussions and examinations of diversity and representation.

Taken together, these works contribute to a fuller, more nuanced understanding of mediated critical communication pedagogy. Each opens space for educators to examine their own assumptions about the intersections of media/

technology, teaching and learning, and power and privilege. We encourage you to invite these insights to influence your own pedagogy, and, as they influence your teaching, be sure to share what you learn.

REFERENCES

Allen, B. J. (2011). Critical communication pedagogy as a framework for teaching difference and organizing. In D. K. Mumby (Ed.), *Reframing difference in organizational communication studies: Research, pedagogy, practice* (pp. 103–25). Thousand Oaks, CA: SAGE.
Atay, A. (2018). Mediated intercultural communication pedagogy. In A. Atay & S. Toyosaki (Eds.), *Critical intercultural communication pedagogy* (pp. 179–94). Lanham, MD: Lexington Books.
Atay, A., & Ashlock M. Z. (2016). *The discourse of disability in communication education: Narrative based research for social change.* New York: Peter Lang.
Atay, A., & Toyosaki, S. (Eds.) (2018). *Critical intercultural communication pedagogy.* Lanham, MD: Lexington Books.
Atay, A. & Trebing, D. (Eds.) (2018). *The discourse of special populations: Critical intercultural communication pedagogy and practice.* New York: Routledge.
Calafell, B. M. (2010). When will we all matter?: Exploring race, pedagogy and sustained hope for the academy. In D. L. Fassett and J. T. Warren (Eds.), *The SAGE Handbook of Communication and Instruction* (pp. 343–60). Thousand Oaks, CA: SAGE.
Cummins, M. W., & Griffin, R. A. (2011). Critical race theory and critical communication pedagogy: Articulating pedagogy as an act of love from Black male perspectives. *Liminalities, 8,* 85–106.
De La Mare, D. M. (2013a). Communicating for diversity: Using teacher discussion groups to transform multicultural education. *The Social Studies, 105,* 138–44.
De La Mare, D. M. (2013b). Dialogue across lines of difference: Acknowledging and engaging diverse identities in the classroom. *Communication Teacher, 27,* 71–75. doi: 10.1080/17404622.2012.752511
DePietro, P. (2013). *Transforming education with new media: Participatory pedagogy, interactive learning and Web 2.0.* New York: Peter Lang.
Endres, D. & Gould, M. (2009). "I am also in the position to use my whiteness to help them out": The communication of whiteness in service learning. *Western Journal of Communication, 73,* 418-436. doi: 10.1080/10570310903279083
Fassett, D. L. (2011). Critical reflections on a pedagogy of ability. In T. J. Nakayama and R. T. Halualani (Eds.), *Handbook of critical intercultural studies* (pp. 461–471). New York: Wiley-Blackwell Publishing.
Fassett, D. L. & Morella, D. L. (2008). Remaking (the) discipline: Marking the performative accomplishment of (dis)ability. *Text and Performance Quarterly, 28,* 139–56. doi: 10.1080/10462930701754390
Fassett, D. L. & Rudick, C. K. (2018). Critical communication pedagogy: Toward "hope in action." In *Oxford Encyclopedia of Communication and Critical Studies.* Oxford University Press. doi:10.1093/acrefore/9780190228613.013.628
Fassett, D. L. & Warren, J. T. (2007). *Critical communication pedagogy.* Thousand Oaks, CA: Sage.
Fox, S. A. (2000). The uses and abuses of computer-mediated communication for people with disabilities. In D. O. Braithwaite & T. L. Thompson (Eds.), *Handbook of communication and people with disabilities: Research and application* (pp. 319–36). Mahwah, NJ: Lawrence Erlbaum Associates.
Gust, S. W., & Warren, J. T. (2008). Naming our sexual and sexualized bodies in the classroom: And the important stuff that comes after the colon. *Qualitative Inquiry, 14,* 114–34. doi: 10.1177/1077800407308819
Hao, R. N. (2011). Rethinking critical pedagogy: Implications on silence and silent bodies. *Text and Performance Quarterly, 31,* 267–84. doi: 10.1080/10462937.2011.573185

Jenkins, H. (2008). *Convergence culture: Where old and new media collide*. New York: New York University Press.
Jones, R. G., & Calafell, B. M. (2012). Contesting neoliberalism through critical pedagogy, intersectional reflexivity, and personal narrative: Queer tales of academia. *Journal of Homosexuality, 59*, 957–81. doi: 10.1080/00918369.2012.699835
Kahl, D. H., Jr. (2013). Critical communication pedagogy and assessment: Reconciling two seemingly incongruous ideas. *International Journal of Communication, 7,* 2610–30.
Kahl, D. H., Jr. (2018). Critical communication pedagogy as a response to the petroleum industry's neoliberal communicative practices. *Communication Teacher.* doi: 10.1080/17404622.2017.1372600
Khanud, M. (2005). Enhancing student learning: A multimedia case study. In G. Chiazzese, M. Allegra, A. Chifari, & S. Ottaviano (Eds.), *Methods and technologies for learning* (pp. 113–119). Southampton, England: WIT Press.
LeMaster, B. & Johnson, A. L. (2018). Unlearning gender: Toward a critical communication trans pedagogy. *Communication Teacher, 33,* 1–10. doi: 10.1080/17404622.2018.1467566
McConnell, K. F. (2012). Connective tissue, critical ties: Academic collaboration as a form and ethics of kinship. *Liminalities, 8,* 12–29.
Rudick, C. K. (2017). A critical organizational communication framework for communication and instruction scholarship: Narrative explorations of resistance, racism, and pedagogy. *Communication Education, 66,* 148–67. doi: 10.1080/03634523.2016.1265137
Rudick, C. K., & Golsan, K. B. (2016). Difference, accountability, and social justice: Three challenges for instructional communication scholarship. *Communication Education, 65,* 110–12. doi: 10.1080/03634523.2015.1096947
Rudick, C. K., & Golsan, K. B. (2018). Civility and white institutional presence: An exploration of white students' understanding of race-talk at a traditionally white institution. *Howard Journal of Communication.* doi: 10.1080/10646175.2017.1392910
Simpson, J. S. (2010). Critical race theory and critical communication pedagogy. In D. L. Fassett & J. T. Warren (Eds.), *The Sage handbook of communication and instruction* (pp. 361–84). Thousand Oaks, CA: Sage.
Warren, J. T. & Toyosaki, S. (2012). Performative pedagogy as a pedagogy of interruption: Difference and hope. In N. Bardhan & M. P. Orbe (Eds.), *Identity research and communication: Intercultural reflections and future directions* (pp. 3–20). Lanham, MD: Lexington Books.

Chapter One

Questioning Dialogue, Arguing Dissemination, and Cultivating Generative Doubt

Marcy R. Chvasta

I did not want to write this chapter. Though I have spent decades thinking, writing, and teaching about media, "critical pedagogy"[1] had not been an area of study or inquiry for me since I was in graduate school. I always have respected the work, however, and consider my work in the classroom to align with the goal espoused by critical pedagogues to challenge oppressive institutions, discourses, and practices. I have argued for the need to incorporate praxis in the classroom, but I did not frame my argument within the literature of critical pedagogy, nor cite critical pedagogues such as Paolo Freire for whom praxis is central to the theorizing (Chvasta, 2005). Frankly, in my limited engagement with the literature over the past 25 years, I have maintained a skeptical stance in relation to "critical pedagogy," and that skepticism extends to the shared fundamental assumptions of "critical communication pedagogy." So, at first, when my colleague suggested I do so, I did not want to write this chapter. But with encouragement and some critical self-reflection, it occurred to me that my doubts and doubt itself—as an epistemological and ontological force that is currently wreaking havoc in the United States—are precisely why I should write this chapter.

As I write this sentence, the 45th president of the United States and his administration have been aggressively cultivating doubt for 17 months. While the mode of cultivation may vary from rally to interview to tweet, the message from the White House remains the same: Mainstream media cannot be trusted. The president's incessant labeling of mainstream news media as "fake news"—characterizing negative coverage about him as untruth—has been taken up by his supporters and vehemently resisted by opponents, profoundly constricting the pathways toward productive democratic participation by the people and their representatives alike. Absolutism on all sides is transforming doubt into denial, and dialogue—however ideally envisioned—seems now impossible. The President's disseminated attack on "The Media" is an attack on communication itself.

In this chapter, I share my doubts and revisit Ellsworth's (1989) foundational critique of the valorization of dialogue in the foundational discourse of critical pedagogy. Though 30 years have passed, her criticisms remain relevant and are perhaps even more pressing as the inhabitants of this country are embattled with each other and a demonizing administration. I then offer an account of the limits of dialogue on my own campus when confronted with the immediate presence and nationwide actions of a neofascist, thereby demonstrating that despite long-recorded criticisms of dialogue (by Ellsworth and others), we still hold it up as an ideal, I fear, to our detriment. With the help of Peters (1999), I argue that "dialogue" and "dissemination" must be rethought in our digital age, and the introductory media classroom is the appropriate place to consider critically these intertwined modes of communication. This is also the classroom to take a microscopic view of doubt and the generative and debilitative force it has on our ways of being and knowing in the world. I answer Fassett and Warren's call to rethink the introductory media course with an aim toward a "pedagogy of relevance" (2008)—a pedagogy that recognizes "the need for understanding the role of communication as constitutive (and, thus, constraining) of our understandings and relationships" (p. 5). Finally, like others, I argue that this is the classroom where critical media literacy should be taught—but perhaps not in the way we have been thinking. And if you follow along with me, know that, although I did not want to write this chapter, I came to realize that I needed to, at least for my own sake as I try to be a productive educator in a time that is terrible and terrifying for so many.[2]

CRITICAL (COMMUNICATION) PEDAGOGY AND DOUBT

I was first introduced to critical pedagogy via the work of Paulo Freire while in my master's program in the mid-1990s. It was the beginning of my teaching career and my critical consciousness was burgeoning. I was drawn to Freire's ideas about the classroom as a site for cultivating transformational processes that lead to emancipation, but I struggled to find ways to put his philosophy into practice in the public speaking classroom. Certainly, I stressed the importance of speech in democratic participation, and I encouraged my diverse students to give speeches about issues that affected them because of their place in the world. Nevertheless, I still heard so many speeches on the importance of recycling—which is very important, but the speeches themselves often sounded recycled, if you know what I mean.

What I struggled with most was the imperative of dialogue. For Freire (1970/1993), dialogue is necessary for the development of critical consciousness, which is necessary for transformation, which is necessary for liberation. Dialogic engagement is the antithesis of the "banking model" of education in which the teacher deposits knowledge into the passive students, thereby maintaining and reinforcing oppressor-oppressed as the dominant social relationship. I certainly did not want to play the role of oppressor in my classroom (or anywhere else), so I worked hard to engage in dialogue with my students. But it was 1994 and I was a 23-year-old heterosexual able-bodied white woman from an upper-middle-class upbringing in West Virginia who was teaching in a diverse classroom in the San Fernando Valley of California. This is a very different context than the Brazilian classrooms that Freire taught in and wrote about decades prior.

I grappled with my positionality. I knew I had power as The Instructor, as well as power in my privileged demographic markers. However, I also felt deeply insecure in my inexperience as an instructor and in my seemingly limited life experiences. Even in my first year of teaching, though, I think I succeeded in cultivating a caring classroom environment in which students found me supportive and attentive to their needs. Nevertheless, I do not think I created the classroom Freire envisioned. Forefront in my efforts was teaching the material I was meant to teach as instructed by my supervisor. I did not dare devote extensive classroom time to dialogue centered on the students' or my own experiences of oppression. Most days, I barely got through the textbook topic scheduled for the day. But I remained committed to the idea of dialogue, perhaps even believing it was an elixir for all social ills—at least, for a while.

It was in my graduate seminars in the position of student that I began to have doubts. In particular, it was my experiences in graduate seminars focused on critical theory and pedagogy that led me to question the efficacy of methods proposed by Freire and others, including North American critical pedagogues Peter McLaren and Henry Giroux. While McLaren and Giroux both addressed issues of heterogeneity that applied more directly to the classrooms I inhabited, I still found their work to be frustratingly abstract and devoid of complex consideration of power dynamics in the classroom. I wish I had been aware at the time of Ellsworth's (1989) now foundational essay, "Why Doesn't This Feel Empowering? Working through the Repressive Myths of Critical Pedagogy."[3] Though she offers what some might consider a scathing critique of the most prominent discourses making up critical pedagogy at the time, I would have found some comfort in her critique and concerns because I would have learned that I was not alone. In fact, in a time when there is "a serious erosion of the discourses of community, justice, equality, pubic values, and the common good" (Giroux, 2016, par. 5—written just after Trump was elected), I wish more educators today would revisit or find their way to this essay to recognize that "dialogue"—as a cure for societal ills—may not be what it seems.

In the essay, Ellsworth builds her critique by weaving her interpretation of the prominent discourses with a reflexive narrative of her experience teaching a course designed to confront and intervene against racist actions on her campus. This weaving was (and remains) significant because, as she notes from her extensive review of the literature, "educational researchers who invoke concepts of critical pedagogy consistently strip discussion of classroom practices of historical and political position" (p. 298). This is an omission that frustrated me as a student of critical pedagogy. I was—and remain certain—that Freire's classrooms (and those of the then-middle-aged white male full professors McLaren and Giroux) were very different from mine. I had trouble envisioning how his methods would play out in my classrooms. Nevertheless, I was taught that I should strive to bring about the aims of critical pedagogy. And I wanted to. I had faith in them.

Though, prior to the course, Ellsworth may also have had faith in key, if problematically abstract, components of critical pedagogy discourse—"namely, 'empowerment,' 'student voice,' 'dialogue,' and even the term 'critical'"—ultimately, she concludes that the class "produced results that were not only unhelpful, but actually exacerbated the very conditions we were trying to work against, including Eurocentrism, racism, sexism, classism, and 'banking education'" (p. 298). To support this conclusion, Ellsworth provides several arguments, all of which, as I see it, speak to the "repressive myth" of dialogue.

Noting that dialogue "has been defined [by theorists including those mentioned above] as a fundamental imperative of critical pedagogy and the basis of the democratic education that insures a democratic state," Ellsworth identifies the "ground rules" of dialogue as they have emerged from the literature to "include assumptions that all members have equal opportunity to speak, all members respect other members' rights to speak and feel safe to speak, and all ideas are tolerated and subjugated to rational critical assessment against fundamental judgments and moral principles" (p. 314). These rules—anchored in myths of rationality, equality, and safety—are problematic in several ways, perhaps most foundationally in terms of dialogue being predicated on rationality.

Employing the work of Aronowitz (1987/1988), Ellsworth advances poststructuralist critique of rationality and argues that if we demand dialogue of our students, we "force students to subject themselves to the logics of rationalism and scientism which have been predicated on and made possible through the exclusion of socially constructed irrational Others—women, people of color, nature, aesthetics" (p. 305). Every classroom I have ever been in has comprised a multiplicity of complex subjects in varying positions of power. Like Ellsworth, I have come to know through observation and participation that dialogue—in the form of rational deliberation and debate—is not a neutral endeavor. Those who have been constructed as irrational cannot enter into dialogue with equal opportunity and, if they do, they will be judged by logics from which they have been historically excluded, thereby reinscribing the oppressive relations critical pedagogues seek to dismantle.

A second component of dialogue that Ellsworth dissects is equal voice, not only in terms of each dialogic participant having equal time to speak in a dialogue, but also in terms of the constitution of an individual's voice—of the individual being. That is, every individual comprises a multiplicity of voices that cannot be equally shared in any given encounter. When Ellsworth was writing her essay, "intersectionality" was not a central concept in critical theory as it is today; however, she recognized it and the ways in which it problematizes rationalist dialogue. She shares the sources of the "pain, confusion, and difficulty in speaking" that her students and she suffered in the course she designed to confront and intervene in campus racist practices:

> Women found it difficult to prioritize expressions of racial privilege and oppression when such prioritizing threatened to perpetuate their gender oppression. Among international students, both those who were of color and who were White found it difficult to join their voices with those of U.S. students of color when it meant a subordination of their oppressions as people living under U.S. imperialist policies and as students for whom English was a second language. Asian American women found it difficult to join their voices with other students of color when it meant subordinating their specific oppressions as Asian Americans. I found it difficult to speak as a White woman about gender oppression when I occupied positions of institutional power relative to all students in the class, men and women, but positions of gender oppression relative to students who were White men, and in different terms, relative to students who were men of color. (p. 312)

No doubt, there are even more difficulties from different subject positions that Ellsworth could have listed. From context to context, instant to instant, we are all both oppressor and oppressed. This dualism is perhaps most evident in moments framed explicitly as dialogic; however, knowing that one is the embodiment of both positionalities does not necessarily enable the dialogue, though it might be a first step toward understanding self and others.

In addition to Ellsworth's students having difficulty with choosing which voice to prioritize, they experienced instances in which they did not feel safe to express themselves. The classroom as a "safe space" is another strand of Ellsworth's critique of the imperative of dialogue—and, in this day and age of bigotry motivating verbal and physical violence on campuses (and everywhere, really)—it warrants revisiting.

A critical pedagogy that insists on equal participation in dialogue, that advocates unconditionally for the un-silencing of all students, is a pedagogy that ignores the complex reasons a student may choose not to participate, not to speak. It is a pedagogy that does not come to terms with the fact that the oppressed may choose to speak elsewhere. On this point, Ellsworth offers bell hooks' challenge to the notion of the silenced woman, a notion that, hooks suggests, arose out of white feminist perspectives. Ellsworth quotes hooks explaining that in Black communities (and in other diverse ethnic communities) women have not been silent. Their voices can be heard. Certainly for Black women our struggle has not been to emerge from silence to speech but to change the nature and direction of our speech. To make a speech that compels listeners, one that is heard (as cited in Ellsworth, 1989, p. 313).

This kind of speech hooks is referring to is disseminative, not dialogic. For hooks and her community, "dialogue, the sharing of speech and recognition, took place not between mother and child or mother and male authority figure, but with other Black women" (as cited in Ellsworth, 1989, p. 313). For hooks, dialogue occurs among peers away from the ears of authority. Moreover, this dialogue away from authority is preparatory for dissemination. "It was in that world [of dialogue with peers] and because of it that I came to dream of writing, to write" (as cited in Ellsworth, 1989, p. 313). The classroom is a space imbued with authority—not just the authority invested in the teacher, but also the authority invested in dominant subject positions. Whether or not a student or teacher speaks is directly related to one's perception of these relational dynamics: "What they/we say, to whom, in what context, depending on the energy they/we have for the struggle on a particular day, is the result of conscious and unconscious assessments of the power relations and safety of the situation" (p. 313).

Over the years since Ellsworth's calling out of the repressive myths of critical pedagogy, others have extended and critiqued her critiques and worked to refine notions of dialogue. I briefly outline a bit of that work here to make it clear that Ellsworth's essay is not the last word on dialogue in the critical educator's classroom. Yet it is remarkable how her arguments are consistently summoned—implicitly or explicitly by name—by theorists struggling to find ways to make the classroom a space to engineer a dismantling of oppressive social structures.

In 1998, *Educational Theory* published a special issue in which scholars respond to two lead essays, one by Peter McLaren and one by Ilan Gur-Ze'ev. McLaren calls on critical pedagogues to return to a commitment to historical materialism and work toward the redistribution of property and dismantling of global capitalism. Gur-Ze'ev criticizes the utopianism of critical pedagogy and argues instead for social transformation via philosophical negativism. Their positions are complex, steeped in philosophical discourse, and noteworthy here, first, because of their impassioned positions that critical pedagogy, as it had been conceptualized and embraced until that point (by themselves and others), is not doing enough to abolish or challenge oppression. Second, their positions are noteworthy for their implicit and explicit stances on dialogue: McLaren finds use for it in the service of dismantling capitalist structures; Gur-Ze'ev explicitly calls it out for its roots in rationalism. Third, their positions are noteworthy for their omission of Ellsworth, despite incorporating the criticisms she raised well prior to various critical pedagogues they do cite. This is not the case with several of the respondents, three out of five of whom incorporate and extend Ellsworth's arguments regarding dialogue. All of the respondents, however, maintain some amount of faith in dialogue (as does Ellsworth, as she rearticulates it as "communicative dialogue" in a later book, *Teaching Positions* [1997]), especially in the sense of its impossibility, its generative open-endedness and surplus of meaning (Carlson, 1998; Kohli, 1998; Lather, 1998).

Continuing a critical yet cautiously and conditionally optimistic consideration of dialogue, Burbules (2000) offers a synthesizing account of the ways "dialogue" has been conceptualized in educational theory. In a section titled "The Fetishization of Dialogue," he organizes the ways according to "six dominant traditions" (p. 252): liberal views of dialogue (in the footsteps of John Dewey or Benjamin Barber); some feminist views characterized by a rejection of antagonistic dialogue (e.g., as seen in work by Deborah Tannen and Mary Belenky); Platonic views (in the tradition of the Socratic search for "Truth"); hermeneutic views (in line with the theorizing of Hans-George Gadamer and Martin Buber); critical educator views (in line with Freire); and postliberal views (as espoused especially by Jürgen Habermas). Burbules details the promise and limitations of these views—in theory and in practice—with substantial attention paid to Ellsworth's considerations, perhaps especially because he disagrees with her consideration of his prior work. Ultimately, he finds that

> the criticisms posed against dialogue by Ellsworth and others have had a tremendously constructive benefit in unsettling the prescriptive account that has predominated in educational discussions. Her challenges to the silences, exclusions, and coercive or co-opting elements in dialogue, which challenge its self-conception as something open, neutral, and inviting to all, need to be addressed directly. What these criticisms have done is to refocus attention on the *practice* of dialogue. (p. 269)

Though he admits that it is an "overly sharp distinction," Burbules distinguishes between prescriptive and practical perspectives on dialogue: The prescriptive perspective is "represented by formal, idealized models," and the practical by "situated, politically critical analysis" (p. 270). Though it may seem from this miniscule presentation here that Burbules would be a wholesale advocate for the practical perspective, he has his doubts about it, too. He ends the essay with a caution: "[T]hose modes of dialogue that put the greatest emphasis on cruciality and inclusivity may also be the most subtly co-opting and normalizing. Such a recognition unsettles critical pedagogies of all sorts, whether feminist or Freirean, rationalist or deconstructionist" (p. 271). I am unsettled, indeed. The troubles Ellsworth called out so long ago—dialogue is rooted in the oppressive logic of rationalism, and even if we say it is not, we fall into rationalistic tendencies; dialogue does not and cannot afford equal voice for all; and dialogue is not a safe endeavor—remain.

Even as I turn to critical communication pedagogy as conceived by my beloved colleagues Deanna Fassett and John Warren (whom I so miss personally and professionally), I find dialogue valorized in ways that I cannot embrace—at least, I do not think I can, not right now, not fully. According to Fassett and Warren (2007), "Critical communication pedagogy is social justice, as defined, explored, and implemented within a community of caring and generous believers in freedom, and justice, and love—for all, all the time" (p. 128). Though any one person may have a very strong sense of what "freedom," "justice," and "love" may mean, the terms are disconcertingly abstract and utopian in the Ellsworthian sense. (In my own senses, those terms have developed deeply negative connotations since patriotism became compulsory post-9/11.) My colleagues anticipate the Ellsworth critique early in the book: "We do not fully know the end result we would like to see, and in that sense, we fall into a similar trap as those overly abstract and utopian critical educators (Ellsworth, 1989)" (Fassett & Warren, 2007, p. 9). Nevertheless, even their more detailed definitional moves maintain a Freirean utopianism and faith in dialogue:

> We contend in this book that one's desire to engage critical communication pedagogy is inherently Freirean: It is about fulfilling a call to do the work of social justice, it is about learning to listen and see in self-reflexive ways, it is about speaking carefully and humbly and recognizing that it is the job of the critical scholar to open rather than shut doors of possibility, it is about engendering hope in the world rather than dwelling in stubborn immobility. In our writing, we imagine critical communication pedagogy that fulfills Freire's call to us as communicators. (Fassett & Warren, 2007, p. 108)

I want to share in their vision of a "community of caring" and "engendering hope in the world"; however, in this terrible and terrifying time for too many, I have my doubts, in others and myself.

I have had my doubts since graduate school—as a student and instructor in the classroom. I have found validation in reading nuanced critiques that articulate those doubts in and against the discourse I had difficulty embracing. And I have tried to remain hopeful over the years, even though I would not argue with you if you were to characterize me as a doubtful person. But the last few years have put a strain on my already-limited reserves of optimism. I will tell you one of the complex reasons why and hope that in my telling I can begin to see a way through the debilitating doubt toward a generative doubt. And I will remember the wise reminder of Alanis (2006): "Hope entails suffering, joy, fear, and being loved; it is a yes and no; it is both rigor and playfulness; it is up and down and in between" (p. 181).

THE WHITE SUPREMACIST AND (NO) DIALOGUE AND (YES) DISSEMINATION

In late fall of 2016, a stack of fliers were placed outside my department's main office after hours. At the top of the paper, it reads, "WARNING TO THE PUBLIC: KNOWN WHITE SUPREMACIST AND VIOLENT OFFENDER IN A CONVICTED HATE CRIME NATHAN BENJAMIN DAMIGO IS CURRENTLY ENROLLED AT CSU STANISLAUS."[4] The flier also contains images of Damigo and a flier that promotes Identity Evropa, the white supremacist group that he founded. The flier at our doorstep contained the following directive and warning:

> Arm yourself—with knowledge! Nathan Damigo is a well-known white supremacist who was dishonorably discharged from the military after he chased down and robbed a cab driver at gunpoint for 'looking Iraqi' in 2007. He served over 5 years in prison and was released in 2014. Since then, he has hosted an alt-right podcast and served as chaiman [sic] in the extremist National Youth Front, a position he aquired [sic] after the previous chair was forced out by death threats over to [sic] his interracial marriage. He also founded the fascist group Identity Evropa (IE), which is based out of Oakdale as Damigo is majoring in social sciences at the nearby CSU Stanislaus. Keep racism off our streets and out of our schools!

The flier also includes Damigo's P.O. Box address, his date of birth, and his Twitter handle. It took some investigation, but my colleagues and I learned that the flier was produced by It's Going Down, a group that describes themselves as "a digital community center for anarchist, antifascist, autonomous anticapitalist and anticolonial movements. Our mission is to provide a resilient platform to publicize and promote revolutionary theory and action."[5]

My colleagues and I are not naïve. We know that we have bigoted students of whatever persuasions in all of our classrooms, though they mostly remain silent even as—or, especially when—we teach about systemic oppression. But we were unnerved by the flier. None of us ever saw one of the IE fliers, but we were now faced with unforgiving knowledge of the existence of them, here and on other campuses, as well as the resistance to them. And even though too many of us and our students have experienced others' hatred in our lives, so many of us (want to) consider our campus a safe space.

Neither our students nor we could continue on dealing with organized hatred in the abstract, or as something that exists outside of the campus perimeter.

The immediate question was (and remains), how do we deal with hatred in the classroom? A then-colleague in the Ethnic Studies department, Fela Uhuru, organized and hosted a symposium in December 2016 in which Damigo "was able to present his political social ideas while also being challenged by students with differing viewpoints as a way to offer insight and some form of understanding" (Campbell, 2017). As it was reported, however, the experience for some students did not end in understanding:

> "In person, Damigo's language is more circumspect than it is in the digital realm, frustrating students in the ethnic studies class. Uhuru, the instructor, asked him about the fliers on campus that characterized him as a white supremacist.
>
> "Language like, you know, 'racist,' 'supremacist,' many of those words have become so horribly loaded that oftentimes they've gotten to the point where I personally will consider some of that language, if they're used in a sense of moralizing a situation and used *to obfuscate from an actual empirical argument*, I would actually see that as antiwhite hate speech," he said.
>
> His answers to the students' questions about his views were *long-winded and complex*. He said [he] called himself an "identitarian," not a white supremacist.
>
> One frustrated student replied, 'You saying you're an identitarian is the same thing as just saying, "I'm a politician." That doesn't tell you where your values lie. . . . *you're masking what you're actually standing for*.' (emphasis mine; Branson-Potts, 2016)

Though Uhuru's reported intent was for "his students to have a frank dialogue about race and identity with someone whose presence on campus has stirred controversy" (Branson-Potts, 2016), Damigo's deployment of seeming rationality left students frustrated and stymied. As nonsensical and fallacious as Damigo's statements ever are to someone educated in argument, he engages the discourse of rationality to silence his interlocutors.

If dialogue is dependent upon the co-participation of rational beings mutually committed to understanding, then what happened during that symposium? I am pretty confident that critical pedagogues of any particular type (from rationalist to feminist to poststructuralist to any combination thereof) would not characterize what happened as dialogue. By many personal accounts, Damigo dominated the discussion and the students left demoralized. Yet Damigo performed in the form of rationality at the invitation for dialogue. Was this encounter worth it?

On April 15, 2017, during a free speech rally in Berkeley, California, Damigo was caught on video punching an antifascist protester (a 95-pound woman, if that matters to you). A reporter from *Mother Jones* met with him in the weeks following:

When I approach Damigo and ask him about the response he's received to the video of the assault, he says it's been 'great.' Recruitment for Identity Evropa has 'gone through the roof' since Trump's inauguration, he adds, growing from just 12 people last year to more than 450 members across dozens of campuses. Cal State Stanislaus, where Damigo is a social sciences major, launched an 'immediate investigation' after the video was posted online. Damigo says he thinks the investigation is 'funny.' (Bauer, 2017)

The reporter does not share in his amusement and presses him on issues:

As we talk, he forces a smile, but his quivering lip betrays an underlying frustration. He repeats catchwords like 'radical diversity,' 'radical inclusion,' and 'multiracialism' throughout our interview. He speaks like someone who has practiced his talking points—a skill he teaches other white nationalists—but he hasn't quite learned how to integrate them into a back and forth with a reporter. (Bauer, 2017)

The characterization of "catchwords" may seem dismissive; however, those terms are ambiguous, if not abstract. It is for this very reason that Damigo can throw them about for the purpose of dismissing what they signify. Bauer may recognize that Damigo's rhetoric is empty, in a sense; however, that rhetoric is forceful in its emboldening of believers. It appears to operate within the logics of rationalism and it is uninvitational, even as Damigo accepts invitations from others to engage in dialogue about his views. Socrates may condemn him as a sophist teaching "talking points," but Damigo's form looks an awful lot like the Socratic dialogues.[6]

While I respected—and still do—Uhuru's motive for hosting Damigo, I never would have invited him into my classroom for an event. I would not have subjected my students to his speech, to his immovability. You may believe that someone else, perhaps yourself, could have facilitated better the "dialogue," allowing for more voices to be heard. But even if that were the case, I do not believe the outcome would have been different. Everyone in the room would have maintained their position and even held more firmly their convictions. And that is exactly what I want for the those in the room who opposed Damigo's position. It is in this way that I would characterize the "dialogue" a success. But, again, I would not have hosted such a dialogue in the first place.

What I did do, instead, was invite my students to talk about how they were processing and experiencing the messages and events coming from and surrounding Damigo. I believed this would be a more productive way to engage the issues in a safer space than in the face of the embodied Oppressor. I am adept at generating classroom discussion and I am not afraid to broach controversial subjects. I felt confident that I could provide them the opportunity to process the headlines surrounding their fellow student and our campus in terms of their experiences of oppression. But here's the thing: My students did not engage. Over three semesters, in all of my classes from freshman to senior level, my students remained nearly completely silent. The only contributions were dismissive comments like "That dude is fucked up." The only concerns expressed were a sprinkling of questions about his whereabouts and whether or not the university could expel him. The energy only increased when we talked about the university president's campus- and community-wide message that the university would not—could not—expel him. This was the message that visibly incensed some (but not most) students. The students did not want to have a dialogue about Damigo's messages or actions or reasons. Perhaps, they did not want to have that dialogue with me, in particular, their middle-aged white female professor. Perhaps their silence was an act of agency, denying the oppressor any time or space in our classroom. As Hao (2011) argues compellingly, silence is complex and is not necessarily a sign of apathy. They did not say one way or the other why they did not want to discuss the oppressor, and I—someone with matching skin color with the oppressor—did not press them to explain. They just wanted him gone. What they wanted to talk about was how to make that so.

In the spring and fall of 2017, there were a handful of protests in which students and community members demanded the expulsion of Damigo and accused our president of "harboring a racist"—to no avail, at least in terms of expulsion. Nevertheless, those moments of direct action, of disseminated messaging, did have force. Student demands for safety led to our president creating the Diversity Center where staff "work to empower underserved communities while challenging systems, hegemonic thinking and policies, and traditions that maintain inequities in our society."[7] Those actions were the most direct political action that this campus has seen in its history, one action seemingly begetting the next with the broader target being the new White House. They were animated with an anger that proved efficacious at the local level, in terms of both causing institutional change as well as strengthening cohesion among participants (Chvasta, 2006). Even if I was dismayed that the students in my classroom were not willing to discuss Damigo as an agent of oppression, I was comforted by their presence in the Quad. And I believe they were comforted by being in the presence of each other, without having to share their personal experiences but speaking in a unified voice. They chose dissemination over dialogue.

In *Speaking into the Air: A History of the Idea of Communication*, Peters (1999) provides an extensive overview of how communication has been understood implicitly and explicitly in Western thought from the time of the Ancient Greeks onward. One chapter in particular resonated strongly with me as I read it at the start of this millennium, and it has resurfaced repeatedly in memory as I thought about my students' actions over the course of the last few semesters. Peters argues that we can understand dialogue and dissemination as the two categorical modes of communication as it has been conceptualized over time. He traces the understanding of these modes to two figures: Socrates (as presented by Plato) and Jesus (as presented in the synoptic Gospels). In short, "Socrates in the *Phaedrus* favors dialogue; Jesus in the synoptics favors dissemination" (p. 51). Over the centuries, and in current times, dialogue, conceived as "reciprocal speech acts between live communicators," has become a "strenuous standard" for authentic and just communication (p. 34). Peters finds the roots of this perception in the Socratic dialogues in which dialogue is associated with face-to-face and soul-to-soul communication, and dissemination was associated with mediation (writing, back then) that invites distrust. However, as Peters argues, the synoptics counter this view with a conceptualization of dissemination as a "rhetoric of sowing and harvesting" that is epitomized in the parables of Jesus, in particular the parable of the sower that "celebrates broadcasting as an equitable mode of communication that leaves the harvest of meaning to the will and capacity of the recipient" (p. 51). To the point, Peters informs that "dialogue can be tyrannical and dissemination can be just" (p. 34). It is on this point that I want to rethink how and what we teach in introductory media courses—especially because, in our mediated society, as Peters notes across the body of his work, dialogue and dissemination are intertwined.[8] In the following section, I offer alternatives to the standard content found in introductory media courses and provide ways, through posing specific kinds of questions, that an instructor may cultivate generative doubt to combat debilitative doubt, destructive certainties, and misinformation in these terrible and terrifying times.

THE INTRODUCTORY MEDIA CLASSROOM AND DOUBT

Communication scholars and teachers have work to do—perhaps most urgently in introductory media courses. These courses typically cover the histories and industries of various media. While a chronological account of media has value, I have come to doubt its place in the introductory course that, at least on my campus, is taken by both majors and non-majors. For many students, it is the only course they will take that is focused on media. Given the current social, cultural, and political conditions, we would benefit better our students if we set aside the innovation-to-industry model and focus, instead, on media convergence (Jenkins, 2006), recognizing the multiplicity of platforms, processes, logics, and products of media consumption and production—and recognizing that these foci cannot be considered in a vacuum. More fundamentally, the course could provide students the opportunity to consider carefully dialogue and dissemination as intertwined modes of communication in our digitally mediated society. Most critically, the course could be a concentrated study of the generative and debilitative effects of doubt in our digitally mediated society and would result in critically media-literate citizens.

The push for critical media literacy has occupied the pages of scholarly journals and curricular policies at all levels of education for decades. I, for one, have long been a fan of the work of Douglas Kellner and Jeff Share (2007, in particular in this context) and have followed their guidance and assigned their writing in my classrooms. Currently, scholars, policy-makers, and think-tank members are scrambling (with careful and deliberative thought) to counter the effects of media manipulation that threaten our ability to engage in democratic ideals (e.g., Jolls & Johnsen, 2018), as well as analyze the ways in which media manipulation affects public perception and understanding of information (e.g., Kavanaugh & Rich, 2018). These are worthwhile endeavors, and the recommendations are worthy of implementation. However, I agree with danah boyd (2018) when she argues that they are not enough, that doubt has been weaponized for political gains, and that educators need to teach across epistemologies.

When the current President of the United States consistently demonizes mainstream news sources, it is not enough to instruct students to "evaluate news sources" (boyd, 2018). We must teach students about the logics of media platforms, the roles of news industries, and the motivations of senders. We can do this in ways that are consistent with dialogical ideals by beginning with an invitation to the students to share what they (think they) know in broad and specific terms. What does it mean to have a President who tweets daily? What do you make, if anything at all, of his tweets? What do you think about the reactions in the Twitterverse? Do you ever talk with anyone, face-to-face, about the President? This type of questioning must not fall into *mythocentric* voice, as Carlson (1998) warns, "a voice that is about telling stories of people's lives, including our own, but in which very little effort is [made] to link personal stories to broader and more generalizable contexts of meaning" (p. 553). Rather this type of questioning should lead to guided instruction on topics such as the "death of local news" (Schmelzer, 2003) and radicalization as the "social process of affective networking" (Johnson, 2018).

We need to teach students how to determine the epistemological assumptions from which messages are constructed. Messages include all media content from news reports to social media posts to memes to movies to music to *every single bit of media content*. Teach them to ask of message producers, "How did you come to know this?" Teach them to ask themselves, "How did I come to know this?" More pointedly, teach them to ask, "Why do they believe this? Why do I (not)?" Though boyd does not have faith in educators' ability (or, perhaps, willingness?) to teach across epistemologies, educators could endeavor to cultivate generative doubt by asking questions designed to raise epistemological assumptions to the surface. We can teach our students to ask of themselves and others, is information factual because it is the result of, say, dialogical engagement, or empirical investigation, or discursive deconstruction, or experience, or faith, or solipsism, or some combination? We can teach them that different epistemological assumptions require different methods for producing knowledge—and knowledge is, indeed, produced.

Class time should be devoted to careful consideration of media logics, perhaps most important these days, the logics of social media platforms. What are the explicit and emergent rules of various platforms? (For example, in terms of emergent rules, my students taught me that one should never "like" a photo on Instagram that is over a month old, lest one wants to be considered a stalker.) What are the capabilities and limitations of various platforms? More important, what are the effects of such? (A president being able to communicate anytime with the people via 280-character messages *seems* like a groovy idea. Yet . . .)[9]

In addition to guiding students in the consideration of epistemological assumptions, we need to make clear that what we (think we) know affects—and effects—who we are. If we allow our doubts in others' ideas to become denial, we perform a kind of erasure. The curt phrase of denial, "I don't believe you," has epistemological and ontological force; it is an invalidation of both message and messenger (Chvasta, 2013). We can ask students to reflect on their experiences of being disbelieved. We can ask them whether there are any messages worthy of erasure. We can ask them to study the comments section of any news story on any site to identify messages that operate as erasures, and then study the responses of those who are targeted. Students can also study particularly ferocious instances in which the rhetorical erasure morphs into life-threatening behaviors (for example, Gamergate). Doing so will provide concrete examples of the interplay between "micro practices" and "macro structures" that constitute oppressive discourse and perpetuate suffering (Fassett & Warren, 2008).

Throughout the course, in the context of each of these questions, we need to confront the ways in which capitalism is shaping platforms, processes, logics, and products of media consumption and production. We can stress Jenkins' (2006) observation: "In the world of media convergence, every important story gets told, every brand gets sold, and every consumer gets courted across multiple media platforms" (p. 3), as well as his argument that the "circulation of media content—across different media systems, competing media economies, and national borders—depends heavily on consumers' active participation" (p. 3). We can ask students to contemplate whether and, if so, how such convergence of systems, economies, and borders is contributing to a "serious erosion of the discourses of community, justice, equality, public values, and the common good" (again, Giroux, 2016, par. 5). We can ask them if they agree with Jürgen Habermas' concern that the splintering effect of [the] internet has changed the role of traditional media, particularly for the younger generations. Even before the centrifugal and atomic tendencies of the new media came into force, the commercialization of public attention had already triggered the disintegration of the public sphere. (as quoted in Hermoso, 2018)

Twenty years ago, I would not have thought it possible for Habermas' faith in the democratic capacity of the "public sphere" to be shaken. Yet here we are. Perhaps, Habermas has come to realize that rationality is not enough, maybe it never was, and maybe the logic itself has become its own undoing. Perhaps McLaren (1998) is right in his argument that educators must devote their energy to teaching toward the stymying and dismantling of the globalization of labor and capital, as it has been "accompanied by technological innovation" (p. 432). But I have my doubts. I have faith, though, that I can get a better sense of where we are and where we might go if I ask students what they (think they) know and share with them what I (think I) know from my own experiences and the teachings of others, highlighting the generative possibilities of doubt as we might achieve it through permissive dialogue and welcoming dissemination.

NOT-FINAL WORDS

From Montessori though high school, I was educated formally mostly by Catholic nuns and a few priests. One of the greatest fundamental lessons I learned was this: *There is no faith without doubt*. In the last several paragraphs, I offer a lot of "we would benefit," "the course could provide," "we must," "we can," "should lead," "we need to," "teach them," "we can teach," "class time should," "we can ask," and "will provide." My language is indicative. Not only do I still believe what the clergy taught me (at least, that particular lesson that they taught me), that there is no faith without doubt; I also believe *that there is no doubt without faith*. Though I question the professed promises of "dialogue" as embraced by critical pedagogues, my questioning has led me to pursue alternatives. And I have doubts in those, too. If we cannot rely on the promise of "dialogue"—as it has been defined by the ideologues of critical pedagogy, we can at least promise ourselves to embrace, and engender in others, a generative doubt and an acceptance of the possibility of dissemination. In our digital age, after all (and arguably long before the Internet), these modes are intertwined, and in our digital age, we cannot ignore their inextricability. I will not have doubt without faith.

NOTES

1. I recognize that "critical pedagogy" is a broad label that is taken up variously by various scholars from various disciplinary traditions. For the most part, I am referencing the work of Paolo Freire and those who have followed his lead. I do so primarily because of the influence his work has had on critical communication pedagogy as conceived by Fassett and Warren (2007).
2. As I write, it is July 2018. Google the headlines for this month. They are terrible and terrifying and I am loathe to commit any of the new stories to print here lest you think I think one terrible event or action committed by the current White House is more terrible than another. And now you know my political orientation.
3. Alanis (2006) refers to this essay as "the first formidable critique of critical pedagogy" (p. 174); Burbules (2000) characterizes Ellsworth as "the major contemporary critic of the prescriptive model of dialogue and its virtually unquestioned role in critical pedagogy" (p. 265); and Google Scholar reports that this essay has been cited nearly 4,000 times.
4. An image of the flier can be found here: https://itsgoingdown.org/nathan-damigo-exposed-identity-evropa-leader-operating-csu-stanislaus/
5. https://itsgoingdown.org/about/.
6. For fun, I Googled "Socrates was an asshole" and was not disappointed. Perhaps my favorite find is a post written by Charles Blattberg, a political philosopher at Université de Montréal, that contains this: "Socrates was an asshole. Imagine how frustrating it must have been to try and explore ideas with this elenchic-obsessed wanker who never, ever listens. Don't believe them when they tell you that he raised his questions in good faith! In fact, not once in all of Plato's so-called dialogues does Socrates say something like 'you're right, I was mistaken' or 'I never thought of it that way before' or 'thank you, I've really learned something here.' One translation of the ancient Greek *'dia-'* is 'between,' which tells us that genuine dialogue requires at least two interlocutors (since only that way can there be a between) *each* of whom is open to being changed by what they hear. Otherwise, you get only unidirectional monologue." http://digressions.angstpatrol.com/adversarialism-in-philosophy-a-prosecution/.
7. California State University–Stanislaus Diversity Center webpage: https://www.csustan.edu/student-affairs/diversity-center.
8. See, for example, "The Uncanniness of Mass Communication in Interwar Social Thought," in which Peters (1996) argues: "The fostering of 'we-ness,' intimate address, and dialogic inclusion generally has remained at the core of broadcast discourse in radio, television, and advertising to this day" (p. 111). Of course, the interactivity of the Internet has heightened this fostering and, ironically and arguably, has led to divisiveness. I address this more directly later in the chapter with a sad acknowledgment of Jürgen Habermas' concerns.
9. One might even ask one's students why people tend to tweet around the original limit of 140 characters. Product manager Aliza Rosen reported in a blogpost: "We—and many of you—were concerned that timelines may fill up with 280 character Tweets, and people with the new limit would always use up the whole space. But that didn't happen. Only 5% of Tweets sent were longer than 140 characters and only 2% were over 190 characters." https://blog.twitter.com/official/en_us/topics/product/2017/tweetingmadeeasier.html.

REFERENCES

Alanis, J. (2006). "How much are you willing to risk? How far are you willing to go?" *Critical Studies—Critical Methodologies*, *6*(1), 166–84.
Aronowitz, S. (1987/1988). "Postmodernism and politics." *Social Text*, *18*, 99–115.
Bauer, S. (2017, May 7). "I met the white nationalist who 'falcon punched' a 95-pound female protester." *Mother Jones*. Retrieved from https://www.motherjones.com/politics/2017/05/nathan-damigo-punching-woman-berkeley-white-nationalism/.

boyd, d. (2018). "You think you want media literacy . . . do you?" *Points: Experimental collection from data & society*. Retrieved from https://points.datasociety.net/you-think-you-want-media-literacy-do-you-7cad6af18ec2.

Branson-Potts, H. (2016, December 7). "In diverse California, a young white supremacist seeks to convert fellow college students." *Los Angeles Times*. Retrieved from http://www.latimes.com/local/lanow/la-me-ln-nathan-damigo-alt-right-20161115-story.html.

Burbules, N. C. (2000). "The limits of dialogue as a critical pedagogy." In P. P. Trifonas (Ed.), *Revolutionary pedagogies: Cultural politics, education, and discourse of theory* (pp. 251–73). New York: Routledge.

Campbell, J. (2017, April 21). "Stan State launches investigation on white supremacist who punched a woman at a Berkeley rally." *The Signal*. Retrieved from https://www.csusignal.com/campus_culture/article_be80e306-2654-11e7-a3bb-9f2981424352.html.

Carlson, D. (1998). "Finding a voice, and losing our way?" *Educational Theory, 48*(4), 541–54.

Chvasta, M. (2005). "Remembering praxis: Performance in the digital age." *Text and Performance Quarterly, 25*(2), 156–70.

Chvasta, M. (2006). "Anger, irony, and protest: Confronting the issue of efficacy, again." *Text and Performance Quarterly, 26*(1), 5–16.

Chvasta, M. (2013). "Sinéad O'Connor: The collision of bodies." In M. Pedelty & K. Weglarz (Eds.), *Political rock*. London: Routledge.

Ellsworth, E. (1989). "Why doesn't this feel empowering? Working through the repressive myths of critical pedagogy." *Harvard Educational Review, 59*(3), 297–324.

Ellsworth, E. (1997). *Teaching positions: Difference, pedagogy, and the power of address*. New York: Teachers College Press.

Fassett, D. L., & Warren, J. T. (2007). *Critical communication pedagogy*. Thousand Oaks, CA: Sage.

Fassett, D. L., & Warren, J. T. (2008). "Pedagogy of relevance: A critical communication pedagogy agenda for the 'basic' course." *Basic Communication Course Annual, 20*(6), 1–34.

Freire, P. (1970/1993). *Pedagogy of the oppressed*. New York: Continuum.

Giroux, H. (2016, December 23). "Militant hope in the age of the politics of the disconnect." *Counterpunch*. Retrieved from https://www.counterpunch.org/2016/12/23/militant-hope-in-the-age-of-the-politics-of-the-disconnect/.

Gur-Ze'ev, I. (1998). "Toward a nonrepressive critical pedagogy." *Educational Theory, 48*(4), 463–86.

Hao, R. N. (2011). "Rethinking critical pedagogy: Implications on Silence and Silent Bodies." *Text and Performance Quarterly, 31*(3), 267–84.

Hermoso, B. (2018, May 25). "Jürgen Habermas: For god's sake, spare us governing philosophers!" *El País*. Retrieved from https://elpais.com/elpais/2018/05/07/inenglish/1525683618_145760.html.

Jenkins, H. (2006). *Convergence culture: Where old and new media collide*. New York: New York University Press.

Johnson, J. (2018). "The self-radicalization of white men: 'Fake news' and the affective networking of paranoia." *Communication, Culture and Critique, 11*(1), 100–15.

Jolls, T., & Johnsen, M. (2018). "Media literacy: A foundational skill for democracy in the 21st century." *Hastings Law Journal, 69*(5), 1379–1408. Retrieved from http://www.hastingslawjournal.org/wp-content/uploads/Jolls-69.5.pdf.

Kavanaugh, J., & Rich, M. D. (2018). *Truth decay: An Initial Exploration of the Diminishing Role of Facts and Analysis in American Public Life*. Santa Monica, CA: RAND Corporation. Retrieved from https://www.rand.org/content/dam/rand/pubs/research_reports/RR2300/RR2314/RAND_RR2314.pdf.

Kellner, D., & Share, J. (2007). "Critical media literacy is not an option." *Learning Inquiry, 1*(1), 59–69.

Kohli, W. (1998). "Critical education and embodied subjects: Making the poststructural turn." *Educational Theory, 48*(4), 511–19.

Lather, P. (1998). "Critical pedagogy and its complicities: A praxis of stuck places." *Educational Theory, 48*(4), 487–97.

McLaren, P. (1998). "Revolutionary pedagogy in post-revolutionary times: Rethinking the political economy of critical education." *Educational Theory, 48*(4), 432–62.

Peters, J. D. (1996). "The uncanniness of mass communication in interwar social thought." *Journal of Communication, 46*(3), 108–23.

Peters, J. D. (1999). *Speaking into the air: A history of the idea of communication.* Chicago: University of Chicago Press.

Schmelzer, P. (2003, April 23). "The death of local news." AlterNet. Retrieved from https://www.alternet.org/2003/04/the_death_of_local_news/.

Chapter Two

Mitigating Pedagogical Marginalization

Critically Assessing the Use of Mediated Communication with Special Populations of Students

David H. Kahl, Jr.

The classroom is a site of learning, but it is also a site of struggle. In this sense, students experience both empowerment in their learning while experiencing concomitant hegemony. Although most students experience some degree of marginalization in their learning, some experience more hegemony than others. These students are more likely to be left out of parts of the learning process because of characteristics that they do or do not possess. Groups that are especially vulnerable to pedagogical marginalization are special populations of students. Special populations of students are those "whose social location is not understood . . . whose life circumstances are not known and not considered; whose voice is not heard or has been silenced; whose needs have been left unfulfilled; whose promise is not recognized and whose protest is ignored" (Dei & Rummens, 2010, para. 6). These groups of students include those who have disabilities, those who lack economic resources, single parents, children of single parents, children of gay or lesbian parents, LGTBQ students, students of color, immigrants, refugees, nonnative English speakers, and first-generation college students. These students lack the advantages that privileged students enjoy and do not experience learning in the same ways as those students who are white, male, and affluent and have a high level of fluency in the English language.

Although special populations possess abilities and experiences that can enrich learning (Kahl, 2018), instructors may (un)intentionally view and treat them differently. Instructors may unknowingly do this because they often do not examine the implications of the pedagogical decisions they make and the assignments they create, which can determine whether instructors marginalize special populations of students. Any teaching method or aspect of the classroom has the potential to be hegemonic, depending on the intent (or lack thereof) of the instructor.

Hegemonic pedagogical practices resemble what Freire (1970) calls the banking concept of education. The banking model, and the neoliberal society from which it derives, value a one-way transfer of information from instructor to student. In this traditional system, instructors are considered the all-knowing masters and students are considered merely empty vessels waiting to be filled with information. Freire (1970) likens such a system to a banking transaction, in which the instructor deposits information in the minds of the students. The banking system teaches students to believe in a Capital-T Truth, to believe that knowledge is fixed and non-nuanced, and to become better prepared to become a pawn in a neoliberally driven consumer society (Giroux, 2014). To counter the banking system, educators need to learn to critically examine their pedagogy, ultimately leading them to become critically minded instructors.

Critically minded instructors realize that power can manifest itself in manifold ways. One way in which power can manifest itself is through the ways in which instructors use mediated communication. Because of the proliferation of technology in contemporary classrooms, mediated communication now holds an almost ubiquitous presence in schools. Instructors can unreflectively utilize mediated communication in ways that facilitate marginalization. Special populations of students are often the recipients of this pedagogical marginalization when attempting to utilize technology. Because of the potential for instructors to use mediated communication in ways that are marginalizing, instructors should examine the ways in which they use mediated communication in the classroom to ensure that their assignments do not (unintentionally) subjugate students.

Here I will provide an overview of mediated communication and will present several examples of the ways in which the uncritical use of mediated communication can marginalize students. Then, I argue that instructors should view mediated communication through the lens of critical communication pedagogy (CCP) and critical assessment. Examining mediated communication through critical lenses allows instructors and students to understand how mediated communication can be empowering and how they can use it to provide opportunities to resist hegemonic structures in the classroom.

MEDIATED COMMUNICATION

Mediated communication includes both new and traditional media and often lacks some elements of nonverbal communication (Waldeck, Kearney, & Plax, 2013). Thus, the medium does not always provide interlocutors the opportunity to communicate using the full accoutrement of nonverbal communicative practices usually available to them. For example, physical appearance, haptics, kinesics, and paralanguage may be absent in some forms of mediated communication. Speaking pedagogically, mediated communication can include any electronic medium that has the potential to enhance communication between instructors and students. Examples of mediated communication include course management systems (e.g., Blackboard and Canvas), social networks (e.g., Facebook, Twitter, and Instagram), websites, Skype, social media sites (e.g., YouTube), videos, online games, personal response systems, and other computer-based technologies.

The majority of research in the area of mediated communication and pedagogy is social scientific in nature. Social scientific research into the pedagogical efficacy of mediated communication sheds light on the ways in which instructors can use it to aid in student learning. This work attempts to determine if and how mediated communication is pedagogically effective at the affective and cognitive levels. Although its findings are pedagogically useful, social scientific research tends not to investigate the ways in which mediated communication can be marginalizing for students. Thus, critically minded instructors recognize the need to critically examine the ways in which their use of mediated communication in the classroom may be marginalizing for students. To better understand this critical perspective the following section will examine the intersections of mediated communication, power, and pedagogy.

CRITICALLY EXAMINING MEDIATED COMMUNICATION

A critical perspective examines power and its effect on diverse student populations. Critically minded instructors need to be aware of the potential hegemony inherent in the pedagogical decisions they make when using mediated communication, especially when interacting with special populations of students. Therefore, it is important to view mediated communication through a critical lens by applying critical theory and critical thought to the pedagogical use of mediated communication in the classroom. A critical perspective examines the use of mediated communication to determine how it might be empowering or marginalizing for special populations of students.

Mediated Communication as a Contributor to Classroom Hegemony

As previously stated, instructors often hold the belief that mediated communication in the classroom is simply a pedagogical tool (Resnyansky, 2002). In actuality, "no technology is neutral or value free. Historical evidence demonstrates that technology use carries social meaning; social values and practices develop around the use of a new technology" (Murray, 2000, p. 406). Scholars have likened mediated communication to Foucault's (1979) description of the panopticon in that it can act as a method of "surveillance and control" (Spears & Lea, 1994, p. 438). Following this analogy, some forms of mediated communication allow for a "panoptic sort" in which hegemons (in this case, instructors and possibly privileged students) can watch and inform on each other, especially on students from special populations, which can reinforce power differences in the classroom (Spears & Lea, 1994, p. 439).

For example, the panopticon-like nature of mediated communication may influence students, especially those from marginalized groups, to apply self-imposed restrictions on the information they divulge or how they respond to questions, believing that they may be under a type of pedagogical surveillance by instructors. These types of self-regulatory actions can be explained by Gramsci's (1971) notion of ideological hegemony, which explains how ruling elites use tools—in this case, mediated communication—to enhance/enact their own power by imposing surveillance measures on students.

One example of this can be found in course management systems used by universities. Course management systems often provide instructors with the means to surveil their students' usage of the medium. Instructors are able to view the number of times that students log into the system to view and work on assignments and are able to view the amount of time that students spent working on them. Special populations of students who might have limited access to the Internet are often unable to spend as much time online as privileged students. Thus, these surveillance-like tools may cause instructors to display an implicit bias against special populations of students whose financial situations may prevent them from spending as much time interacting with the medium. Thus, instructors may be more likely to (un)consciously penalize these students when grading their work.

Thus, power is inherent in pedagogical uses of mediated communication. Because of this, critical theories of communication and media can help instructors to understand the power inherent in mediated communication. One of these perspectives, critical media theory, unpacks the intersections of power, capitalism, neoliberalism, and marginalization.

Critical Media Theory

Critical media theory is a broad theoretical perspective that takes into account many diverse theories regarding the hegemonic effects of media. Critical media theory speaks about injustice, marginalization, and hegemony driven by media (in many forms). A key tenet of critical media theory is that "there is a close relationship between the media, politics and the economy" (Fourie, 2007, p. 134). Critical media theory posits that those who own and disseminate media in any form influence the content of the message in ways that support a particular ideology in ways that marginalize others and their own ideologies. Deriving from the Frankfurt School and Marxist thought, critical media theory also views media as a capitalist endeavor that constructs messages in ways that allow "the ideological perspective of the elite class to dominate over all others" (Tuman, 2010, p. 172). Thus, it criticizes media for silencing subaltern classes in society by not presenting or giving voice to their viewpoints. Critical media theory draws on other critical assumptions about neoliberal, capitalist society as well. It posits that media is produced to benefit capitalism and profit by discouraging critical thought and perpetuating the belief that commodification of everything leads citizens to the assumption that consumption will bring happiness and satisfaction in life (Taylor & Harris, 2008).

Critical media theory draws on politics, culture, and economics to explain why media serves to legitimize elite voices and silence others. Applied to the classroom, critical media theory explains why the use of some media, although it can provide opportunities of access to students, may also have unintended hegemonic effects on students, namely special populations of students who are most susceptible to being marginalized. Understanding critical media theory is important as it provides broad, foundational knowledge about the ways in which media can serve plutocratic voices in society. As I will discuss later, a connection exists between critical media theory, the hegemony that it uncovers, and CCP, which strives to understand how the use of communication as pedagogy can be marginalizing. I will examine the ways in which the knowledge gleaned from critical media theory can be viewed through the lens of CCP to determine how to respond to the hegemony that mediated communication (un)intentionally produces.

Critical media theory is useful in that it provides knowledge about mediated communication and hegemony. Another important theory relating to the effects of mediated communication use in the classroom is intersectionality theory. Intersectionality builds upon critical media theory by providing more detail as to the specific ways that special populations can be marginalized through the use of media in the classroom.

Intersectionality

The notion of intersectionality explains that special populations of students are not marginalized by one characteristic alone but, instead, face greater marginalization because of a confluence of characteristics that distance them from privileged students. These characteristics include students' ethnic background, skin color, sex, gender, economic status, appearance, clothing, and speech patterns. Thus, marginalization becomes exacerbated as characteristics overlap (Crenshaw, 1989). Shields (2008) explains that examining marginalization through the lens of intersectionality is useful because it provides "a language for the glaring fact that it is impossible to talk about (one characteristic) without considering other dimensions of social structure/social identity" (p. 303). The following examples illustrate some unintended marginalizing effects of mediated communication that are exacerbated by intersectionality.

Examples of Intersectionality

Special populations of students can experience the negative effects of intersectionality when interacting with mediated communication in the classroom. To illustrate the interrelatedness of mediated communication use and intersectionality, this section will focus on one special population—economically disadvantaged students. Many mediated communication assignments require Internet access. Economically disadvantaged students, however, do not have the same access to Internet in their homes as economically privileged students. To illustrate, at least 55 million Americans either do not have the Internet in their homes or lack reliable access (Daley, 2015). Thus, when these students are asked to complete such an assignment, they may face extreme difficulty doing so. In her examination of the struggles that marginalized groups in Pennsylvania face related to Internet access, Daley (2015) tells the story of an adult student, a 47-year-old single mother of two. Because her family cannot afford Internet access in their home, she is forced to go the laundromat with her school-aged daughter so that they can both complete their schoolwork in the Wi-Fi-enabled environment. Further contributing to the marginalization of these special populations is the fact that students who have to complete Internet-related work due to mediated communication-related assignments often have to stay after school to do so. When this occurs, students come home after dark, which increases the danger that they face (Daley, 2015).

Another problem with mediated communication technology is its use of English as a lingua franca. Economically disadvantaged students may be immigrants who are not proficient in English and may have difficulty utilizing and interpreting communication technology. For this reason, "participants who are not competent in English may be excluded from a potentially influential medium of communication or, worse still, may experience the use of English as a tool of power" (Murray, 2000, p. 408). Additionally, some students who are economically disadvantaged also have special learning needs in the classroom. Students with special needs learn best through close interaction with an encouraging teacher who uses both verbal and nonverbal cues to help them concentrate more effectively (Williams, 2009). While some forms of mediated communication can encourage and facilitate marginalized groups' participation through the availability of translators, the absence of nonverbal cues in some forms of mediated communication creates another learning gap for these students. Thus, intersectionality theory demonstrates that the very assignments that are designed to be empowering can marginalize some students.

The previous sections have discussed the ways in which critical media theory and intersectionality as a framework explain how special populations of students can be marginalized by mediated communication. Critical media theory explains how media can be hegemonic by expanding a neoliberal economic system that exploits the marginalized and furthers elitist ideologies. Intersectionality, on the other hand, expands on this by explaining that, in this case, using mediated communication in the classroom can have the effect of subjugating special populations of students in numerous, intersecting ways.

These theories show that the use of mediated communication can be subjugating to students. Because of this potential subjugation, critically minded instructors should examine their own use of mediated communication to ensure that their assignments are not (unintentionally) subjugating. Critically minded instructors can resist hegemony by viewing mediated communication through the lens of critical communication pedagogy (CCP). Viewing their mediated assignments through the lens of CCP can serve as an important means for instructors to respond to hegemony in the classroom. Instead of fostering hegemony, power, and isolation, CCP can assist instructors in using mediated communication to encourage all students in recognizing and responding to hegemony by learning about difference, tolerance, respect, and acceptance.

CRITICAL COMMUNICATION PEDAGOGY

Critical communication pedagogy (CCP) is radical pedagogy. It is radical in the sense that is does not accept nor adhere to the status quo of traditional modes of education. It does not accept prevailing ideologies that instructors are all knowing and that students are simply passive vessels who must be filled with knowledge (Freire, 1970). It does not accept dominant neoliberal ideals that students must be silent observers in the classroom in order to memorize copious amounts of material that must be regurgitated on standardized tests. It rejects the neoliberal notion that any discussion of activism, societal change, and social and economic betterment for special populations of students should be absent from class discussions (Giroux, 2014). CCP rejects the belief that we live in a post-racial society and that discussing subjects such as race, class, sex, gender, wealth inequality should not be part of the classroom. CCP is "political pedagogy" (Giroux, 2014, p. 50), meaning that it does not inculcate beliefs, but instead poses difficult questions that challenge students to think about their classroom and society.

CCP is a pragmatic response to hegemony (Kahl, 2011). CCP accepts as a central tenet that "educational processes are not neutral; they can either domesticate or liberate" (Allen, 2011, p. 104). Thus, it focuses on the ways in which language and meaning can be empowering or marginalizing (Kahl, 2013a; Simpson, 2010). To do so, CCP examines social interaction to determine ways in which instructors and students can resist the disparities in power that language creates (Fassett & Warren, 2007). Overall, CCP is pedagogy that examines how communication marginalizes some and empowers others by viewing interpersonal interaction as the site at which power originates (Allen, 2011).

CCP challenges instructors to examine the ways in which they use mediated communication in their classrooms. In order to do so, they must analyze the (potential) marginalizing effects of their pedagogical choices. As I have illustrated, mediated communication as pedagogy can result in hegemonic effects for students; however, mediated communication as pedagogy can also serve as a response to power. For instructors to use mediated communication effectively, they must critically assess the ways in which they use this medium in the classroom.

CRITICAL ASSESSMENT OF MEDIATED COMMUNICATION

Instructors need to have a means by which to determine the effectiveness of their own pedagogy. Assessment procedures are important because they answer the questions for instructors who "constantly question if and how the educative process is working" (Cooks, 2010, p. 307). Thus, critically minded instructors who embrace CCP and mediated communication as a means to teach students about intersectionality, difference, tolerance, and power must determine the degree to which their critical pedagogical techniques have the intended effects of assisting students to become engaged citizens of the world (Kahl, 2013b). Critical assessment must be designed to assess not only content knowledge, but also the application of content knowledge to ameliorate effects of hegemony. Importantly, instructors engaging in the critical assessment of their mediated assignments should determine how they can create "a critical awareness of how privilege and oppression become normalized through our everyday interactions" (Rudick, Golsan, & Cheesewright, 2018, p. 43).

Critical assessment, unlike traditional neoliberal modes of assessment, is generally free of prescription. Freire (1970) explains the marginalization inherent in prescription, saying:

> One of the basic elements of the relationship between oppressor and oppressed is *prescription*. Every prescription represents the imposition of one individual's choice upon another, transforming the consciousness of the person prescribed to into one that conforms with the prescriber's consciousness. (pp. 46–47)

Because the assessment procedures I will describe regarding the use of mediated communication follow CCP, I will not offer prescriptive or formulaic examples of assessments that may or may not be hegemonic. Rather, I will offer assessment procedures that critically minded instructors may choose to follow to assess whether or not their mediated assignments are a contributor to classroom hegemony or a response to it. These procedures can be formative, assessment during the learning process, and summative, assessment after the learning process (Harlen & James, 1997). Critically minded instructors need to determine the degree to which their use of mediated communication as pedagogy is accomplishing the critical goals that they set for it. Thus, instructors can use CCP to develop assessment procedures to determine if their use of mediated communication encourages critical change. CCP assessment asks the following questions: Is this empowering for my students? Why or why not? How do I know? I suggest following a three-step critical assessment procedure that allows instructors to examine whether or not their assignments are empowering or marginalizing. This process consists of reflexivity, dialogue, and praxis.

Step 1: Reflexivity

Reflexivity is an important process that allows instructors to determine the effect that their pedagogical choices involving mediated communication have on students, especially marginalized special populations of students. Unlike simply being reflective, which only recounts the past, reflexivity involves concomitantly looking back and looking forward. This process is an "important motion, back and forth, between one's actions and how those implicate one in social phenomena" (Denzin, 1997, p. 48).

Reflexivity challenges instructors to consider how their past use of mediated communication may affect current and future pedagogical decisions. Unfortunately, pedagogical decisions are often made with haste. Haste can lead to careless pedagogy. Reflexivity challenges instructors to avoid haste and "to slow down, to subject our experiences to critical examination, to expose life's mundane qualities for how they illustrate our participation in power" (Fassett & Warren, 2007, p. 103). The knowledge gleaned from reflexivity about the use of mediated communication as pedagogy can illuminate how the instructor "is both product and producer of culture" and how the instructor's "very (in)actions create and sustain complex social phenomena, including how s/he understands identity, power, and culture" (Denzin, 1997, p. 47).

Application of reflexivity

In the case of mediated communication use in the classroom, instructors could act reflexively by carefully considering the following: past assignments involving mediated communication, rationale for choosing those assignments, and how those assignments might have been subjugating to special populations of students. The following questions can assist instructors in considering the effects of their pedagogical choices.

Reflexive Questions

- How do I choose the mediated communication that I use in the classroom?
- Which procedures do I use to make these decisions?
- What are my intended outcomes? What are the actual outcomes?
- How might the technology that I have chosen be marginalizing for special populations of students? How might the assignments/assessment procedures be marginalizing? How might they be empowering?
- Are they a move toward or away from the banking model?
- Am I using technology as a panopticon-like system in which students may feel surveilled? How so?
- Am I silencing my students' voices by using mediated communication technology?
- How am I using mediated communication to extend social connections among students?

Considering these questions can assist instructors in looking back on past action with the intention of gaining insight that can be applied to future assignments. I suggest that instructors can work toward this goal by dialoguing with students to share what they have discovered to foster future change.

Step 2: Dialogue with Students

A critical (communication) pedagogical model favors liberating, horizontal communication, in which instructors are equals and dialogue can flow freely between instructor and student (Freire, 1973). In contrast, the neoliberal model of education favors oppressive, vertical communication, in which the instructor gives students information and is anti-dialogic. Therefore, critical (communication) pedagogues place great importance on dialogue. They view dialogue as a means to resist power and collectively make meaningful change. Puiggrós (1994) discusses the fact that Freire recognized importance in "dialogical education," which is the "possibility of a pedagogical discourse emerging from articulation of differences" (p. 171). Thus, dialogue is a central tenet of critical communication pedagogy as it allows for diverse learners to share their varied perspectives about their classroom experiences. At this point, instructors have gained knowledge about their pedagogical missteps through the process of reflexivity that they undertook in step one. Step two provides an opportunity for instructors to dialogue with students about mediated assignments to determine if/how they have experienced hegemony.

Questions for Dialogue

Instructors might consider using the following questions as a starting point for dialogue.

- Do you feel that you have been empowered or marginalized through the mediated communication assignments that I have designed? How so?
- How have you felt empowered? How have you felt marginalized? How have mediated communication assignments negatively affected you?
- In what ways do you feel that the mediated communication assignments helped you/hindered you as a student? How could assignments using mediated communication be better designed to learn course content and learn about hegemony?
- How could mediated communication assignments better help you to recognize and respond to hegemony in society?

After engaging in dialogue and reflexivity, instructors should possess an understanding of the hegemony present in assignments utilizing mediated communication.

Step 3: Praxis

Critical assessment of the pedagogical efficacy of assignments involving mediated communication would not be complete without praxis. Praxis is the implementation of change; it is putting the knowledge gleaned from reflexivity and dialogue into action. Praxis is embodied in Freire's (1970) notion of conscientization, which is a response to hegemony. Action cannot occur without dialogue, as "action for action's sake negates the true praxis and makes dialogue impossible" (Freire, 1970, p. 88). Dialogue can facilitate praxis in that it necessitates collective action, between instructor and students. In this sense, praxis is transformative because it is not done *"for* another," but instead, is "the right of everyone" to make change (Freire, 1970, p. 88).

In a Freirean sense, praxis involves the collective. It is not change made solely by the instructor, but instead collectively developed change that will reduce hegemony for special populations of students. Thus, now that instructors and students have acted reflexively about the (hegemonic) role of mediated communication in the classroom, they can begin to take collective action and can employ praxis by using knowledge to make change. Freire (1970) explains that "there is no transformation without action" (p. 87). In this case, transformation can occur by responding to the hegemony that has previously been present in mediated communication assignments.

Praxis can be accomplished in a myriad of ways. I suggest that instructors pose the following questions to students to facilitate the co-creation of future assignments that will ameliorate hegemony and allow for positive pedagogical experiences with mediated communication.

Questions That Facilitate Praxis

- How should mediated assignments be developed and implemented so as not to marginalize special populations of students in our class? Would these changes create extra work/new challenges for some/all students?
- Would assignments need to be different for some members of the class? Would doing so be fair for everyone? Why/why not?
- How would we communicate differently as a class if these changes took place? How would we be resisting traditional and neoliberal models of education if we enacted these changes?
- How would you view the classroom differently if we enacted these changes? Would these changes create a positive educational experience for you?

CONCLUSION

Technology, especially in the form of mediated communication, is largely ubiquitous in the contemporary classroom. Mediated communication has the potential to be a pedagogically useful means of empowering students in the classroom. It can allow students to interact with course material in ways that allow for both affective and cognitive learning. However, as I have argued, the pedagogical use of mediated communication, without examination, can result in the opposite effect—the marginalization of some special populations of students, particularly students from economically subjugated backgrounds. Therefore, to ameliorate these subjugating effects, educators must make a commitment to act as critically minded instructors and assess the potential hegemonic effects of their use of this type of technology in the classroom. Building on critical media theory and intersectionality, in this chapter I have elucidated ways in which critically minded instructors can employ intentionality in their choices to use mediated communication in the classroom. Additionally, I have demonstrated how critically minded instructors can follow a CCP perspective by employing critical assessment procedures—namely reflexivity, dialogue, and praxis—to determine the ways in which assignments utilizing mediated communication are empowering and ways in which they are marginalizing.

Overall, viewing mediated communication through the lens of critical communication pedagogy can assist instructors in reframing the ways they view mediated communication in the classroom. When instructors become willing to understand the ways in which special populations are marginalized by intersectionality, instructors recognize the need to challenge pedagogical norms and create a pedagogy of exploration and empowerment. When instructors engage in mediated communication assessment that rejects traditional and neoliberal practices that decimate the learning environment and deny difference (Freire, 1970), critically minded instructors can make interpersonal connections with special populations of students who, each day, face pedagogical injustices.

REFERENCES

Allen, B. J. (2011). Critical communication pedagogy as a framework for teaching difference and organizing. In D. K. Mumby (Ed.), *Reframing difference in organizational communication studies: Research, pedagogy, practice* (pp. 103–25). Thousand Oaks, CA: Sage.
Cooks, L. (2010). The (critical) pedagogy of communication and the (critical) communication of pedagogy. In D. L. Fassett & J. T. Warren (Eds.), *The Sage handbook of communication and instruction* (pp. 293–314). Thousand Oaks, CA: Sage.
Crenshaw, K. W. (1989). Demarginalizing the intersection of race and sex: A black feminist critique of antidiscrimination doctrine, feminist theory and antiracist politics. *Chicago Legal Forum, 140*, 139–67.
Daley, E. (2015). At least 1.1 million Pennsylvania homes lack Internet access, *PublicSource*. Retrieved from http://publicsource.org/investigations/least-11-million-pennsylvania-homes-lack-internet-access#.V-AZv0kVDIU.
Dei, S. G. J., & Rummens, J. A. (2010). Including the excluded: De-marginalizing immigrant/refugee and racialized students. *Education Canada, 50*. Retrieved February 26, 2016, from http://www.cea-ace.ca/education-canada/article/including-excluded-de-marginalizing-immigrantrefugee-and-racialized-student.
Denzin, N. K. (1997). *Interpretive ethnography: Ethnographic practices for the 21st century.* Thousand Oaks, CA: Sage.
Fassett, D. L., & Warren, J. T. (2007). *Critical communication pedagogy.* Thousand Oaks, CA: Sage.
Foucault, M. (1979). *Discipline and punish: The birth of the prison.* New York: Vintage Books.

Fourie, P. J. (2007). Theoretical approaches to the study and research of mass communication. In P. J. Fourie (Ed.), *Media studies: Media history, media and society* (2nd ed.). (pp. 115–183). Cape Town, South Africa: Juta.
Freire, P. (1970). *Pedagogy of the oppressed* (M. B. Ramos, Trans.). New York: Herder and Herder.
Freire, P. (1973). *Education for critical consciousness.* New York: Continuum.
Giroux, H. A. (2014). *Neoliberalism's war on higher education.* Chicago: Haymarket Books.
Gramsci, A. (1971). *Selections from the prison notebooks.* New York: International Publishers.
Harlen, W., & James, M. (1997). Assessment and learning: Differences and relationships between formative and summative assessment. *Assessment in Education: Principles, Policy & Practice, 4,* 365–79.
Kahl, D. H., Jr. (2011). Autoethnography as pragmatic scholarship: Moving critical communication pedagogy from ideology to praxis. *International Journal of Communication, 5,* 1927–46.
Kahl, D. H., Jr. (2013a). Critical communication pedagogy and assessment: Reconciling two seemingly incongruous ideas. *International Journal of Communication, 7,* 2610–30.
Kahl, D. H., Jr. (2013b). Viewing critical communication pedagogy through a cinematic lens. *Communication Teacher, 27,* 99–103.
Kahl, D. H., Jr. (2015). Analyzing masculinist movements: Responding to antifeminism through critical communication pedagogy. *Communication Teacher, 29,* 21–26.
Kahl, D. H., Jr. (2018). Autoethnography as a catalyst for pedagogical change for special populations of students. In A. Atay & D. Trebing (Eds.), *The discourse of special populations: Critical intercultural communication pedagogy and practice* (pp. 23–38). New York: Routledge.
Murray, D. E. (2000). Protean communication: The language of computer-mediated communication. *TESOL Quarterly, 34,* 397–421.
Puiggrós, A. (1994). Politics, praxis, and the personal: An Argentine assessment (F. Taler, Trans.). In P. L. McLaren & C. Lankshear (Eds.), *Politics of liberation: Paths from Freire* (pp. 154–72). New York: Routledge.
Resnyansky, L. (2002). Computer-mediated communication in higher education: Educators' agency in relation to technology. *Journal of Educational Enquiry, 3,* 35–59.
Rudick, C. K., Golsan, K. B., & Cheesewright, K. (2018). *Teaching from the heart: Critical communication pedagogy in the communication classroom.* San Diego, CA: Cognella.
Simpson, J. S. (2010). Critical race theory and critical communication pedagogy. In D. L. Fassett & J. T. Warren (Eds.), *The Sage handbook of communication and instruction* (pp. 361–84). Thousand Oaks, CA: Sage.
Shields, S. A. (2008). Gender: An intersectionality perspective. *Sex Roles, 59,* 301–11.
Spears, R., & Lea, M. (1994). Panacea or panoticon?: The hidden power in computer-mediated communication. *Communication Research, 21,* 427–59.
Taylor, P. A., & Harris, J. Ll. (2008). *Critical theories of mass media: Then and now.* New York NY: McGraw-Hill.
Tuman, J. S. (2010). *Communicating terror: The rhetorical dimensions of terrorism* (2nd ed.). Los Angeles, CA: Sage.
Waldeck, J. H., Kearney, P., & Plax, T. G. (2013). *Business and professional communication in a digital age.* Boston, MA: Cengage Learning.
Williams, D. S. (2009). *The role of verbal and nonverbal communication between students with special needs and their teachers in middle school* (Doctoral dissertation). Walden University: Minneapolis, MN.

Chapter Three

Learning from One Another

Con/Divergences with/in/between Online Pedagogy, Andragogy, and Critical Pedagogy

Julie L. G. Walker

Several years ago I started my first journey into teaching public speaking online. I based my course on the well-conceived online classes I took in graduate school. I wanted to achieve the same carefully curated readings, the pre-slotted announcements, and dropboxes neatly arranged prior to the semester start. Feverishly, I recorded lectures, created assignment descriptions, and mastered the new learning management system (LMS). After several long days, my class sat ready. My readings, assignments, announcements, rubrics, and space were all created before the semester launched. Before stepping a digital foot into a discussion board, before students enrolled in the course were automatically slotted by the LMS, I built a class. I controlled all aspects of the course without regard for prior knowledge or experience students brought to the course. My first announcement should have read, "Get ready for my knowledge deposit."

My teaching approach fit many "best practices" in the online realm, but I completely abandoned my critical pedagogy foundation. Prior online class experiences as a student informed how I created the online space, but I did not recognize the prescriptive teaching model I unthinkingly espoused. Critical communication pedagogy (CCP) played a pivotal role in my graduate school coursework, but I failed to discern the gap between power-disrupting aspects of my pedagogy and the professor-dictated nature of my online space. Research into transitioning from the physical to the digital CCP classroom yielded few exemplars. Critical pedagogy scholars typically situate practices in face-to-face situations. Online pedagogy research covered a vast array of topics, but most approaches focused on the context (mediated spaces). Assessment data and course completion rates? Yes! Ways to prevent cheating online? Absolutely! Co-created learning havens whereby we practice fighting for equality? Error 404: File not found. Only a few pieces focused on mediated critical pedagogy (e.g., Caruthers & Friend, 2014; DeVoogd, Loveless, & Yelland, 2000; Duffelmeyer, 2000, 2002; Kalogeras, 2013; and McCurry, 2000).

Instructors face increasing pressures and opportunities to teach in mediated spaces. A 2018 U.S. Department of Education report found about 30 percent of students take at least one online course; 14 percent of students enroll in completely online degree programs. We have a responsibility as instructors to adapt our critical communication pedagogy practices to the digital context as much as we adapt to each individual group of students with which we have the privilege of working.

Pedagogical practices privilege one aspect of teaching over others. Online pedagogy primarily emphasizes contextually specific strategies. Critical pedagogy utilizes dialogic instruction efforts to fight power structures within/outside the classroom (Wink, 1997). However, despite clear definitions, praxis shows pedagogy does not fit neatly into a single category or perspective; we draw from multiple experiences to fit student and content needs. But how do we balance the best practices in online classrooms while implementing critical pedagogical principles effectively? Preparing to teach in new contexts requires reflexive examination of our experiences and prevailing practices. When we focus solely on the context (online pedagogy) or on power (critical communication pedagogy), we neglect rich colloquy. We need to bridge our approaches to situate critical pedagogy in mediated spaces effectively.

Andragogy overlaps effective practices in online pedagogy and critical communication pedagogy. Successful online pedagogy relies on andragogical principles (Morrison, 2015). Effective application of critical pedagogy has likewise been linked to andragogical principles (e.g., Schapiro, 2003). Despite not being a clean syllogism, andragogical principles provide useful guides for addressing difficulties transitioning critical pedagogy online. In the United States, Knowles (1962) elevated the term "andragogy" to highlight theory focused on teaching adult learners. He focused on the type of learner first over the context or the authority figure. Knowles (1984) argued, "The pedagogical [teaching theory designed for children] and andragogical models result in two very different approaches to the design and operation of educational programs" (p. 13). Adult learners use education as a tool to achieve a goal, and they seek more control over the learning process (Knowles, 1962). Creating classroom spaces where adults thrive requires instructors to acknowledge relevant student experiences, co-create course objectives with students, and explain how assignment components build to end goals.

By looking to the con/divergences with/in/between online pedagogy, andragogy, and critical pedagogy we may thoughtfully embrace the challenges and opportunities of mediated communication instructional spaces. Therefore, the following chapter uses andragogy to bridge the divergences between critical pedagogy and best practices touted by online pedagogy. The frameworks may guide our initial forays into digitally mediated critical communication pedagogy.

DIVERGENT PERSPECTIVES

Researchers refer to pedagogy in online learning contexts as web-based instruction (e.g, Donlevy & Donlevy, 2000), online learning (e.g., Palloff & Pratt, 2009), e-learning (e.g., Chapnick & Meloy, 2005), digital pedagogy (e.g., Barber, King, & Buchanan, 2015), web-enhanced or web-based education (Lavooy & Newlin, 2003), and online pedagogy (e.g., Hart, 2014). Since 1979 the U.S. education system included various forms of mediated instruction (Knowles, 1962). Today, mediated instruction typically involves Web 2.0 components (Solomon & Schrum, 2010) and utilizes completely (a)synchronous online classes, hybrid courses (half-virtual, half-physical classrooms), and web-enhanced course formats (Cargile Cook & Grant-Davie, 2005; Fordham University, n.d.; and University of Arkansas, Fort Smith, n.d.). Instructors developed online pedagogy when they realized physical classroom teaching strategies do not directly translate to virtual spaces (Cargile Cook, 2005; O'Brien, 2009; Terblanché, 2015). Even instructors with years of physical classroom experience might "become novices" online (Coppola, 2005, p. 97), including critical communication pedagogues.

Regardless of degree of mediation, current Web 2.0 LMSes promote objectivist, teacher-centered learning. Freire (1970/2010) described objectivist instruction as the banking style of education, where "the teacher issues communiqués and makes deposits which the students patiently receive, memorize, and repeat" (p. 72). Cargile Cook (2005) suggested widely used LMSes, like Blackboard or Moodle, easily facilitate situations where "students read course materials, complete self-paced activities and pretest, and then take final tests to assess their learning" with limited student-peer or student-instructor interactions and LMS-enforced learning patterns (p. 52). For instance, online pedagogical literature often argued effective online spaces rely on prescribed learning patterns from which learners are not allowed to deviate. Hodge, Collins, and Giordano (2011) suggested instructors should "outline the entire course [including] content, assignments, interaction, assessment, and evaluation methods [to] identify appropriate materials [and] determine the tools you will need to effectively deliver *your* content" (p. 221, emphasis added). Most online instructors control content, justification for learning, acceptable student behaviors, and assessment in their digital spaces. Despite a few scholars (e.g., Palloff and Pratt, 2009) origin that student control of learning and assessment increases engagement in online classes, most emphasize control for ease of student navigation and reduction of instructor workload (Chapnick & Meloy, 2005; Conceição & Lehman, 2011). While online pedagogy literature focuses on ways to help students through learning challenges, most literature currently does not address power structures built into the widely accepted instructional practices. Much of the online pedagogy literature diverges from critical pedagogy practices.

Critical communication pedagogy prioritizes dialogic instruction efforts "by people concerned with education to embrace profound ideological difference and socioeconomic context as constitutive of what happens in schools and classrooms" (Fassett & Warren, 2007, p. 26).[1] Critical pedagogy contrasts in profound ways from the largely teacher-centered online pedagogy best practices. On a fundamental level, critical pedagogues prioritize how the societal structures underlying classrooms' function as an integral part of instructional design. Shor (1992) suggested that "the learning process is negotiated, requiring leadership by the teacher and mutual teacher-student authority" (p. 16). Critical pedagogues recognize students who spend years submitting to the authority of teachers create society members untrained to fight injustice, thus denying "citizen status as members of democracy" (Shor, 1996, p. 31).

The divergent nature of the pedagogical practices initially appears difficult to overcome. Critical communication pedagogy manifests as instruction with the intent to encourage the skills needed to dissent and fight injustice, and online pedagogy starts with context. Critical pedagogy emphasizes dialogic exchange, which is touted as important by many online pedagogy scholars (e.g., Richardson, 2010). In practice, online pedagogues often forsake dialogue for instructor planning and student ease of navigating the online context (e.g., Johnson-Curiskis, 2006). Online pedagogy scholars justify objectivist practices as necessity, while critical pedagogues find banking-model notions implacable.

Outright dismissal of alternative teaching practices ignores important learning opportunities. Mediated contexts are often new learning and professional communication spaces for students. Despite a digital native[2] status, many students find navigating LMSes difficult, and the lack of face-to-face communication makes mediated classrooms challenging for many students. Students must manage time and learning more actively than in passive, lecture-based classroom spaces. Critical pedagogues similarly challenge students to engage in their own education through co-creating learning spaces and taking ownership of the learning process. In this way, an online space opens a unique context for critical pedagogy to thrive. Students create new learning habits in online spaces; here, critical communication pedagogy can influence how learners self-advocate for more effective teaching strategies across all education contexts. Andragogy provides a useful scaffold across the divergence between pedagogical perspectives by balancing the needs of the learner with the context and who has authority over the content and learning space.

In the United States, Knowles (1962) elevated the concept of andragogy to address the surge of adult learners and their learning motivations (Peterson, 1979). Knowles (1970) argued children's dependence on the resources of others underlies traditional childhood learning environments. The passive, obligatory nature of pedagogical spaces does not match adult self-reliance. Adults depend on their own resources to survive and thrive, including in education spaces. Sogunro (2015) explained, "Generally, adult learners perceive learning as a means to an end" (p. 29). Adults require active learning spaces based on end goals rather than obligation (Knowles, 1984). Knowles, Holton, and Swanson (1998) reported adult learners need to know and be motivated by the purpose of the learning, to feel in control, to have their previous experience valued in the learning process, to apply knowledge gained in everyday tasks, and to be driven by internal motivation. Espousing andragogy usually means rethinking typical classroom structures to accommodate the alternative learning styles adults prioritize.

Remodeling from a pedagogy-focused to an andragogically grounded classroom requires the same type of perspective shift required to convert from agentic to critical pedagogy practices. Similarly, transferring face-to-face classes to online contexts requires more than rote transcription of oral practices. While similarities exist between physical/digital, pedagogy/andragogy, and objectivist/critical pedagogy classrooms, the language and structure fundamentally change when the instructor engages in effective translation. Translating to digitally mediated critical communication pedagogy spaces is informed by applying effective online pedagogy and andragogy principles.

Praxis demonstrates theory in tangible ways (Wink, 1997), but no isolated practice creates effective learning situations, regardless of whether the focus is on context, learner, or authority. The application of a single andragogical practice (e.g., learning contracts) does not make a classroom adult-learner focused. Fassett and Warren (2007) bemoan the articulation of critical classroom practices as foolish. Decontextualized classroom actions are not, prima facie, critical, andragogical, or effective online pedagogy in nature. Removing the instructor, students, and learning environment from the action may fundamentally shift pedagogical implementation. Critical pedagogy examples are not critical without the proper context. Similarly, context drives effective mediated pedagogy, and learner motivations influence andragogy application. However, moving from theory to praxis for classroom diversity digitally mediated classrooms requires discussion of practices. Therefore, the following sections lay out possible classroom acts a teacher might take to more effectively create critical digital learning spaces.

Classroom preparation does not look the same for any two people much less any two instructional approaches. However, relying on the con/divergences with/in/between online pedagogy, andragogy, and critical communication pedagogy (CCP) provides a theoretical framework for thoughtful, reflexive praxis. For the purpose of simplicity, the following framework assumes the course is a fully online, mostly asynchronous (read: can have a minimal number of synchronous meetings during the semester, but students expect few situations where they compulsorily must attend during a specific time frame), and a typical three and a half month class with one instructor.

IDENTIFYING WHERE STUDENTS (AND PROFESSORS) ENTER THE SPACE

Online pedagogy scholars emphasize the online readiness model as an important way to gauge student success within the online context (e.g., Cigdam & Yildirim, 2014; Johnson-Curiskis, 2007; Rude, 2005; and Sherblom, Withers, & Leonard, 2013). Yu and Richardson (2015) noted online readiness should assess social, communication, and technological competencies, due to their influence on student learning outcomes. Closely examining the available tools in an online class can help instructors "understand learners' needs and preempt problems"; a learner readiness profile presents such an opportunity (Conceição & Lehman, 2011, p. 85). Many universities require students to complete an online readiness questionnaire or course prior to enrolling in online classes to help students recognize their own potential pitfalls. Online readiness assessments may be administered via an LMS quiz option or an alternative university-standard tool. Assessing student digital literacy and technology hard/software opens or closes communication and learning opportunities professors can embed within the course.

Unfortunately, after gathering information about students' hardware and technology savvy, many online pedagogues stop assessing initial knowledge. CCP ideally begins by identifying existing and desired knowledge. Co-created learning spaces blossom based on student knowledge of concepts, what students want to learn, and how students want to learn. Online readiness measures channel aptitude. CCP seeks the information as part of the way we attempt to subvert disempowering objectivist practices. Andragogy bridges the differences between CCP and online pedagogy.

Andragogues contend instructors must value adult learners' prior experiences; unvalued prior experience decreases adult engagement with content.

The individualized learning environment creates a customer-service education model based in productivity and efficiency. Personalized content engages students more readily than prepackaged, one-size-fits-none pedagogy applied semester after semester without updates or renovations. CCP uses similar pedagogical approaches, but the subversive learning practices attempt to disrupt reduplication of hierarchical oppression. Rather than prioritizing capitalist notions, CCP approaches learning contexts as co-created spaces whereby dialogic principles are utilized to explore content while simultaneously exploring practices to displace injustice. Many students learning in a new mediated context seek the familiarity of the physical classroom; students look to instructors for clarity as a way to combat their insecurities in online spaces. CCP overwhelms students steeped in objectivist situations whose school experiences always included the instructor-as-dictator models. Co-justifying baseline knowledge as a way to connect learning to individual goals bridges the already uncertain student to the CCP approach. Instead of requiring students to leap from objectivist to anarchist pedagogy, the andragogical justifications for baseline gathering help students recognize the value of alternative pedagogical approaches without requiring immediate dismissal of all prior learning environment expectations.

Simultaneously, online CCP instructors need to identify their own motivations, strengths, weaknesses, and goals for the course. When students face the challenges of learning in a new context with a new pedagogical style, they rely upon the instructor to be the expert. Bawa (2016) found online retention suffered when professors were ill equipped to address technological issues. Gillette (1999) rightfully pointed out, "We often take the [physical] classroom for granted. We are surrounded by a wide assortment of technologies that we use so often with such precision and lack of forethought, that we have internalized them and begun to think of them as part of our own teaching" (pp. 23–24). Online classrooms require knowledge and setup of new resources. Physical classroom spaces provide limited methods for conveying content, but online classrooms convey content to meet multiple student learning styles (Carter & Rickly, 2005). Chapnick and Meloy (2005) cautioned multiple learning paths increase course chaos and advocated instructors limit learning path options.

Online pedagogy literature identifies numerous ways content can be conveyed online, including research about effective lectures (e.g., Lyons, Reysen, & Pierce, 2012; Pflugfelder, 2013; Smith, 2008) and the benefits/detriments between a/synchronous communication media (e.g., Finkelstein, 2006; Hood & Lander, 2016). Online teachers use tools such as virtual worlds (e.g., Hodge, Collins, & Giordano, 2011) or media platforms like blogs, wikis, and social networks (e.g., Richardson, 2010; Solomon & Schrum, 2010) to reach students. Determine which of these learning resources you have competence in using and in which you need to develop confidence. Instructors need to seek training in online teaching tools (e.g., Finkelstein, 2006; Hodge, Collins, & Giordano, 2011; MERLOT.org, n.d.; Richardson, 2010; Solomon & Schrum, 2010).

The three pedagogy perspectives converge to suggest learner profiles provide an important starting point for mediated CCP, and andragological justifications provide students a more palatable way to overthrow expected objectivist practices. Learner profiles may seek information about student background knowledge of the content, learning styles, educational success criteria, learning expectations and motivations, available hardware, software skills, computer-mediated communication competence, and obligations outside the classroom (Fassett & Warren, 2007; Grady & Davis, 2005; Kincheloe, 2008; and Shor, 1996). While CCP recognizes students' preexisting knowledge and motivations for entering a classroom, neither highlight the readiness for learning specifically. Critical pedagogues may benefit in physical and digital spaces from engaging in a critical pedagogy readiness assessment. Students well versed in subversive teaching strategies where they participate in co-creating the classroom may require fewer justifications and explanations of CCP, whereas students whose education existed only in objectivist spaces may need more guidance early in the semester to understand expectations. Future research may design potential instruments to help students assess their CCP readiness, and implementation of said instruments may be vital to helping students recognize their roles in CCP classrooms online. Following the results of the instruments (especially in online settings), instructors may find learners benefit from introductory activities to explain and motivate participation in CCP (e.g., Walker & Brunner, 2017).

ADDRESSING THE AMBIGUITY AND ANXIETY

Ambiguity in computer-mediated classroom spaces exists for students and instructors. Physical classroom participants benefit from the physical classroom affordances (e.g., the ability to immediately ask clarifying questions), but most significantly, nearly all learners have experience learning in a physical space. Carter and Rickly (2005) contended online learners need to overcome the muscle memory of learning in a classroom without "all the physical trappings of pursuing learning" (p. 130). They described the physical aspects of class (e.g., the weight of a backpack, designated learning spaces and times) as a notable difference between physical and virtual classrooms. In essence, online learners are mastering course content and "learning how to learn" in mediated spaces (Chapnick & Meloy, 2005, p. 35). CCP explores ways to break students out of typical learning experiences to topple oppressive educational structures (ideally with students heading the wrecking crew). Because students already engage in a new learning space in online classrooms, CCP is uniquely positioned to embed democratic processes and shared learning responsibilities into the learning environment if the students can overcome the ambiguity.

Online retention must inform the ways CCP is engaged online. Bawa's (2016) comprehensive literature review of online retention found 40 to 80 percent of online students drop out of their online classes and programs. Bawa noted a wide variety of reasons, but key components dealt with ambiguity and increased student accountability. The ambiguity of an online classroom with the typically nonverbal-impoverished communication channels may make students feel anxious or unprepared. Students expect online classes to be completely self-paced, intuitive, and asynchronous (Bawa, 2016; Hickey, 2014), even if students are not equipped or ready for that level of responsibility. Compounded by the anxiety of learning in a new space and the increased accountability to complete tasks without physical reminders, many students seek clear structure and routine in online spaces. Online learning, then, becomes less about content and more about completing the carefully laid out to-do lists within the meticulously crafted cyberspace classroom provided by instructors.

Many professors respond by providing carefully pre-slated course spaces where assignments and resources are provided before even speaking with students. Though unreflexive, pre-created courses respond to the ambiguity students loathe. Coincidentally, professors also benefit from less ambiguity in online classes. Conceição and Lehman (2011) identified administrative, facilitative, and evaluative as categories of instructor tasks that happen while conducting the class. Administrative tasks exist regardless of teaching approach (e.g., taking attendance, inputting grades). Online pedagogues Caplan and Graham (2008) reminded their readers that online professors spend more time creating learning resources (e.g., online lectures, assignment descriptions) before they actually teach the class. The communication requirements and time spent assessing learning during the class mirror typical classroom teaching, so the overall amount of time needed to teach an online course far exceeds a typical face-to-face course.

The first few weeks of a physical CCP classroom include co-creating some or all of the course, from objectives to resources to assignments to assessments. The synchronous conversations and face-to-face interactions help mitigate anxiety students face in CCP classrooms when they are asked to eschew prior pedagogical training. The context-based anxiety coupled with the pedagogical anxiety may spur students to drop or withdraw when the course does not meet expectations. To respond to student needs, critical pedagogues need to take a lesson from andragogy: connect the minutiae to the big picture in conscious ways.

Andragogy recognizes adults do not engage in learning for the sake of learning. Instead, adults tend to engage in learning to accomplish specific tasks. After andragogues gather baseline data about adult learners during the student identification stage, andragogues move students toward course objectives through co-created learner contracts. Knowles (1984) suggested learning contracts should include learning objectives (connected to knowledge, skills, or other acquirable concepts), the paths and evaluation methods through which objectives will be met, and the timeline for objective completion. The self-directed nature of learning contracts help adults feel respected for their knowledge and goals while providing self-directed learning opportunities.

Andragogical structure provides ways for mediated CCP to overcome the absent physical classroom space while still dissolving oppressive power structures. Online pedagogy necessarily includes self-directed, autonomous learning, so online CCP instructors may choose to utilize learning contracts. Having gathered information during the readiness section of the course, online CCP instructors can have students co-create learning contracts describing the ways students plan to achieve learning objectives. Posting the learning plans and course progress in online discussion boards may be a way for students to visually see how other students are learning/engaging the material while also providing a level of responsibility to the other students. When students know peers will see their work, the stakes get higher and the work tends to be more engaged. Additionally, knowing the learning plans of peers creates more of a sense of community while still providing a self-directed, learner-centric learning environment. Learning contracts need to include certain components: specific objectives, ways students intend to reach the objectives, and a schedule to complete the objectives. CCP may use learning contracts to help students control the ways they master content while decreasing the ambiguity of the online learning space. However, students will not complete any work if they do not feel motivated.

CREATING SPACE FOR (SELF-)MOTIVATION

The "to-do" list model of online pedagogy emphasizes accessibility of homework over self-motivated learning. CCP relies on establishing trust via making authentic connections with students to encourage full participatory creation and engagement. The nonverbal-deficient computer-mediated context makes establishing trust and authentic connections more difficult to build. Learner analysis in andragogy centers student motivation in understanding the learner and their external motivations. Andragogy emphasizes the importance of learner motivation for pursuing education as justification for course objectives. However, andragogy relies on authority-based classroom management creating a climate of trust and respect (Knowles, 1970). While not as subversive as CCP, andragogues do not enter the classroom space assuming students will submit to their authority. Andragogues assume they must earn the trust of students by demonstrating mutual respect for prior learning, while simultaneously providing high-quality information and leadership *related to the adults' goals for the course.*

Online CCP may benefit from utilizing the focus andragogy puts on student motivations when co-creating the course. Prior sections described how learning contracts create more certainty for students to combat the contextual issues faced in online spaces. Online CCP instructors may choose to provide reminders (or better yet, have students create reflections each week) describing the ways their tasks associate with the goals for the course and larger life goals set by the student. Ideally, CCP instructors will find ways to develop internal motivation beyond students saying, "I wanna get a good job." Instead, during the initial learner profiling, instructors can ask questions about life goals as humans (not just as productivity monkeys). How do you want to change the world? How do you want to change your community? How will this class impact your path toward those goals? By helping the students recognize the ways the activities they created connect to larger life goals, the students may feel motivation beyond the to-do list.

FROM THEORY TO PRAXIS

Andragogy, online pedagogy, and critical pedagogy are three teaching approaches focused on three different things: learner motivation, context, and smashing power structures. Scholars have connected andragogy to critical pedagogy (e.g., Schapiro, 2003) and andragogy to online pedagogy (Morrison, 2015), but exploring the con/divergences with/in/between all three provides insights into ways to apply critical pedagogy in online contexts. Until more reports are widely shared about online critical pedagogy, we must look to existing theory to inform praxis so we can begin to create theory that will inform better reflexive praxis. Through identifying where students and professors enter the space, addressing the ambiguity of the context, and specifically prioritizing the notion of motivation, instructors may find better success into initial forays into mediated critical communication pedagogy.

NOTES

1. Kincheloe (2008) argued, "Descriptions of critical pedagogy . . . are shaped by those who devise them and the values they hold . . . many will agree with it . . . while others will be disappointed—even offended—by what was included and what was left out" (pp. 5–6). I recognize selecting a single definition for critical communication pedagogy is problematic, but I provide a working definition for the purposes of dialogue.
2. "Digital natives" is admittedly a very problematic term. Despite the inherent privilege associated with access to technology, digital native status implies the individual intuitively

understands all CMC. In reality, many digital natives still struggle in educational settings (e.g., academic database searches).

REFERENCES

Barber, W., King, S., & Buchanan, S. (2015). Problem based learning and authentic assessment in digital pedagogy: Embracing the role of collaborative communities. *Electronic Journal of e-Learning, 13*(2), 59–67.

Bawa, P. (2016). Retention in online courses: Exploring issues and solutions—A literature review. *Sage OPEN*, (1), 1–11. doi: 10.1177/2158244015621777

Caplan, D., & and Graham, R. (2008). The development of online courses. In T. Anderson (Ed.), *The theory and practice of online learning* (2nd ed., pp 245–63). Edmonton, Alberta, Canada: AU Press.

Cargile Cook, K., & Grant-Davie, K. (2005). *Online education: Global questions, local answers*. Amityville, NY: Baywood.

Carter, L., & Rickly, R. (2005). Mind the gap(s): Modeling space in online education. In K. Cargile Cook & K. Grant-Davie (Eds.), *Online education: Global questions, local answers* (pp. 123–39). Amityville, NY: Baywood.

Caruthers, L., & Friend, J. (2014). Critical pedagogy in online environments as thirdspace: A narrative analysis of voices of candidates in educational preparatory programs. *Educational Studies: Journal of the American Educational Studies Association, 50*(1), 8–35.

Chapnick, S., & Meloy, J. (2005). *Renaissance eLearning: Creating dramatic and unconventional learning experiences*. San Francisco, CA: Pfeiffer.

Cigdam, H., & Yildirim, O. G. (2014). Effects of students' characteristics on online learning readiness: A vocational college example. *Turkish Online Journal of Distance Education, 15*(3), 80–93.

Conceição, S. C. O., & Lehman, R. M. (2011). *Managing online instructor workload: Strategies for finding balance and success*. San Francisco, CA: Jossey-Bass.

Coppola, N. W. (2005). Changing roles for online teachers of technical communication. In K. Cargile Cook & K. Grant-Davie (Eds.), *Online education: Global questions, local answers* (pp. 89–99). Amityville, NY: Baywood.

DeVoogd, G. L., Loveless, A. M., & Yelland, N. (2000). In search of the revolutionary power of critical pedagogy: Issues of ideology, power, and culture in technology teacher education. Paper presented at the Society for Information Technology and Teacher Education international conference.

Donlevy, J. G., & Donlevy, T. R. (2000). Concept to classroom: Web-based workshops for teachers. *International Journal of Instructional Media, 27*(2), 129–32.

Duffelmeyer, B. B. (2000). Critical computer literacy: Computers in first-year composition as topic and environment. *Computers and Composition, 17*(3), 289–307.

Duffelmeyer, B. B. (2002). Critical work in first-year composition: Computers, pedagogy, and research. *Pedagogy, 2*(3), 357.

Fassett, D. L., & Warren, J. T. (2007). *Critical communication pedagogy*. Thousand Oaks, CA: Sage.

Finkelstein, J. (2006). *Learning in real time: Synchronous teaching and learning online*. San Francisco, CA: Jossey-Bass.

Fordham University. (n.d.). Types of online learning. Retrieved from http://www.fordham.edu/info/24884/online_learning/7897/types_of_online_learning.

Freire, P. (1970/2010). *Pedagogy of the oppressed* (M. Bergman Ramos, Trans.). New York, NY: Continuum.

Gillette, D. (1999). Pedagogy, architecture, and the virtual classroom. *Technical Communication Quarterly, 8*(1), 21–36.

Grady, H. M., & Davis, M. T. (2005). Teaching well online with instructional and procedural scaffolding. In K. Cargile Cook & K. Grant-Davie (Eds.), *Online education: Global questions, local answers* (pp. 101–22). Amityville, NY: Baywood.

Hart, Z. P. (2014). Hybrid online teaching: Pathway to success for "traditional" universities. *Kentucky Journal of Communication, 33*(1), 40–51.
Hickey, R. (2014, December 5). 5 most common misconceptions about online education. Retrieved from https://www.petersons.com/college-search/5-most-common-misconceptions-about-online-education.aspx#/sweeps-modal.
Hodge, E., Collins, S., & Giordano, T. (2011). *The virtual worlds handbook: How to use Second Life® and other 3D virtual environments*. Sudbury, MA: Jones and Bartlett.
Hood, S., & Lander, J. (2016). Technologies, modes and pedagogic potential in live versus online lectures. *International Journal of Language Studies, 10*(3), 23–42.
Johnson-Curiskis, N. (2006). Online course planning. *Journal of Online Teaching and Learning, 2*(1), 42–48.
Johnson-Curiskis, N. (2007). Pre-registration for online courses. *Journal of Online Learning and Teaching, 3*(2), n.p.
Kalogeras, S. (2013). Storytelling: an ancient human technology and critical-creative pedagogy for transformative learning. *International Journal of Information and Communication Technology Education, 9*(4), 113–23.
Kincheloe, J. L. (2008). *Critical pedagogy primer* (2nd Ed.). New York: Peter Lang.
Knowles, M. S. (1962). *The adult education movement in the United States*. New York: Holt, Rinehart and Winston.
Knowles, M. S. (1970). *The modern practice of adult education: Andragogy versus pedagogy*. New York: Association Press.
Knowles, M. S. (1984). *Andragogy in action: Applying modern principles of adult learning*. San Francisco, CA: Jossey-Bass.
Knowles, M. S., Holton III, E. F., & Swanson, R. A. (1998). *The adult learner: The definitive classic in adult education and human resource development* (5th ed.). Houston, TX: Routledge.
Lavooy, M. J., & Newlin, M. H. (2003). Computer mediated communication: Online instruction and interactivity. *Journal of Interactive Learning Research, 14*(2), 157–65.
Lyons, A., Reysen, S., & Pierce, L. (2012). Video lecture format, student technological efficacy, and social presence in online courses. *Computers in Human Behavior, 28*(1), 181–86. doi:10.1016/j.chb.2011.08.025
McCurry, D. (2000). Technology for critical pedagogy: Beyond self-reflection with video. In D. Willis, J. Price & J. Willis (Eds.), *Proceedings of SITE 2000—Society for Information Technology & Teacher Education International Conference* (pp. 6–11). Chesapeake, VA: Association for the Advancement of Computing in Education (AACE). Retrieved from https://www.learntechlib.org/primary/p/15517/.
Morrison, D. (2015, September 25). How to make learning matter to online students [Blog post]. Retrieved from https://onlinelearninginsights.wordpress.com/2015/09/25/how-to-make-learning-matter-to-online-students/.
O'Brien, M. (2009). The e-learning industry: Facing the challenges of Web 2.0. *Rocky Mountain Communication Review, 6*(1), 57–61.
Palloff, R. M., & Pratt, K. (2009). *Assessing the online learner: Resources and strategies for faculty*. San Francisco, CA: Jossey-Bass.
Peterson, R. E. (1979). Present sources of education and learning. In R. E. Peterson, *Lifelong Learning in America* (pp. 13–74). San Francisco, CA: Jossey-Bass.
Pflugfelder, E. H. (2013). The minimalist approach to online instructional videos. *Technical Communication, 60*(2), 131–46.
Richardson, W. (2010). *Blogs, wikis, podcasts, and other powerful web tools for classrooms*. Thousand Oaks, CA: Corwin.
Rude, C. (2005). Strategic planning for online education: Sustaining students, faculty, and programs. In K. Cargile Cook & K. Grant-Davie (Eds.), *Online education: Global questions, local answers* (pp. 67–85). Amityville, NY: Baywood.
Schapiro, S. A. (2003). From andragogy to collaborative critical pedagogy: Learning for academic, personal, and social empowerment in a distance-learning PhD program. *Journal of Transformative Education. 1*(2), 150–68.

Sherblom, J. C., Withers, L. A., & Leonard, L. G. (2013). The influence of computer-mediated communication (CMC) competence on computer-supported collaborative learning (CSCL) in online classroom discussions. *Human Communication, 16*(1), 31–39.

Shor, I. (1992). *Empowering education: Critical teaching for social change*. Chicago, IL: The University of Chicago Press.

Shor, I. (1996). *When students have power: Negotiating authority in a critical pedagogy*. Chicago, IL: The University of Chicago Press.

Smith, R. M. (2008). *Conquering the content: A step-by-step guide to online course design*. San Francisco, CA: Jossey-Bass.

Sogunro, O. A. (2015). Motivating factors for adult learners in higher education. *International Journal of Higher Education, 4*(1), 22–37.

Solomon, G., & Schrum, L. (2010). *Web 2.0: How-to for educators*. Eugene, OR: International Society for Technology in Education.

Terblanché (2015). Deciding to teach online: Communication, opportunities and challenges for educators in distance education, *Communicatio, 41*(4), 543–63, DOI: 10.1080/02500167.2015.1115416.

University of Arkansas, Fort Smith. (n.d.). Types of online classes. Retrieved from http://academics.uafs.edu/distance-learning/types-online-courses.

U.S. Department of Education. (2018). National Center for Education Statistics, integrated postsecondary education data system (IPEDS), spring 2016 and spring 2017, fall enrollment components. Retrieved from https://nces.ed.gov/programs/digest/d17/tables/dt17_311.15.asp?current=yes.

Walker, J. L., & Brunner, K. M. (2017). Getting critical communication pedagogy *Accepted*: Using a popular culture portrayal of the education system to encourage a critique of the banking system. In K. C. Rudick, K. Golsan, & K. Cheesewright (Eds.), *Teaching from the heart: Critical communication pedagogy in the communication classroom* (pp. 132–39). San Diego, CA: Cognella.

Wink, J. (1997). *Critical pedagogy: Notes from the real world*. White Plains, NY: Longman.

Yu, T., & Richardson, J. C. (2015). An exploratory factor analysis and reliability analysis of the student online learning readiness (SOLR) instrument. *Online Learning, 19*(5), 120–41.

Chapter Four

New Media, New Possibilities

Engaging Diversity

Ahmet Atay

I left my office in a hurry, carrying my computer, our textbook, printed copies of our additional class reading, the class folder, one piece of milk chocolate, one piece of dark chocolate, and a bottle of water. As I struggled to carry everything, I managed to close my office door with my foot, causing a passing student to giggle at my perhaps not so scholarly act. As I walked through the hallway, I remembered that I had an electronic copy of the class reading and the textbook on my computer. On the short walk to the classroom, I quickly realized that I was "that professor," a generational hybrid—a little bit of Generation X and a little bit of Millennial. I often tried to incorporate technology into every aspect of my academic life, including teaching, but days like this reminded me that I was not a "digital native" in the traditional sense. As I walked into my regular orange-colored classroom, I noticed that most of my students were occupied with the cyber world, using either their smartphones or laptops to consume the latest news, play an online game, text message, or tweet. I set my large pile of belongings down as I greeted them. They noticed me and said a quick "hi" as if they were lost in a haze. I spent the next couple of minutes turning on the classroom computer and projection system and connecting my computer to the Apple TV. As I located my Power-Point presentation, I quickly checked the links I had embedded in the slides. I also opened the college's electronic film database and another film in the media text provider to find the materials I wanted to screen in class. As I was completing the last tasks before we began, my body was tickled by my smartphone in my left pocket. I was wired. I was ready to teach the class.

We live in a highly wired and a fast-paced culture, and we now expect that we embody and perform the technological expectations of this culture. Most of our everyday interactions are mediated in some form or another. As academics, we spend most of our waking hours in front of a screen, writing research papers and reports, preparing class notes, and sending and receiving non-stop e-mails. Most of us also use other technologies simultaneously, ranging from smartphones to tablets and wearables. We also spend a significant portion of our time talking on the phone, sending and receiving text messages, and interacting with technology or people through new (computers, laptops, smartphones, and wearables) or legacy media technologies (radio, television, and other technological devices prior to the development of new media technologies). For example, we pay for our coffees and lattes at the campus café with our credit cards, and we open our electronic doors or check out books with our college IDs. We pay our bills, scan our grocery items, measure our weight, and calculate our steps or calorie intake with a digital device, and we even wake up in the morning to a digital alarm sound. We use new media technologies to access information as well as write our papers and documents, and we attend to most of our academic duties through cyber technologies. We teach with these technologies, and similarly, our students conduct their academic lives with and through these technologies.

I don't fully believe that our technologies determine the development of our social structures and cultural values. However, I realize that technological tools and platforms, particularly new media technologies, increasingly occupy more significant roles in our lives. I believe that knowing and understanding both the positive and negative aspects of technology and mediated communication are important if we are to effectively function in today's highly wired culture, but I also think it is important to make informed decisions about our technology use in our professional lives as educators as well as in our everyday lives. Mediated critical communication pedagogy (MCCP) as an approach recognizes the importance of these interrelated social and cultural issues, and provides pedagogical and cultural tools to empower faculty and students by educating them about both the positive and negative potential of traditional and new media technologies. Hence, I argue that while new media technologies might produce new cultural and social anxieties, they also provide new opportunities for marginalized individuals to express their voices and new opportunities to empower students who learn differently. In this chapter, my goal is to illuminate some of these cultural forces as well as several social and academic issues. More specifically, I discuss the role of new media technologies in the lives of historically marginalized students and faculty, including international students and faculty, and I develop a new pedagogical approach that connects and truly embodies the link between diversity and mediated critical communication pedagogy. In order to offer mediated critical communication pedagogy as a pedagogical approach, which is infused with national and transnational sensibilities, I first discuss the notion of both national and transnational diversity. Second, I define the idea of mediated diversity. Finally, I focus on the role of mediated dialogue in the context of cultural diversity. As I use these ideas to further develop mediated critical communication pedagogy, in this essay, I also attempt to answer the following two questions related to this pedagogical approach: What is the role of diversity in MCCP? And what are some of the benefits and drawbacks of MCCP for diversity?

DIVERSITY AND POSITIONING MYSELF

Media technologies and cyber platforms occupied a paramount role in my educational experiences and social life as an international student in U.S. higher education. Technologies such as the Internet, online messengers, social network sites, research databases, online dictionaries, and online grammar sites shaped my experiences in positive ways. Like the other international students, I came to the U.S. to seek a higher education. The certain aspects of the academic culture I encountered encouraged us to use not only new media technologies but also online resources, such as education technologies and library databases, to enhance our learning and improve our social lives as part of our cultural adaptation process. The same technologies also enabled me to keep in touch with my parents, members of my extensive family, and friends around the world. These technologies connected my cultural worlds and helped me function in U.S. higher education. For example, sometimes I used web-based translators to look up the academic words I was hearing for the first time. Sometimes I used ESL- (English as a Second Language) or ELL- (English Language Learning) related websites to look up a sentence structure or the grammatical use of words, or to ensure that my APA or MLA citations were correct. I am sure I was only one of the thousands of international students who depended on new media technologies to function in the academy. I am equally certain the technologies that students in general and international students in particular use have changed and evolved as has their role in our students' lives.

I started this section with my own story to position myself as a scholar within the discourse of diversity. I am a transnational queer scholar who analyzes media texts and produces critical and cultural studies scholarship. This positionality informs my pedagogical approaches and teaching methods regardless of the course content. I live the diversity; hence, I am committed to diversity within and outside of the classroom. Furthermore, I am also committed to opening up spaces within the classroom as well as in higher education in general to allow historically marginalized faculty and students to articulate their voices. Regardless of the criticism of new media, cyber technologies, and digital platforms, I believe these technologies allow teachers to teach differently and enable students, specifically international students, to learn differently.

Diversity often refers to non-mainstream identities, cultures, and ways of being and knowing. Within the U.S. context, diversity refers to people who belong to historically marginalized groups and occupy such positions as they live their lives within the mainstream culture, including within higher education (Martin & Nakayama, 2014; Yep, 2002). Hence, "diversity" is an umbrella term that encompasses individuals who may be of a different race or gender, who have a different ethnicity, sexual orientation, ability, or disability, or who come from a different socioeconomic or class backgrounds. Within the discourse of diversity, we have to differentiate those individuals who represent national (or domestic) and international diversity. Individuals who come from different national and linguistic backgrounds or occupy different immigration and citizenship statuses are often described as diverse within the U.S. context by administrators. Some individuals can also belong to multiple identity categories in many ways; thus they can be described as having multiple diversity descriptions or positions. For example, as a former international student and now transnational scholar, I occupy different linguistic, nationality, ethnic, gender, sexuality, and class categories, many of which often intersect, overlap, or contradict each other depending on who is describing me and in what context. In this essay, I consistently move between these constructions and try to articulate how educators can use mediated critical communication pedagogy as an approach to speak to or educate the student groups we define and describe as nationally or internationally diverse within the context of U.S. higher education. Even though I recognize that there are differences in national and international diversity in U.S. higher education, due to linguistic and citizenship differences, I take an intersectional perspective in this essay to recognize the overlapping nature of our identities, standpoints, and oppressions (Crenshaw, 1991; Yep, 2013; Yep & Lescure, 2019).

EXPERIENCING DIVERSITY IN ACADEMIA

There are two possible ways to discuss the link between mediated pedagogies and diversity. One is to look at the mediated representations of diversity in television, film, news, advertising, or other forms of traditional and new media. For example, instructors could have a rich discussion about how varying media texts represent racial minorities or LGBTQ+ individuals. Presumably, these discussions will make the ideologies embedded in such mediated representations more apparent. Jennifer Bondy and Lisa Pennington (2016) write, "Scholars in the fields of cultural studies, critical media literacy, and critical pedagogy have argued that media texts are a powerful educator that organize, shape, and disseminate values, meanings, and ideas about the world" (p. 103). It is important to recognize that in a very highly mediated culture, media texts often function as teachers or educational materials for multiple groups of people, mainly for the college-age students.

The second way to look at the relationship between diversity and media is to focus on how the students with different backgrounds and identity standpoints use new media technologies in and outside of the classroom to learn and interact with course content. Their modes of interaction might be different than our conventional ways; nevertheless, through these new media technologies, these students can still mindfully engage in the course content and they can also gain unexpected insights. Although I value both these approaches, in this essay, I will focus on the latter to discuss the link between diversity and MCCP. My goal is to discuss the ways in which historically marginalized and international students as well as faculty might use new media technologies to teach and to learn.

Building on Paulo Freire's (1970) work, critical communication pedagogy (CCP) focuses on creating cultural change by both recognizing the existing power dynamics in our classrooms and by identifying ways students can empower themselves, including students from historically marginalized communities. In their book, Deanna Fassett and John Warren (2007) see tremendous possibilities for engaging in advocacy work in the classroom by inviting students to articulate their voices and cultural standpoints. They write, "Pedagogy is advocacy" (p. 32). Therefore, as CCP scholars, we see the communication classroom as a venue where we can cultivate a community of learners who are committed to social justice, diversity, and equity. Fassett and Warren offer ten different commitments of CCP. In their very first commitment, Fassett and Warren acknowledge the link between the cultural identities we occupy and perform in the classroom and the classroom as a physical and intellectual space. They argue that "in critical communication pedagogy, identity is constituted in communication" (p. 39). Similarly, in their second commitment, they postulate that "critical communication educators understand power as fluid and complex" (p. 41). In both commitments, the authors highlight the importance of how our cultural identities are constructed, negotiated, and performed even in the classroom, and they reiterate that the communication we engage in is never free of the power structures that either empower or disempower us. Both of Fassett and Warren's commitments guide my thinking in relation to diversity and mediation. Now allow me to connect the dots.

Most of our current students are either part of the Millennial generation or Generation Z; hence, they are known for being technologically savvy even though they might be simply users of technologies without critically understanding their power or mechanical compositions. They also make up the most diverse generations in the history of the U.S. Nowadays, while members of the older generations are also heavily using new media technologies, Millennials and the members of Generation Z are different because they were born into a highly wired, media-driven, digitalized culture (boyd, 2014; Jenkins, 2006). According to JingJing Jiang, in a 2018 article titled "Millennials Stand Out for Their Technology Use, but Older Generations Also Embrace Digital Life,"

> More than nine-in-ten Millennials (92%) own smartphones, compared with 85% of Gen Xers (those who turn ages 38 to 53 this year), 67% of Baby Boomers (ages 54 to 72) and 30% of the Silent Generation [generation before the Baby Boomers] (ages 73 to 90), according to a new analysis of Pew Research Center data. Similarly, the vast majority of Millennials (85%) say they use social media. For instance, significantly larger shares of Millennials have adopted relatively new platforms such as Instagram (52%) and Snapchat (47%) than older generations have.

These numbers are fascinating but also very telling about the nature of our highly wired and digitalized culture.

Dimcok (2019) describes Generation Z as "anyone born from 1997 onward" and "part of a new generation." Similar to millennials, Gen Zers were born into a highly wired culture. Unlike the members of the millennial generation, they also grew up with smartphone technologies, tablets, and other portable electronic devices, social network sites, and global online streaming technologies and platforms, such as Hulu, Netflix, and Amazon Prime. Dimock writes,

> In this progression, what is unique for Generation Z is that all of the above have been part of their lives from the start. The iPhone launched in 2007, when the oldest Gen Zers were 10. By the time they were in their teens, the primary means by which young Americans connected with the web was through mobile devices, Wi-Fi and high-bandwidth cellular service. Social media, constant connectivity and on-demand entertainment and communication are innovations Millennials adapted to as they came of age. For those born after 1996, these are largely assumed.

Unlike previous generations, the members of Generation Z grew up with complete connectivity. The digital divide still certainly exists because still people who are in a particular financial bracket can afford technologies or access to the Internet or other serves. However the vast majority of the younger generations owns a smartphone of some sort thanks to the affordability of such technologies. For example, most if not all of our international students possess high-tech gadgets, such as smartphones or tablets. However, a digital divide still exists and students from particular counties can have easier access to these technologies compared to students from other contries. Over the years because of the market-driven needs, most of the technological devices depending on their models or capabilities are priced differently, making it affordable to people from different socioeconomic backgrounds. Hence, these technologies are making all of us wired, highly connected, and even global.

Millennials are the most demographically diverse U.S. generation. According to Richard Fry, Ruth Igielnik, and Eileen Patten (2018),

> In 2017, fewer than six-in-ten Millennials (56%) were non-Hispanic whites, compared with more than eight-in-ten (84%) Silents. The share who are Hispanic is five times as large among Millennials as among Silents (21% vs. 4%), and the share who are Asian has also increased. However, the share who are black has remained roughly the same.

However, the latest demographic numbers now suggest that Generation Z is the most diverse generation of all time. Richard Fry and Kim Parker (2018) suggest that the "new Pew Research Center analysis of Census Bureau data finds that the 'post-Millennial' generation is already the most racially and ethnically diverse generation, as a bare majority of 6- to 21-year-olds (52%) are non-Hispanic whites." These numbers clearly suggest that most of our students represent some type of ethnic, racial, class, gender, or sexual orientation diversity.

Our student body is more complex, diverse, and highly wired. Considering that we are predominantly educating the members of the Millennial Generation and Generation Z, we must pay closer attention to their demographics as well as their cultural complexities, needs, desires, and expectations, especially within our communication classrooms. In addition to the increase in domestic diversity that is due to the shifts in U.S. demographics, U.S. universities are also experiencing an increase in the number of international students. According to the Power of International Education website, there are more than 1.09 million international students on our campuses. Along with the historically marginalized students (such as racial and ethnic minorities, women, LGBTQ+, students with disabilities, and students who come from less privileged socioeconomic backgrounds), these international students are also turning our classrooms and campuses into diverse cosmopolitan spaces.

Within these cosmopolitan spaces, there are also historically marginalized as well as international faculty, some of whom are millennials themselves and educating a very diverse student population. Like our students, these faculty are also wired, technologically savvy, and globally connected. All of these forces are collectively influencing and changing the ways we teach, the ways our students learn, and how we are positioned and evolve within academia. To thread all of these forces and issues together, at the moment, we are educating very diverse and highly wired students who are fully immersed in the digital culture. They communicate differently. Their understanding of community, cultural identity, and belonging are different, often fluid, and also digitally constructed and performed. They grew up writing with new media technologies alongside pens and pencils, and they read e-books instead of their printed versions. They use online technologies to access information or translate and new media technologies to socialize, access information, and learn.

In the next section, I present two cases studies where I use a mediated critical communication approach to make sense of the link between diversity and the usage of new media technologies in the classroom. These two personal stories, separately and together, offer examples of how new media technologies were used by students who either came from different cultural backgrounds or had different education experiences to seek for information or translate. These two stories also embody cultural sensitivities toward the difference that mediated critical communication pedagogy approach is committed to.

DIVERSITY AND MEDIATED CRITICAL COMMUNICATION PEDAGOGY

Case 1

It was another class period in my Visual Communication and Culture course. Following the suggestions provided in my last student evaluations, I incorporated many photos, video clips, and other visual materials to provide examples and context for some of the concepts and theories we would discuss during the semester. This way I can also embody a mediated critical communication pedagogical approach to provide students tools to critically analyze mediated texts. On this particular day, we were covering the link between impressionism and photography, and our goal was to create a lineage of how art movements and visual culture technologies had informed each other. For this class period, I decided to use my notes, a long PowerPoint presentation to show the high number of images of important paintings, and two in-class activities. I found that in-class analysis with focused activities was very useful in this class. I began by asking the students if they had taken any college-level courses in art history or visual culture. Based on the hands in the air, I figured not many had. I began defining impressionism as an art movement and mentioned some key names and paintings before analyzing them in depth. As I was covering Eduard Manet, I noticed two of my students were frantically typing on their cell phones. I politely asked them to put their phones away. They did. As I moved on to talk about Renoir's famous **Bal du moulin de la Galette***, I noticed that they were back to typing on their cell phones. At that point, I decided to address the issue after class.*

At the end of the class, I asked the students to chat with me briefly, something I hardly ever did. I asked them why they were so busy text messaging and if everything was ok. Their answers were simple. They both stated that they had been a bit lost in the discussion of impressionism, and they were looking up more information about the artists and paintings we were talking about. We spent the next half an hour talking about their high school education. They wanted to share with me that they respected me too much to text during class, but they really wanted to access their devices to look up the information they did not have. I simply asked them why they chose not to ask me for clarification. They both very firmly stated that they did not want their peers to see them as less than based on their lack of art history information, which most of their peers had. At the end of our conversation, I told them I would try to provide more context and background information in the future. When the class met again, I told the students that they could use their computers and phones to look up more information on the artists, concepts, or artwork we were discussing. I also reminded the students that this would be the only reason for using their devices during the lectures, discussions, or in-class activities.

Case 2

I find teaching Intercultural Communication courses rewarding but also emotionally draining. Teaching topics about diversity is my academic passion despite the fact that it presents challenges, and often I feel heartbroken. This was one of those days.

It was not an ordinary day in my course because our topic was international students and their experiences in U.S. higher education. As a former international student, this subject was a bit too personal. I asked the students to read two narrative-based essays about the cultural barriers and issues around international students. Both of these pieces highlighted the issues around accent discrimination, the lack of empathy by mainstream faculty, and the lack of agency and power in the classroom for international students. Before class, I was worried about the responses of my two international students because they may be called to speak on behalf of all international students and some of these discussions might be fraught with microaggressions. I entered the classroom with some hesitations and a myriad of questions in mind. My memories of being an international student accompanied me into my classroom. As international students and faculty, we often suffer in silence, and I did not want my students to experience that suffering, at least not in my classroom. I asked the students a couple of questions about the readings, one on the issue of "the accent" and the other on language competencies and the cultural experience of "translation." Even though most of the students did not know much about the international students' *experiences and had not even considered these issues since they had not experienced them firsthand, we managed to generate an interesting and complex discussion.*

It was one of those emotionally complex moments when one of my international students raised her hand, volunteering to share her story. First, she told us how she felt very self-conscious about her accent then proceeded to articulate how painful it was for her when her peers asked her to repeat what she said, or when her professors asked for clarification or corrected her English. The silence in the classroom was dense. She also volunteered that she had been prohibited from using her online dictionary to translate. Sometimes, we all fail to mirror our experiences and emotions with the right words in a different language. She felt like a failure. Our education system had failed her. Our students sat in silence, processing her experiences and the heaviness of the moment. We had all failed to translate.

I chose to begin this section with two personal stories. In each, there is a clear connection between diversity and media usage.

MCCP invites a cultural and epistemological shift into our role as educators. Despite the drawbacks and financial costs of new media technologies, I believe they can provide new possibilities that facilitate and even require new critical pedagogical approaches. In the following section, I outline some of the clear connections between new media technologies and critical communication pedagogy as they relate to diversity.

First and foremost, critical pedagogy and critical communication pedagogy emerge from the idea of philosophical and practical classroom shifts that could empower students and introduce new approaches for engaging in advocacy work. These two issues occupy important roles in diversity discussions. To put the crucial elements of this discussion side by side, I return to my previous arguments on diversity and new media technologies: New media technologies can provide new possibilities for students who come from different backgrounds and who may have different educational needs to perform well in the classroom and also they provide new opportunities to express their voices and cultural positions. As faculty, we are currently educating the members of the two most diverse generations in U.S. history, which means that our students are different in terms of their abilities, educational and socio-economic backgrounds, and other demographic categories relating to identity politics. At the same time, their identities are multi-layered and shape-shifting. Furthermore, we also have an increasing number of international students with differing language competencies and cultural variations. Needless to say, the advocacy work that critical pedagogies are committed to might look very different in our communication classrooms and on our campuses at large. I recommend using this chapter to articulate how illuminating power structures looks with these students. A large portion of our diverse students understand and acknowledge their privileges and oppressions, and they are willing to share their experiences if the faculty members provide the right opportunities. Advocacy work that we might employ in the classroom as faculty, and diversity faculty in particular, might look very different than our previous advocacy work due to the changing student and faculty demographics. For example, similar to historically marginalized students, the faculty who come from non-mainstream backgrounds might openly articulate their experiences and connect with their students at a personal and cultural level despite personal risks and emotional labor. This type of advocacy work might also offer possibilities for identity-based community building and mentorships between faculty members and students.

Not only might our students be learning and accessing information differently, but they might also be engaging differently in advocacy work. For example, I began incorporating visual essays and podcasting assignments to connect my class content to everyday media and technologies. Students who might be described as weaker writers might be highly skilled visual storytellers or radio personalities. These types of opportunities not only encourage the students to excel in their stronger areas but also ask them to use the technologies around them to create new knowledge or critically analyze both the production and consumption of media texts and technologies. Moreover, I want to acknowledge that our students might be using new media technologies to engage in novel types of advocacy efforts. Similarly, I also believe that as faculty, we can also incorporate these technologies and digital forms, such as film production, blog writing, or photo essays, to open up multiple possibilities for ourselves and our students to perform civic engagement, social justice, and activism work.

As a media studies scholar, I understand both the issues that new media technologies present as well as the new opportunities they offer. Mediated critical pedagogy, as it engages with the issues of diversity, capitalizes on these opportunities. As I already pointed out, the demographics, skills, interests, abilities, and issues of our students vary and are continuously changing.

I want to emphasize that incorporating new media technologies and digital platforms into the course content would allow the faculty and students to critically reflect on the technologies themselves, how they are being used in our society and in the classroom, who is able to use them, and finally, what people are doing with these technologies. Taking this particular approach and framing the use of new media technologies as part of the class would allow students and faculty to not only engage in the technologies but also make sense of how they are being used or consumed. This framework would help to achieve two goals: 1) offering new media technologies as alternative or new opportunities to invite students to express their issues within and outside of the classroom and to engage in the class material through alternative means, and 2) to generate a discussion on how we can engage in diversity and social justice work by using these technologies. Obviously, these discussions would be much better suited for and more fruitful in certain types of classes, particularly those that grapple with the issues related to diversity. New media technologies and digital platforms, such as social network sites, discussion boards, blogs, and vlogs, would allow historically marginalized and international students to express their voices when they choose not to verbally articulate in traditional classroom settings. Through these alternative venues, these students can dialogue with faculty members and other students, especially in discussion boards, without being physically present in the classroom or worrying about their accents or disabilities that might hinder their participation in class discussions. These technologies also would provide a voice and agency for the students to express their concerns, issues, and struggles more openly than in a classroom setting that they feel is oppressive. I also believe that critically oriented faculty members could take advantage of these opportunities to engage in a larger discussion of how new media technologies and digital platforms potentially provide new opportunities and a voice to historically marginalized individuals so they can engage in diversity and social justice work by amplifying their voices. I also recognized that these technologies exist within the consumer culture and serve capitalistic agendas, but they still offer new possibilities. Without a doubt, the ways in which students might use these technologies to do advocacy work or engage in diversity-related issues might look very different from the conventional ways that exist in the physical classroom. I argue that mediated critical communication pedagogy is interested and invested in these alternative and new possibilities.

New media technologies would allow students to engage with class content more interactively as well as in a more dialogue-based and immersive way. Inviting students to use their laptop or smartphones in the classroom might sound like a radical idea for some or even unacceptable to others. If the students are using these technologies to look up information or translate a word, I think students can enhance their learning experiences. At the same time, they can also be distracted and not follow the class lecture or activity. For example, our students might lack the relevant background or contextual information for the class content, so looking up such information during class would provide them the information they need to better understand the lecture or in-class assignment. These technologies could also allow our students to interact with the class content differently, allowing them to seek additional information about a topic, pull up an image or a video, zoom in and out of an image (especially in media and visual communication), and follow a hyperlink to arrive at another related concept, image, film, or idea. Students could also be exposed to international materials that might not be easily accessible. For example, I encouraged my students to use their computers to look up relevant information for their in-class work when I was teaching the Visual

Communication and Culture course as well as the British Film and Media course. When students feel overwhelmed with the amount of new information they are not familiar with, they might shut down. However, allowing them to access the information they need to better understand this information will help them learn.

The interactive nature of new media technologies would enable our students to engage in a dialogue with one another on discussion boards or blogs. The same technologies would also permit them to interact with the texts and images related to their course content. I believe these technologies could provide new entry points or opportunities for students, and diverse students in particular, to engage in a dialogue. When the classroom settings and the bodies in it are discouraging or uninviting, students might not participate in the dialogue. New media technologies would allow them to dialogue differently, unconventionally, and multilingually.

CONCLUSION

In this chapter, I proposed mediated critical communication pedagogy as a framework to engage with different types of diversity at different levels. I realize that the possibilities provided through new media technologies and digital platforms might be limited, costly, or commercially driven; however, these technologies ultimately provide new ways of learning and participating for historically marginalized students by allowing them to be present and engaged even though their presence might take a digital form. New media technologies could also empower students who learn differently, have different educational needs, and need translators or note takers. These technologies would also allow these students to create a comfort zone that the physicality of a classroom might not always provide.

I returned to my apartment after a long work day. As I reflected on the day, I started to question my performance in the class. I allowed students to use their laptops and phones to complete their group assignment. Typically my colleagues do not allow students to use their laptops during the class. I broke the rules. I set them technologically free.

I began reading my e-mails despite the fact that this semester I was trying not to respond to e-mails after certain hours to achieve a better work-life balance. Her e-mail caught my eye. She was one of the two international students in the class. She e-mailed to thank me because I invited the students to use their technological devices to access information. The next day, she came to visit me in my office, telling me that she often struggles with her English and cultural references that she is not familiar with. Therefore, giving her permission to use her devices meant a lot because throughout the day she felt like she did not belong and she was not going to make it. She confessed she was crying before my class because she was really struggling in some of her classes. After she left my office, I sat back and thought about how many times I felt similarly. In this case, using a technological device really helped the student to access the information that she needed. Regardless of how we feel about the usage of technology in the classroom, experiences like this really inspire me to invite students to incorporate it into their learning.

REFERENCES

Bondy, J. M. & Pennington, L. K. (2016). Illegal aliens, criminals, and hypersexual spitfires: Latin@ youth and pedagogies of citizenship in media texts. *The Social Studies*, 107(3), 102–44.
boyd, d. (2014). *It is complicated: The social lives of networked teens*. New Haven, CT: Yale University Press.
Crenshaw, K. (1991). Mapping the margins. *Stanford Law Review, 43*, 1241–1299.
Dimock, M. (2019). Pew Research Center, Defining generations: Where millennials end and Generation Z begins, https://www.pewresearch.org/fact-tank/2019/01/17/where-millennials-end-and-generation-z-begins/.
Fassett, D. L., & Warren, J. T. (2007). *Critical communication pedagogy.* Thousand Oaks: Sage Publications, Inc.
Freire, P. (1970). *Pedagogy of the oppressed* (M. B. Ramos, Trans.). New York: Herder and Herder.
Fry, R., Igielnik, R., & Patten, E. (2018). How Millennials today compare with their grandparents 50 years ago. *Pew Research Center*. March 16, 2018.
Fry, R., & Parker, K. (2018). Early benchmarks show 'post-millennials' on track to be most diverse, best-educated generation yet. *Pew Research Center*. November 15, 2018.
Jenkins. H. (2006). *Convergence culture: Where old and new media collide*. New York: New York University Press.
Jiang, J. (2018). Pew Research Center, Millennials Stand Out for their Technology Use, but Older Generations Also Embrace Digital Life, http://www.pewresearch.org/fact-tank/2018/05/02/millennials-stand-out-for-their-technology-use-but-older-generations-also-embrace-digital-life/.
Martin, J. N. & Nakayama, T. K. (2014). *Experiencing intercultural communication: An introduction*. New York: McGraw Hill.
The power of international education. The number of international students in the United States reaches new high of 1.09 million. November 13, 2018.
Yep, G. A. (1998). My three cultures: Navigating the multicultural identity landscape. In J. N. Martin, T. K. Nakayama, & L. A Flores (Eds.), *Readings in intercultural communication* (pp. 60–66). Mountain View, CA: Mayfield.
Yep, G. A. (2002). My three cultures: Navigating the multicultural identity landscape. In J. N. Martin, T. K. Nakayama, & L.A. Flores (Eds.), *Readings in intercultural communication: Experiences and contexts* (2nd ed., pp. 60–66). Boston, MA: McGraw-Hill.
Yep. G A. (2013). Queering/quaring/kauering/crippin'/transing "other bodies" in intercultural communication. *Journal of International and Intercultural Communication*, 6(2), 118–26.
Yep, G. A & Lescure, R. (2019). A thick intersectional approach to microaggressions. *Southern Communication Journal*, 84:2, 113–26.

Chapter Five

Critiquing Hegemony through Mediated Critical Communication Pedagogy

Key Questions for Critical Media Analysis

Yannick Kluch and Lara Martin Lengel

Among our favorite class sessions each semester is one that centers around the following activity: In a session on gender norms in American society, Yannick (first author) asks students to review photos of athletes published in *ESPN: The Body Issue*. The annually published special edition of *ESPN The Magazine* was first published in 2009 and features popular athletes in semi-nude and nude photographs. "Let's play a game," he always introduces the activity and adds: "A game called 'Guess the Sport.' I am going to show you a series of photographs of male and female athletes. All you have to do is tell me what sport they play." He starts to show a series of photographs of male athletes first, and students usually identify the sport each pictured athlete is representing easily. The athlete dunking a basketball? A basketball player, of course. The athlete swinging his racket at a tennis ball? A tennis prodigy. The athlete displaying his finesse with a soccer ball? A soccer athlete ready to score a goal. "You're probably wondering why I am having you identify the sport in these rather obvious pictures," Yannick then announces to the class, and he is usually met with a rhythmic sea of nodding heads before he introduces the second part of the activity: "Now let's look at some pictures of female athletes next."

Students' reactions to the pictures of female athletes often offer a stark contrast to their previous response to pictures portraying male athletes. Class members who previously gave rapid-fire answers suddenly turn silent with their facial expressions revealing confusion. There is a picture of a semi-nude woman laying by the pool. There is another one showing a woman seductively staring into the camera. And there's one showing a female athlete preparing burgers on a gas grill, with snowboarding equipment placed in the background. While previously students guessed the sport correctly on the first try, they now shout out multiple guesses before finding the correct answer. "These women don't even look like athletes ... these pictures might as well be from a beauty magazine," students would often say. Leading into the lesson debriefing, Yannick then responds: "Exactly! What does that tell us about gender norms in the United States?"

There is no lack of scholarship arguing for the importance of mediated popular culture, including both "traditional" media such as films, television, and magazines, and "newer" media technologies, in classroom environments (see, for instance, Bumpus, 2005; Erlandson, 2012; Eyestone, 2013; Garcia, Seglem, & Share, 2013; Garrett & Schmeichel, 2012; Grady, Marquez, & McLaren, 2012; Kellner & Kim, 2010). Greenfeld (2007), for instance, calls for more frequent "inclusion of popular culture into the curriculum" as it is "a meaningful vehicle for encouraging educators to become more aware of matters of identity and to implement classroom approaches to best meet the needs of today's learners" (p. 232). Owen, Silet, and Brown (1998) argue for harnessing the expertise of students, who are experienced consumers of television. Eyestone (2013) concurs and, more importantly, poses that "since our students are familiar with the medium, our task becomes easier; we can focus on more critical issues related to genre and difference instead of worrying about teaching them how to 'read the medium'" (p. 2).

As critical scholars of popular culture, we, too, recommend harnessing students' passion for media as a gateway to build their critical thinking skills and their capacity for a lifelong commitment to social responsibility and social justice.[1] While we loathe mainstream media tendencies to essentialize portrayals of race, ethnicity, gender, and sexuality, we argue that mediated stories and popular cultural texts offer fruitful pedagogical opportunities for students to explore hegemonic practices and ideological frameworks at play in intercultural encounters. As researchers and educators, it is our responsibility to inspire students to critically examine these stories and texts, particularly in terms of how these stories are conduits for the representations of gender, race, ethnicity, sexuality, and other markers that shape students' identities.

Centering learning on popular cultural texts becomes particularly important during a time in which social media, Internet-delivered entertainment, and televisual texts dominate many students' social and cultural lives. Evaluating the potential of popular culture to be used in gender studies classes, Weber (2010), for instance, views popular culture as one of the major influences on how members of a culture become socialized into gender norms of that culture. More importantly, she also points out that "though all of us are immersed in popular culture materials, few people consume or produce popular culture with an active and critical knowledge of its ideological [content and capacity]" (p. 129). However, Weber (2010) notes, because popular culture is often deemed entertainment, it can be a powerful carrier of normative codes related to identity markers such as gender.

It is in this context that popular culture becomes particularly suitable for teaching students to critique hegemony, which we define as the economic, political, or cultural dominance or authority of one entity over others, as popular cultural texts often draw from different (inter)cultural clichés to appeal to mass audiences. Pandey (2012) argues popular cultural texts can be valuable to help students decipher other cultures, and "with guidance and help of the instructors, students can learn nuances of cultural theories and constructs very easily by means of films [or other visual media] shown in the classroom" (p. 1). As such, popular media texts can not only be engaging and entertaining but can also encourage interest in and compassion for other identity groups and cultures (Cardon, 2010). For example, Cardon (2010) has shown convincingly that the Academy Award–winning film *Slumdog Millionaire* can be used to critically deconstruct stereotypes about Indian culture and, as such, serve as a tool to promote respect for foreign cultures. Similarly, several intercultural communication and critical pedagogy scholars (see, for instance, Adejunmobi, 2008; Cooper, 2004; Daspit, 2000; Kluch & Lengel, 2015a, 2015b; Morrell, 2002; Sfeir, 2014; Smith, 2000; Weaver & Daspit, 2000) suggest using popular cultural texts as pedagogical tools. Indeed, popular cultural texts can be incorporated into international and intercultural communication curricula to help students explore how these texts can construct cultural identities. In addition, such texts provide scope to analyze why people consume or resist specific popular cultural texts and encourage critique of the relationship between socio-cultural roles and reasons underlying certain popular culture consumption choices.

ANALYZING POWER, CULTURE, AND IDENTITY IN OUR STORIES

In his work "The Spectacle of the 'Other,'" Stuart Hall (1997) analyzes representational practices in popular cultural texts. He argues that "representations sometimes call our very identities into question. We struggle over them because they matter—and these are contests from which serious consequences can flow" (p. 10). Similarly, Paul Hodkinson (2017), in his work on the central role media play in the everyday lived experience in late modernity, suggests mediated cultural texts provide "resources for the forging of identities and imaginations" (p. 2). Indeed, as Jo Hall (2018) notes, Baudrillard and other postmodern scholars have suggested "it is difficult to conceive identity as separate from media image and representation" (p. 55).

Given the emphasis of mediated critical communication pedagogy specifically, and critical pedagogy broadly, on critical awareness of the relationships between power, culture, and identity, we seek "the common ground of education among participants" (i.e., both teachers and learners) that will "serve as a pivotal source for collaboration and learning as they observe and analyze how relations of power develop contextually" (Allen, 2012, p. 110). Often such common ground is found through stories, our own and others. Lincoln and Denzin (2003) suggest scholars must study experiences through their representations, "through the ways in which stories are told" (p. 240). Similarly, Leard and Lashua (2006) suggest stories—both narratives and the representations within these narratives—provide great insight into "how young people draw from a variety of popular media to continually re-define and reposition themselves within the social contexts of their everyday lives" (p. 247).

In this chapter, we focus on critiquing mediated depictions of the intersections of power, culture, and identity with our students. We keep in mind our own journeys while we guide those of our students, sensitive to how developing one's critical skills over time is a process. We draw from our experiences living, learning, teaching, and researching in numerous international contexts, as we analyze the potential of mediated critical communication pedagogy in teaching communication studies courses. Because depictions of power, culture, and identity are often subtle, even nearly imperceptible to an unassuming eye, we draw upon mediated critical pedagogy strategies to highlight "the immediate power of communication, power that may be both oppressive and liberating depending on local contexts" (Nainby, Warren, & Bollinger, 2003, p. 207). Critical pedagogy provides us with a valuable tool, as Allen (2012) reminds us, "to engender learning that leads to raising students' consciousness and empowering them to be change agents" (p. 110).

Based on our own experiences as educators in the communication classroom, it is our goal to empower students to move past the mere consumption stage of the popular cultural text towards a stage of critical reflection of what is seen on screen. This critical reflection, to us, becomes a priority in our use of popular cultural artifacts in the classroom. Because we only have very limited access to the production and consumption stages of the popular cultural texts under analysis (as many students had already seen part of the TV shows prior to being in the class), our focus shifted towards encouraging students to reflect on the texts in order to enable them to effectively critique these texts. Indeed, critical reflection seemed to be a valuable first step in sensitizing students for a lens of rigorous critique. Cardon (2010) used a similar approach when using films to deconstruct intercultural stereotypes. He prompted students to first understand how their own culture was stereotyped, before guiding them in a process to turn their critical lens onto how other cultures' stereotypes were constructed. Both of these foci on students' reflection on and critique of popular cultural texts provided a natural suture with critical communication pedagogy's call for self-reflexivity and dialogue to question taken-for-granted assumptions that make up students' view of the world and reveal how power operates in communication encounters (Fassett & Warren, 2007).

CHOOSING STORIES AND TEXTS FOR CRITICAL INQUIRY

The choice of specific stories and texts can be targeted toward specific courses. For instance, the *ESPN: The Body Issue* example shared in the opening of this chapter is well suited for courses focused on sports communication or related courses. For the purposes of this study, however, we focus on popular television shows due to the texts' short running time, which makes them particularly suitable to be used during a variety of class sessions, and because most students in U.S. colleges and universities tend to be familiar with these texts. We provide examples of how we use situation comedies (hereafter, sitcoms) such as *The Big Bang Theory*, which depicts a group of scientists whose lives get turned upside down when they befriend their free-spirited woman neighbor, and *How I Met Your Mother*, in which protagonist Ted Mosby retrospectively tells his future kids how he met their mother in the New York City of the 2000s. We also draw from our use of the horror drama series *The Walking Dead*, which follows a group of survivors in the aftermath of a zombie apocalypse.

All these shows have achieved international success, and because all three televisual texts under analysis in this chapter originated in the U.S. and have been exported to many countries across the globe, they can be viewed as prime examples of artifacts that both encompass textual elements and audience consumption patterns consistent with global hegemony. Finally, we draw from other media examples we have used successfully in the classroom, such as *Drunk History* and *The Daily Show*, to extend our argument to texts beyond the sitcom and post-apocalyptic genres. While the choice of texts we draw from in this chapter relies heavily on mediated and televisual materials, it is important to emphasize that the key questions for critical analysis as outlined in this chapter can be applied to other popular cultural artifacts as well—such as sports texts, songs and music lyrics, video games, or radio commercials.

PRAXIS: KEY QUESTIONS FOR CRITICAL MEDIA ANALYSIS

We view mainstream popular cultural texts like the ones described above not only as vehicles carrying significant cultural meaning in both national and global contexts, but also as prime tools that enable students to critique hegemony and the lack of equity and inclusivity in mainstream texts. As such, they become tools that can increase cultural awareness, critique hegemony, and enhance social responsibility both in and out of the classroom. Guided by Kahl's (2013) analysis of critical communication pedagogy and assessment, we provide students with an introduction to the concept of hegemony and ask them to view a media text with the following questions in mind so that "they can begin to use their knowledge to work toward praxis. Instructors will assess the ways in which students use their knowledge of hegemony to determine how to respond to the hegemony they encounter" (p. 21). As such, we use our theorizing about hegemony, the relationship of culture and power, and the pedagogical strategies and course content we have developed to "function as a synergy of theory and action" (Fassett & Warren, 2007, p. 112; see, also, Kahl, 2013) and guide students to engage in critical viewing and reading of media texts. As such, by outlining six guiding questions for critical media analysis, we follow Kahl's (2016) call to "transition [critical communication pedagogy] from a discipline of ideas to a discipline of action" (p. 118).

Because we find that many students struggle to uncover underlying hegemonic discourses in popular cultural texts, we focus on the idea of stories—the ones they see, hear, and read through media, as well as their own—to illuminate that struggle. The following key questions encourage students to scrutinize both narrative and stylistic elements of stories in order to carefully examine the underlying assumptions and ideologies conveyed by them. These guiding questions allow opportunities to reflect on their viewing of popular cultural texts. Encouraging students to approach the popular cultural texts with these questions for reflection enables them to move from a state of mere consumption toward a state of cultural critique.

Examining the Face(s) of Power: Analysis of Characters (The "Who")

Who is central and who is marginal? The first key question concerns the centrality and marginality of individuals and groups in popular cultural stories. This question focuses on the central characters of the story; it prompts students to look beyond characters' physical features that characterize their visible presence in the story toward an analysis of how the characters are constructed narratively, psychologically, and behaviorally. Characters are also examined for their relationship with other characters to understand hier-

Key Questions for Critical Media Analysis
Who?   Analysis of characters in the story. Treatment of characters by others in the story.   *Who is central and who is marginal? Who is silenced? Who is being laughed at?*
What?   Analysis of norms, key story points, plot twists.   *What is constructed as "the norm"? What is shown as desirable (not desirable)?*
When?   Analysis of context.   *When is the story set? What are the historical contexts, if any, of the story? When do the texts matter?*
Where?   Analysis of setting.   *Where is the story set? Where does space reveal the global and local contexts of the story?*
Why?   Analysis of story ending and outcome.   *Why do characters end up a certain way? Why does the story advance the way it does?*
How?   Analysis of extent to which audience can relate to story.   *How do viewers relate (or not relate) to the story?*

archies of power. For instance, *The Big Bang Theory* character Raj Koothrappali, a particle astrophysicist from India and the only foreign character featured on the show, is often constructed through the use of underlying assumptions attached to the Other. All the other (white) characters are constituted as superior to Raj professionally, interpersonally, and socially; the power hierarchy of the white characters over Raj provides much of those characters' comedic elements of the series.

Who is silenced? In addition to looking at the characterization of each protagonist, we also encourage students to reflect on the ability of the characters to share their thoughts. Privileged characters (often white, heteronormative men) are those who do most of the talking or who lead the conversation. Again, Raj is a prime example here. For most of the series, Raj is not able to make his voice heard, but instead has to rely on the mercy of his American, white counterparts. Throughout the first six seasons of *The Big Bang Theory*, Raj is not comfortable talking to women unless he is intoxicated. If a woman is present in the room with him and his friends, he whispers in Howard's ear, who then shares Raj's thoughts with the rest of the group. Raj cannot utter his own thoughts but is dependent on the other characters—all of which are heterosexual, white men—to speak for him.

Who is being laughed at? For popular cultural texts situated in the televisual comedy genre, practices of *laughing with* versus *laughing at* become important when examining the power relations shown on the program and the wider cultural landscape. Comedy relies on making audiences laugh, yet practices to do so often reflect characters' unequal power distribution. On *The Big Bang Theory*, the audience laughs *at* Raj along *with* the other characters. A very common stylistic element of the sitcom genre reminds the viewer that Raj is making a fool of himself: the laugh track, which is often placed right after Raj is done talking. For instance, the audience is encouraged to laugh *at* Raj through the use of the track when he says things like "It's like accidently walking into a gay bar and then having no one hit on you. It happened to a friend of mine" ("The Thespian Catalyst") or "I haven't cried this hard since *Toy Story 3*" ("The Apology Insufficiency"). The encouragement of the viewers to laugh at Raj maybe becomes the most obvious when the other characters make jokes directly at his expense. One such example can be found in the episode "The Cooper-Nowitzki Theorem." In this episode, Raj and Leonard talk about going to a social event at their university:

Raj: Isn't there a policy against dating graduate students?

Leonard: No. If you can talk to them, you can ask them out.

Raj: Damn, there's always a catch.

Here, Leonard's words are used to make fun of Raj's inability to talk to women. The use of the laugh track herewith becomes a valuable tool in the identification of ideological underpinnings of the creators of the text. Walsh, Fürsich, and Jefferson (2008) note, in sitcoms, power is usually with those making the jokes, as "the characters who are laughed at hold the undesirable position or function as scapegoats." They suggest "what is considered common sense and acceptable normality remains in the position of those characters who are initiating the jokes" (p. 131). It is not surprising that these characters making the jokes—much like Leonard in the example above—are those holding privileged identities in the context of the show.

When Narrative Constructs the Norm: Analysis of Plot (The "What")

What is constructed as "the norm"? This question points to interrogations of gender, sexuality, and other identity markers inherent in popular cultural stories. Despite prodigious changes in gender representation in mainstream media texts, unfortunately, heteronormativity tropes remain dominant in popular culture (see, for instance, Atay, 2015; Dhaenens, 2014; Kluch, 2015; Kluch & Lengel, 2015b; Lengel & Martin, 2010; Meyer, 2010; Westerfelhaus & Lacroix, 2006). In *How I Met Your Mother* and *The Big Bang Theory*, heterosexuality is constructed as the norm through the portrayal of all main characters of both sitcoms as heterosexual. Hegemonic normative social and cultural hierarchies, including but not limited to heteronormativity, "can be exposed by revealing their inherent frictions, instabilities, and incoherencies" (Dhaenens, 2014, p. 534; see, also, Jagose 1996). "As a representational strategy," Dhaenens (2014) argues, "this strategy of exposure thus makes explicit how assumed natural sexual and gender identities are social constructs that only preserve the authority of the heterosexual matrix while harming and excluding those who do not fit the matrix" (p. 534). By portraying all (or the majority of) main characters on a TV show as heterosexual, heterosexuality is normalized and all sexual identities deviating from this norm are depicted as unnatural.

What is desirable (not desirable)? Dhaenens' (2014) critique of the "heterosexual matrix" (p. 534) is an important and relatively easily identifiable point for students' critical media analysis. There is no lack of televisual and online media texts, advertisements, news channels (both news content and the personalities that present news), and social media commentary to use to teach students critical analysis skills. For example, *How I Met Your Mother* allows us to illustrate another aspect that becomes important when evaluating the potential of popular culture to illustrate and critique hegemony: that of desirability or the lack thereof. We use this televisual text to show our students what characters and behaviors are presented as desirable (and which are not). We often use a gender and sexuality lens for this question, as the show following Ted Mosby on his quest to find "the one" serves as a perfect example for this endeavor. While *The Big Bang Theory* directly features a foreign individual as part of the show's main cast, *How I Met Your Mother* provides a good example of how Western ideals related to gender and sexuality are constructed in a televisual popular cultural text that is distributed globally.

It is very likely that no character on the show has received more attention than *How I Met Your Mother*'s Barney Stinson. For most of the series, Barney can be characterized quite simply: He is physically strong and attractive, and tries to have sexual intercourse with as many women as possible. Most storylines associated with Barney evolve around him trying to have sex with a woman. While trying to do so, he is shown to be aggressive, dominant, and competitive, thus promoting the "image of the young macho-man lifestyle [that] has been strongly static throughout American history, mirroring and perpetuating the hegemonic male ideal" (Krauss, 2011, p. 6). Researchers agree that aggressiveness, assertiveness, and competitiveness are a common stereotype of masculine men (e.g., Hatty, 2000; Mansfield, 2006). Barney's preference for challenges (as can, for instance, be seen in his infamous catchphrase "Challenge accepted!"), his behavior towards other men, his penchant for adventure (as can be seen in his magician skills), as well as his stubbornness when it comes to picking up women are further signifiers that align him with hegemonic notions of masculinity.

It is for these reasons that his group of friends finds it all the more surprising that, at the beginning of the episode "The Stinsons," Barney refuses to pursue three attractive women, even though—as Lily points out—they are his type because they are "three blonde babies drinking bad decision juice at eight o'clock." Instead, he tells the group he has to go somewhere, but is secretive about his plans. Because the group suspects Barney of having a secret girlfriend, they decide to follow him to a house that turns out to be that of his mother, Loretta. When the group is shocked to learn that Barney seemingly has a girlfriend (Betty) and a son (Tyler), Barney reveals they are both actors he hired to play his "perfect family," because he thought this family would make his mother happy. For the dinner following the friends' discovery, Barney even wrote a scene for both his fake wife and son, thus telling both what (and, more importantly, what not) to say.

This scene is crucial, as it can be interpreted as mirroring the character of Barney Stinson in two significant ways. First, it attributes further overtly masculine character traits to Barney: By hiring an actress as his ideal wife, it becomes obvious that Barney's perfect wife is a woman over whom he has complete control. He is the active part in this inauthentic relationship, telling Betty what to do, what to say, and how to behave. As such, his behavior is highly dominating and aligns him with hegemonic masculine ideals, as "the opportunity and capacity to dominate Others is integral to hegemonic masculinity" (Hatty, 2000, p. 181). This power is also reflected by Barney's wealth on the show; after all, he is fortunate enough to pay two actors to play his family. Second, it shows Barney's general attitude towards women: In the traditional gender dichotomy, as represented by this character, a masculine man's wife is shown to be dependent on him and rather passive—just as Betty is in this episode.[2]

Barney's characterization as a successful "ladies' man" who succeeds at having sex with many women throughout the run of the show is particularly significant when asking students to apply a critical lens to the show. In one activity we frequently feature in our classes, we ask students to compare the gender ideals promoted by *How I Met Your Mother* to those of other countries across the globe by examining a text from that country's popular culture. Many students then point out similarities between the ideal propagated by *How I Met Your Mother* and that of other—Western—cultures. Interestingly, our students have also pointed out that on *How I Met Your Mother* women with different cultural backgrounds are attracted to Barney, who is herewith constructed as a global masculine ideal. The show draws a picture of Barney as the ultimate, globally attractive epitome of masculine power and hegemonic masculinity. The example of Barney in *How I Met Your*

Mother, as such, allows students to analyze what and who is desirable in these texts, which enables them to reflect on globalization practices by scrutinizing and evaluating Western ideals of wealth accrued in a capitalistic system, gender and sexuality, all of which are spread across the globe.

History Speaks: Analysis of Context (The "When")

When is the story set? What are the historical contexts? We invite students to interrogate contextual nuances in the stories. McKee (2001) notes texts cannot be analyzed sufficiently without putting them into context. By highlighting social, political, economic, and gendered contexts, among others, we ask students to situate texts in what McKee (2001) describes as "the wider 'semiosphere' (the 'world of meaning')" (p. 149) in which the texts are produced and consumed. For instance, Barney's construction as a "ladies' man" correlates to contemporary ideals of what it means to be a man. When discussing this text with students, we have sometimes asked them to describe how a character like Barney would have been constructed in earlier decades (e.g., the 1950s). Posing questions like these prompts students to understand that these texts are produced in a very specific cultural context.

When do the texts matter? At times, sitcoms cannot sufficiently capture the urgency for literacy in critical analysis among undergraduate students due to their, at times, cartoonish features (as, for instance, illustrated by the characterization of Stinson as hyper-promiscuous). As a philosopher and historian, Freire (1970) considered the challenges of contemporaneity in democratic citizenship and the importance of teaching history to young people. He argued that historical consciousness is necessary to build civic awareness (Simon & Blanch, 2015). Active critique of history is particularly important given many students struggle to see value in studying history and understanding historical contexts (Crabtree, 2001). *The Daily Show* is an excellent text for media literacy (Garrett & Schmeichel, 2012), as it calls out such ignorance in simultaneously hilarious and horrifying ways. For example, on *The Daily Show*, Jordan Klepper has interviewed attendees of Trump rallies in Wisconsin and Ohio. The following is one segment from the interview (*The Daily Show*, 2016):

Rally attendee: "Barack Obama had a big part of 9/11."

Klepper: "Which part?"

Rally attendee: "Not being around; always on vacation."

Klepper: "Why do you think Barack Obama wasn't in the Oval Office on 9/11?"

Rally attendee: "That I don't know. I'd like to get to the bottom of that."

Given the rally attendee's certainty that Barack Obama should have been in the Oval Office on September 11, 2001, rather than George W. Bush, we certainly concur with Freire that students of undergraduate age and younger are not nearly as engaged with history as they should be. It is for this reason that we invite students to examine *when* (not simply *why*) popular cultural texts matter at certain times. Freire's work is also a call to encourage students' historical experience in order to be able to critique the post-truth discourses and fake news that rely on the hegemonically convenient "forgetting" of history, particularly the history of Othering, that illuminates the "reciprocal relationship between truth about the past and justice in the present" (Loewen & Sebesta, 2011, p. 393; see also, Lengel, Newsom & Montenegro, 2017; Lengel & Smidi, in press; Mejia, 2017; Mejia, Beckermann & Sullivan, 2018).

For instance, Comedy Central's *Drunk History* is a prime example that educators can use to strengthen students' ability to examine *when* particular stories matter. In times when history appears to be a rather dry area of inquiry for students, "the show's incoherence and plethora of misstatements are exactly why it can be valuable in the classroom" (Sheumaker, 2015, para. 1). Sheumaker (2015) suggests that "those of us in the business of teaching history and producing historical narrative take as a virtue, not a flaw, the fact that *Drunk History* presents our discipline as entertaining" (para. 4). Students have expressed that "'entertainment' need not imply passively consuming mass culture; instead, they saw the entertainment value of *Drunk History* as moving viewers to assume an active, participatory, and ultimately critical position" (Sheumaker, 2015, para. 4). Any inaccuracies of the inebriated narrators are a call to action for students to serve as active investigators, collaboratively participating in meaning-making with the narratives rather than passively consuming them.

Space Displays Power: Analysis of Setting (The "Where")

Where is the story set? Analyses of context(s) do not only require critics to look at the time in which a story is set or at which a story *matters;* they also prompt us to critically examine the spaces that dominate these stories, as Somerville (2010) reminds us that "our relationship to place is constituted in stories and other representations" (p. 326). Since McLaren (1999) called for the development of a "critical pedagogy of space" there has been a growth of scholarship rich in spatial references and metaphors (Morgan, 2000, p. 273; see also, for instance, Cravey & Petit, 2012; Edwards & Usher, 2000; Gruenewald, 2003; Somerville, 2010). A critical pedagogy of space enables critics to identify the various ways in which spaces "naturalise existing spatial arrangements that favour certain social groups at the expense of others" and "are organised to keep a whole range of 'others' 'in their place' and [. . .] convey to certain groups that they are 'out of place'" (Morgan, 2000, pp. 278–79). Therefore, as Soja (1989) argues,

> we must be insistently aware of how space can be made to hide consequences from us, how relationships of power and discipline are inscribed into the apparently innocent spatiality of social life, how human geographies are filled with power and ideology. (p. 25)

Dystopian narratives are some of the most visually profound and thematically effective popular cultural texts that politicize space. Given increased uncertainties and anxieties since 9/11 and, more recently, the global financial crisis, numerous televisual, filmic, and other artistic texts have centered around narratives of dystopia (see Ahmad, 2014; Bressler & Lengel, 2016; Ndalianis, 2015; Platts, 2013). The spaces of dystopian narratives are far more often than not differentially designated in a strict hierarchy that illustrates the architectures of power. While these spaces are denaturalized and exaggerated, they emphasize the need for political views of space by highlighting the "divisibility and hierarchy of space" (Brown, 2015, p. 99; see also Morgan, 2000).

The AMC hit series *The Walking Dead* is one of the best televisual texts to illustrate the unique spatial considerations of dystopia. In her work on "Space and Place in Zombie Culture," Austin (2011) suggests the undead "undermine the notion of controlled social spaces of behavior" (p. 1). In *The Walking Dead*, as in many zombie narratives, zombies are portrayed as the dangerous Other that does not have a place among the living. Further, one of the dominant themes of the show is the human survivors' efforts to separate themselves physically from the zombies by finding spaces that those zombies do not have access to. For instance, architectural spatial elements such as a razor-wire-topped chain-link fence of a prison (season three) and a 15-foot high wall surrounding the Alexandria Safe Zone (seasons six to nine) serve the purpose to create a physical border between the human individuals and the inhuman threat embodied by the zombie figure.

Where does space reveal the global and local contexts of the story? Connections of the space, place, and architecture of fictional texts to nonfiction phenomena are another way to enact critical media analysis. The fear-mongering and anti-immigration discourses of Donald Trump's 2016 election campaign strategy, for instance, can be linked to the construction of hierarchies through spatial elements on *The Walking Dead*. In his article, "It's official—*The Walking Dead* helped elect Donald Trump," film critic Peter Bradshaw (2016) of *The Guardian* shares "the disturbing news that zombies played a part in the election of Donald Trump" by relying on the notion "that people who thrill to the idea of battling sinister marauding monsters that look human, but aren't really, will also be very sympathetic to building an enormous wall" (para. 1). This example is particularly compelling as it addresses a number of media forms (horror genre television programming, a respective international news organization) as well as serves as international critique of the use of U.S. popular culture for political purposes. Further, it helps students understand that future dystopian narratives like *The Walking Dead* may not be quite as fictional as they first seem.

The End Can Be Revealing: Analysis of Story Outcome (The "Why")

Why do characters end up a certain way? One of the most important narrative elements of each televisual text is related to the outcome of the series and, related to that outcome, the situation in which the characters of the show end up at the conclusion of each episode, season, or series as a whole. It is thus important to scrutinize the way narratives conclude, as often the final situations characters find themselves in reflect the underlying assumptions and norms of the show's universe and, as such, reveal disguised biases of society as a whole. For instance, the conclusion of the main characters' storylines on *How I Met Your Mother* reinforces heteronormative, monogamous behavior as the norm. Ted, Lily, and Marshall all succeed at fulfilling their dreams by the show's final episode: Ted has met the love of his life, and Lily and Marshall have a family with three children while simultaneously succeeding professionally. Robin and Barney, however, as two of the characters who have been portrayed in a promiscuous way, struggle to fulfill their dreams. While Robin does succeed professionally, she struggles maintaining interpersonal relationships. And while Barney does become a father in the final episode as the result of a one-night stand, he struggles to build a meaningful relationship with a significant other. As such, the show validates the dating behavior of Lily, Marshall, and Ted, all of whom find ultimate fulfillment in their heterosexual relationship.

Why does the story advance the way it does? The question of where characters eventually end up becomes particularly important in a post-apocalyptic drama series like *The Walking Dead*, as death is a dominant theme in shows of this dystopian genre. In *The Walking Dead*, many characters die throughout the seasons that have aired to date. Even though both white and racially underrepresented characters die on the show, one thing about the Black characters' demises stands out: the introduction of a new racial minority character shortly after a Black character's death on screen. For instance, Michonne is introduced shortly after T-Dog's death and Noah joins the group of survivors shortly before Tyreese's death. The misrepresentation of African American characters on the show is particularly problematic given that the show is initially set in and around Atlanta, a city with a predominantly Black population. Such (mis-)representation, if critically analyzed and reflected on by students, can serve as a further tool for critiques of hegemony as well as the complex interplay of culture and power.

This Is Me? Analysis of Extent to Which Audience Can Relate (The "How")

How do viewers relate (or not relate) to the story? Recall Stuart Hall's work (1997) on how representations "sometimes call our very identities into question. . . . They define what is 'normal,' who belongs—and therefore, who is excluded" (p. 10). In our careers as teachers and educators, many students in our classes have reported that critically reflecting on popular cultural texts allowed them to not only critique the texts and question the texts' constitutions of "normal," but also better understand how the texts intersect—or do not intersect—with their own lived experience. It is thus important to encourage students to critically reflect on how the depictions on the screen reflect and, more importantly, differ from their own lived experiences.

Critical media analysis is most transformative when students can self-reflexively relate the stories they see on screen to their own lives, as an example from Yannick's (first author) Introduction to Popular Culture class illustrates. When Yannick first started using *The Big Bang Theory* in the classroom, he remembers very clearly how one of his students reflected on the character of Raj on the show. Being friends with Indian international students who had moved to the United States, that student pointed out that Raj is often portrayed in a different way than his white counterparts. As such, Raj's presence on the show provided an apt tool for critical engagement with the text as it was situated within the student's life. We encourage our students to critique these and other popular cultural texts to analyze cultural meaning, identity construction, cultural nuances of metaphor, satire, and symbolism (Champoux, 1999).

Positioning a popular cultural text in one's own life by analyzing the extent to which one can relate (or not relate) to the characters on the screen becomes particularly important for individuals who belong to groups that have been constructed in rather one-dimensional ways in popular culture narratives and that have limited identity scripts available to relate to. In her autoethnographic essay on depictions of Black women on reality television, Boylorn (2008) draws from the works of Stuart Hall and bell hooks to argue for the use of an "oppositional reading" as a form of engagement with what is seen on screen; she offers a "critical and self-reflective gaze at the one-dimensional representation of Black womanhood on reality television" (p. 428). Instead of passively consuming what is seen on screen, Boylorn (2008) prompts Black women to bring their own personal experiences and realities to the forefront to serve as a place and point of comparison. She argues, "[I]f Black women become critics of the depictions of their lived realities and construct their realities beyond stereotypes they can invite representations that acknowledge the diversity of Black women's lives" (p. 430). While Boylorn (2008) focuses on Black women in her autoethnographic piece, we join her in this call for all individuals whose various identities have been constructed in monolithic ways to "construct their realities beyond stereotypes" (p. 430).

CONCLUSION: FROM CONSUMPTION TO REFLECTION AND CRITIQUE

Because many students struggle to uncover the underlying hegemonic messages in popular cultural texts, it has become obvious to us that critical engagement with popular cultural texts cannot be taken for granted in the classroom. Indeed, several of our students throughout the years have indicated that they usually watch programs like *The Big Bang Theory*, *How I Met Your Mother*, *Drunk History*, and *The Walking Dead* for entertainment purposes only. Thus, scholars and educators must teach critical media analysis carefully and rigorously. Popular cultural texts such as the ones used throughout this chapter give students valuable opportunities to discuss and analyze alternatives to dominant cultural norms and constructions, and to critique how texts re-inscribe and reify dominant ideologies and cultural norms.

Many of our students indicate that, after completion of our courses, they view popular culture in a different light, that they were not aware of what popular culture is trying to teach us, and that they could not watch TV the same way they did before. With our six guiding questions as outlined in this chapter, it is our hope that students will be empowered to become critical viewers of popular cultural texts—and the stories embedded within those texts—and strong critics of the hegemonic forces that shape their everyday lives. Drawing from our experience living, learning, teaching, and researching in numerous international contexts, we have aimed here to analyze the impact of televisual texts as critical pedagogy tools. Popular cultural texts can not only be viewed as vehicles that carry considerable cultural meaning in both national and international contexts. Rather, they become prime tools that enable students to move from a state of mere consumption of popular culture to a state of critical reflection and critique of hegemonic processes and, as such, become powerful tools that can increase cultural awareness, social responsibility, and efforts for social justice.

NOTES

1. This chapter is informed by two related projects, the first of which analyzes the potential of popular cultural texts in teaching international and intercultural communication (Kluch & Lengel, 2015a). Through a triangulated methodological approach employing textual analysis, in-depth interviews, and ethnographic viewing experiences, this larger project analyzes how students decode messages of globalization in and engage with a variety of televisual popular cultural texts including, but not limited to, *The Big Bang Theory, How I Met Your Mother, South Park, Drunk History,* and *The Walking Dead,* political satire programs including *The Daily Show,* and films such as *Children of Men* in international, intercultural, and political communication and communication ethics courses. This study also seeks ways to encourage students to critically reflect on the messages presented to them, to accurately assess the potential of televisual popular cultural texts to educate students about how hegemony works, the intersections of culture, identity, and power, and processes of cultural globalization. Our work here is also informed by our critical discourse analysis of social media texts about *The Walking Dead* commenting on representations of masculinity and GLBTQ characters in the series (Kluch & Lengel, 2015b). These two studies led to the development of strategies for praxis for students to engage in critical viewing and reading of media texts, as outlined in this chapter.

2. In the classroom, the portrayal of Barney Stinson's character as a reinforcement of the traditional gender dichotomy can be juxtaposed with the celebrity persona embodied by the actor behind Stinson, openly gay Neil Patrick Harris. For example, instructors can prompt students to analyze how the casting choice of Neil Patrick Harris may provide a further layer of complexity to the character of Barney Stinson, who may seem to be constructed as rather one-dimensional at first sight.

REFERENCES

Adejunmobi, M. (2008). Intercultural and transcultural literacy in contemporary Africa. *Language and Intercultural Communication, 8*(2), 72–90.

Ahmad, A. (2014). Feminist spaces in horrific places. *Offscreen 18*(6/7), 1–13.

Allen, B. J. (2012). Critical communication pedagogy as a framework for teaching difference and organizing. In D. Mumby (Ed.), *Reframing difference in organizational communication studies: Research, pedagogy, practice* (pp. 103–25). Thousand Oaks, CA: Sage.

Atay, A. (2015). *Globalization's impact on cultural identity formation: Queer diasporic males in cyberspace.* Lanham, MD: Lexington Books.

Austin, E. (2011). Space and place in zombie culture: How fictional film inspires dissent, celebration and the Carnivalesque in social spaces. Paper presented at the Zombosium conference, October 28, 2011, University of Winchester, Winchester, England.

Boylorn, R. M. (2008). As seen on TV: An autoethnographic reflection on race and reality television. *Critical Studies in Media Communication, 25*(4), 413–33. doi:10.1080/15295030802327758.

Bradshaw, P. (2016, November 23). It's official—*The Walking Dead* helped elect Donald Trump. *The Guardian* (UK). Retrieved from https://www.theguardian.com/commentisfree/2016/nov/23/walking-elect-dead-trump-immigration-zombies.

Bressler, N., & Lengel, L. (2016). Mothering and/in dystopia: Lone parenting in a post-apocalyptic world. In M. Motapanyane (Ed.), *Motherhood and single/lone parenting: A 21st century perspective* (pp. 19–52). Toronto, Canada: Demeter Press.

Brown, K. (2015). *Dispatches from dystopia: Histories of places not yet forgotten.* Chicago, IL: University of Chicago Press.

Bumpus, M. (2005). Using motion pictures to teach management: Refocusing the camera lens through the infusion approach to diversity. *Journal of Management Education, 29*(6), 792–815.

Cardon, P. W. (2010). Using films to learn about the nature of cross-cultural stereotypes in intercultural business communication courses. *Business Communication Quarterly, 73*(2), 150–65.

Champoux, J. (1999). Film as a teaching resource. *Journal of Management Inquiry, 8,* 206–17.

Cooper, C. (2004). Mix up the Indian with All the Patwa: Rajamuffin sounds in "Cool" Britannia. *Language and Intercultural Communication, 4*(1–2), 81–99.

Crabtree, D. (2001). The importance of history. Retrieved fromhttp://msc.gutenberg.edu/2001/02/the-importance-of-history/.

Cravey, A. J., & Petit, M. (2012). A critical pedagogy of place: Learning through the body. *Feminist Formations, 24*(2), 100–119.

Daspit, T. (2000). Rap pedagogies: "Bring(ing) the noise" of "knowledge born on the microphone" to radical education. In T. Daspit & J. A. Weaver (Eds.), *Popular culture and critical pedagogy: Reading, constructing, connecting* (pp. 163–82). New York: Routledge.

Dhaenens, F. (2014). Articulations of queer resistance on the small screen. *Continuum: Journal of Media & Cultural Studies, 28*(4), 520–31.

Drunk History. (2013–). Comedy Central (Seasons 1–4). Derek Waters, Creator, Derek Waters and Owen Burke, Executive Producers; Produced by Gary Sanchez Productions, Konner Productions.

Edwards, R., & Usher, R. (2000). *Globalisation and pedagogy: Space, place and identity.* London, UK: Routledge.

Erlandson, K. T. (2012). Teaching intercultural awareness with *Star Wars*: A new hope. *Communication Teacher, 26*(1), 17–21.

Eyestone, D. (2013). Feminist aliens, black vampires, and gay witches: Creating a critical polis using SF television in the college composition classroom. Unpublished doctoral dissertation, Iowa State University.

Fassett, D. L., & Warren, J. T. (2007). *Critical communication pedagogy.* Thousand Oaks, CA: Sage.

Freire, P. (1970). *Pedagogy of the oppressed* (M. B. Ramos, Trans.). New York: Herder and Herder.

Garcia, A., Seglem, R., & Share, J. (2013). Transforming teaching and learning through critical media literacy pedagogy. *LEARNing Landscapes, 6*(2), 109–24.

Garrett, H. J., & Schmeichel, M. (2012). Using "The Daily Show" to promote media literacy. *Social Education, 76*(4), 211–15.

Grady, J., Marquez, R., & McLaren, P. (2012). A critique of neoliberalism with fierceness: Queer youth of color creating dialogues of resistance. *Journal of Homosexuality, 59*(7), 982–1004.

Greenfeld, D. (2007). What's the deal with the white middle-aged guy teaching hip-hop? Lessons in popular culture, positionality, and pedagogy. *Pedagogy, Culture & Society, 15*(2), 229–243.

Gruenewald, D. A. (2003). The best of both worlds: A critical pedagogy of place. *Educational Researcher, 32*(4), 3–12.

Hall, J. (2018). *Boys, bass and bother: Popular dance and identity in UK drum 'n' bass club culture.* London, England: Palgrave Macmillan.

Hall, S. (1997). The spectacle of the 'Other.' In S. Hall (Ed.), *Representation: Cultural representations and signifying practices* (pp. 223–90). Thousand Oaks, CA: Sage.

Hatty, S. (2000). *Masculinities, violence and culture.* Thousand Oaks, CA: Sage.

How I Met Your Mother. (CBS, 2005–2014) (Seasons 1–9), C. Bays, Writer, P. Fryman, Director, C. Bays, Producer, Century City, CA: 20th Century Fox.

Hodkinson, P. 2017). Media, culture and society (2nd ed.). London: SAGE.

Jagose, A. (1996). *Queer theory: An introduction.* New York: New York University Press.

Kahl, D. S. (2013). Critical communication pedagogy and assessment: Reconciling two seemingly incongruous ideas. *International Journal of Communication, 7,* 2610–30.

Kahl, D. S. (2016). Addressing the challenges of critical communication pedagogy scholarship: Moving toward an applied agenda. *Journal of Applied Communication Research, 45*(1), 116–20.

Kellner, D., & Kim, G. (2010). YouTube, critical pedagogy, and media activism. *Review of Education/Pedagogy/Cultural Studies, 32*(1), 3–36.

Kluch, Y. (2015). 'The man your man should be like': Consumerism, patriarchy and the construction of twenty-first-century masculinities in 2010 and 2012 Old Spice campaigns. *Interactions: Studies in Communication & Culture, 6*(3), 361–77. doi:10.1386/iscc.6.3.361_1

Kluch, Y., & Lengel, L. (2015a). Critiquing globalization through popular cultural texts: Communication education for social responsibility. Refereed paper presented at the 10th Global Communication Association Conference, July 18, 2015, Berlin, Germany.

Kluch, Y. & Lengel, L. (2015b). "If it were the end of civilization what good would gays be?" Ruptures and reinscriptions of heteronormative masculinity in season 5 of *The Walking Dead*. Refereed paper presented for the LGBTQ Communication Studies Division of the National Communication Association, November 19, 2015, Las Vegas.

Krauss, K. (2011). Boys will be boys: The male image in Old Spice advertising in the 1950s and 2000s. *Media Report to Women, 39*(4), 6–20.

Leard, D. W., & Lashua, B. (2006). Popular media, critical pedagogy, and inner city youth. *Canadian Journal of Education, 29*(1), 244–64.

Lengel, L., & Martin, S. C. (2010). Gender and critical intercultural communication. In T. Nakayama & R. Halualani (Eds.), *Handbook of critical intercultural communication* (pp. 334–47). Oxford, UK: Blackwell.

Lengel, L., Newsom, V., & Montenegro, D. A. (2017). White religio-nationalism, post-truth populism, and Muslim Othering. Paper presented at the International Communication Association preconference: Populism, Post-Truth Politics and Participatory Culture: Interventions in the Intersection of Popular and Political Communication, May 25, 2017, San Diego.

Lengel, L., & Smidi, A. (in press). How affect overrides fact: Anti-Muslim politicized rhetoric in the post-truth era. In L. Zhang & C. Clark (Eds.), *Emotion, affect, and rhetorical persuasion in mass communication: Theories and case studies*. New York, NY: Routledge.

Lincoln, Y. S., & Denzin, N. K. (2003). *Turning points in qualitative research: Tying knots in a handkerchief*. London, UK: Sage.

Loewen, J. W., & Sebesta, E. H. (2011). Concluding words. In J. W. Loewen & E. H. Sebesta (Eds.), *The Confederate and neo-Confederate reader: The "great truth" about the "lost cause"* (pp. 392–93). Jackson, MS: University of Mississippi Press.

Mansfield, H. C. (2006). *Manliness*. New Haven, CT: Yale University Press.

McKee, A. (2001). A beginner's guide to textual analysis. *Metro, 127/128*, 138–49.

McLaren, P. (1999). Revolutionary pedagogy in post-revolutionary times: Rethinking the political economy of critical education. *Educational Theory, 48*, 432–62.

Mejia, R. (2017). Post truth, or the cultural logic of late racism. In Media Res, January 27, 2017. Retrieved from http://mediacommons.org/imr/2017/01/28/post-truth-or-cultural-logic-late-racism.

Mejia, R., Beckermann, K., & Sullivan, C. (2018). White lies: A racial history of the (post)truth. *Communication and Critical/Cultural Studies, 15*(2), 109–26.

Meyer, M. D. E. (2010). Representing bisexuality on television: The case for intersectional hybrids. *Journal of Bisexuality, 10*(4), 366–87.

Morgan, J. (2000) Critical pedagogy: The spaces that make the difference. *Pedagogy, Culture & Society, 8*(3), 273–89.

Morrell, E. (2002). Toward a critical pedagogy of popular culture: Literacy development among urban youth. *Journal of Adolescent & Adult Literacy, 46*(1), 72–77.

Nainby, K., Warren, J. T., & Bollinger, C. (2003). Articulating contact in the classroom: Towards a constitutive focus in critical pedagogy. *Language & Intercultural Communication, 3*(3), 198–212.

Ndalianis, A. (2015). Genre, culture and the semiosphere: New horror cinema and post-9/11. *International Journal of Cultural Studies 18*(1), 135–51.

Owen, D. B., Silet, C. L. P., & Brown, S. E. (1998). Teaching television to empower students. *The English Journal, 87*(1), 28–33.

Pandey, S. (2012). Using popular movies in teaching cross-cultural management. *European Journal of Training and Development, 36*(2–3), 329–50.

Platts, T. (2013). Locating zombies in the sociology of popular culture. *Sociology Compass, 1*(14), 547–60.
Sfeir, G. (2014). Critical pedagogy through popular culture. *Education Matters, 2*(2), 15–25.
Sheumaker, H. (2015). "Downhill from there": *Drunk History* in the classroom. *Perspectives on History*, newsmagazine of the American Historical Association, October 2015. Retrieved from https://www.historians.org/publications-and-directories/perspectives-on-history/october-2015/downhill-from-there-drunk-history-in-the-classroom.
Simon, C. B., & Blanch, J. P. (2015). Paulo Freire, ensino, história e os desafios da contemporaneidade. *Dialogos, 19*(1), 117–42.
Smith, D. (2000). Outlaw women writers, (un)popular popular culture, and critical pedagogy. In T. Daspit & J. A. Weaver (eds.), *Popular culture and critical pedagogy: Reading, constructing, connecting* (pp. 183–99). New York: Routledge.
Soja, E. (1989). *Postmodern geographies*. London, UK: Verso.
Somerville, M. J. (2010). A place pedagogy for "global contemporaneity". *Educational Philosophy and Theory, 42*(3), 326–44.
The Big Bang Theory. (CBS, 2007–), (seasons 1–12), Lorre, C., & Prady, B. (Writers), & Cendrowski, M. (Director). (2008). The Cooper-Nowitzki Theorem [Television series episode]. In C. Lorre, B. Prady, & S. Molaro (Producers), Burbank, CA: Warner Home Video.
The Daily Show. (Comedy Central, 2016, September 21). "Conspiracy Theories Thrive at a Trump Rally", Jordan Klepper, Producer, Fingers the Pulse. Retrieved from https://www.youtube.com/watch?v=eFQhw3VVToQ.
The Walking Dead. (AMC, 2010–) (Seasons 1–9). Robert Kirkman, Creator, Executive Producer, and Writer. Glenn Mazzara, and Scott M. Gimble, Executive Producers/Writers; David Alpert, Gale Ann Hurd and Tom Luse, Executive Producers; Greg Nicotero, Executive Producer/Special Effects Make-Up Designer. Produced by AMC Productions, Circle of Confusion, Darkwood Productions, Valhalla Motion Pictures, Valhalla Entertainment, and Idiot Box Productions.
Walsh, K. R., Fürsich, E., & Jefferson, B. S. (2008). Beauty and the patriarchal beast: Gender role portrayals in sitcoms featuring mismatched couples. *Journal of Popular Film & Television, 36*(3), 123–32.
Westerfelhaus, R., & Lacroix, C. (2006). Seeing 'straight' through *Queer Eye*: Exposing the strategic rhetoric of heteronormativity in a mediated ritual of gay rebellion. *Critical Studies in Media Communication, 23*(5), 426–44.
Weaver, J. A., & Daspit, T. (2000). Critical pedagogy, popular culture and the creation of meaning. In T. Daspit & J. A. Weaver (Eds.), *Popular culture and critical pedagogy: Reading, constructing, connecting* (pp. xiii–2). New York: Routledge.
Weber, B. R. (2010). Teaching popular culture through gender studies: Feminist pedagogy in a postfeminist and neoliberal academy? *Feminist Teacher, 20*(2), 124–38.

Chapter Six

Critical Engagement or Critical Mistake?

Social Media, Ethics, and Critical Communication Pedagogy

E. Michele Ramsey

As Web 2.0 technologies and platforms have developed over the past decade or so, I have watched as those we might (too simplistically) categorize as technophiles or Luddites discuss and debate the positives and negatives of various social media platforms and computer-assisted educational tools. While the reasons for movement toward the use of Web 2.0 technologies are often as varied as the ways these tools are used, my experience has been that the arguments in favor of movement in this direction tend to fall somewhere within two primary camps—institutional encouragements to use technology in classes simply because those technologies exist, and a desire to increase student engagement in courses by "meeting students where they are" and redirecting their in-class technology use toward educational goals.[1] Administrators and instructional technology staff, anxious to make their marks on their institution, push a variety of new technologies to promote alternative means of interpersonal communication/communication of information between students and faculty, and leave in their wake scores of "smart boards," "clickers," and similar new technologies that, like a toy outgrown by a child, are ultimately placed in a corner somewhere, rarely ever played with again. And faculty working to find ways to engage students more effectively often seem to move quickly from one new platform or tool to another and may not concern themselves with deeper questions about the use of such tools in the classroom before jumping into a new platform with both feet.

Neither of these camps (nor most others, I assume) are "wrong," per se, but both seem to (mis)understand communication, and especially computer-mediated communication, in very important ways. Most significantly, both groups tend to assume that more communication is always a good thing. But as a late mentor reminded me for years, we rarely need more communication in this world as much as we need *better* communication. And one place where perhaps this statement is most true is in communication classrooms where issues of social justice, diversity, and marginalization are important elements of the curriculum. Requiring, or even just encouraging, the use of social media platforms in courses such as these can be problematic when we assume that *more* communication is always better. Moreover, faculty interested in critical communication pedagogy may find these tools at odds with their good intentions, despite the constant refrain of the Internet as a great democratizing tool.

With their possibilities for immediate comment and feedback on *the* day's events and the oversimplified arguments that herald their ability to level the "marketplace of ideas," to many, social media platforms seem ripe for the kind of critical education Freire (1968) encourages—a type of learning that Fassett and Warren note means "entering into the problem" and "feeling the moment of possibility" (2007, p. 26). But these common *prima facia* assumptions about social media platforms in the academy as a means of democratizing or encouraging discussions are fraught with internal and external issues of ethics that all faculty, but especially faculty invested in critical communication pedagogy, should consider.

While too dense to explicate fully here, important ethical and pragmatic concerns about the use of social media that are relevant to my argument have already been recognized. There are familiar worries about the impact of social media posting on job searches, careers, and online bullying and harassment in the age of Web 2.0 that are long-standing, as are recognitions that the truncated nature of social media communication encourages confrontation (Junco and Chickering, 2010). In addition, Silicon Valley entrepreneur, Andrew Keen (2007), shares the concerns of some academics, noting that the so-called "democratization" of the Internet damages our culture by replacing higher quality sources of information with user-generated content that can be unreliable, unethical, and dishonest. We only need look at the latest Facebook privacy debacle—the Cambridge Analytica scandal and its effects on our election process—to realize that Keen was on to something early. His position is made clear when he says, "What happens when ignorance meets egoism meets bad taste meets mob rule? The monkey takes over." And he adds that only the "loudest and most opinionated voices survive" (p. 9). Lovink (2011) notes concern about the personal and governmental ability to track Internet traffic. He also critiques "comment culture," where the goal is to "be heard, to achieve any impact, and leave behind a mark" rather than to simply correct a statement or contribute to "general intellect" (p. 53). In other words, he argues, there is a "widespread unwillingness to reach consensus and to come to a conclusion in a debate" (p. 58). Discussing the use of social media for political participation, Dahlgren (2014) argues that the "discursive contribution" of social media tends to deflect politics from people "without an already existing political sense of self" and thus doubts its ability to promote "democratic political life" in society as a whole.

Scholars also note that users have little control over the access to their information and posts, making even those who are aware of the dangers of social media usage unable to do much about those problems on their own (Hundley & Shyles, 2010; Lewis & West, 2009). Research also indicates that college students report compulsively checking social media sites (Lewis & West, 2009) and that addiction to the Internet can be linked to depression, loneliness, and social anxiety (Caplan, 2007; Skoric et al., 2009). Without using the word, Lowry et al. (2016) seem to point to the tendencies of people we typically refer to as "trolls" in their research, which showed that cyber bullying among adults was more strongly linked to time spent online than to anonymity.

These well-known concerns raised about social media use in general should be considered carefully when thinking about its use in the classroom, especially given the popularity of using these tools in the classroom. In fact, in a study of 1,920 faculty, Moran, Seaman, and Tinti-Kane (2011) found that 91 percent of surveyed faculty used social networking for professional and/or educational purposes, that 70 percent viewed social networking as a valuable tool for teaching, and that 58 percent believed that social networking platforms could positively impact collaborative learning. More broadly, current research on the use of social media platforms in classes includes discussions of social media as a means of encouraging engagement with the course content and better or worse grades (Dayter, 2011; Dyson et al., 2015; Gagnon, 2015; Junco, Elavsky, & Heiberger, 2013; Junco, Heibergert & Loken, 2010; Kuznekoff, Munz, & Titsworth, 2015; Parcha, 2014a; Reed, 2013; Suit et al., 2015; Tyma, 2011), the challenges and ethics of using social media in classrooms (Aragon et al., 2014; Chang & Gray, 2013; Gray, 2008; Jouneau-Sion & Sanchez, 2013), and scores of assignments linked to social media in many disciplines. Research on the efficacy of using social media has produced mixed results, but important issues of ethics (e.g., concerns about privacy, ignorance of the impact of public communication on one's own career prospects, the impact of trolling in educational contexts, and putting students in situations where the mistakes they might make in the classroom are put on public display) generally are not considered in this research. Indeed, many of the published assignments based in social media ignore issues like these and, instead, take for granted the inherent virtue of social media. But just as it is a mistake to assume that there is always inherent value in communication ("We just need *more* communication!"), it is a mistake to assume that social media use in class has inherent value as well.

There are important internal and external issues of ethics surrounding the use of social media in the classroom that faculty must consider, especially faculty interested in a critical communication pedagogy that recognizes "profound ideological difference in socioeconomic context as constituent of what happens in schools and classrooms" and attempts to "reflect and act upon the world in order to transform it, to make it a more just a place for more people, to respond to our collective pains and needs and desires" (Fassett & Warren, 2007, p. 26). To the end of considering social media platforms as a means of interrogating oppression in the classroom and outside of it, I will focus on what I call the internal ethical issues—perceived anonymity and the impact that may have on student judgment, problems linked to fallacious notions of the First Amendment protection of expression, and the problematic notion that students can "just delete" problematic posts without consequences. From those discussions I will move into an examination of what I consider the external issues of ethics related to the use of social media in class, including how possible future employers and/or internship supervisors may use data from social media, concerns about student privacy, and whether social media allows for a recognition of context in discussing important questions of communication as it relates to social justice and critical thinking.

INTERNAL AND EXTERNAL CONCERNS ABOUT SOCIAL MEDIA IN THE CLASSROOM

Internal Concerns

The first internal concern to consider is the impact of *perceived anonymity* on student behavior and the behavior of non-students who may also engage in these public conversations. Foundational research on computer-mediated communication points to its lack of social context cues and its tendency to encourage a neglect of social conventions while also encouraging aggression (Kiesler, Siegel, & Mcguire, 1984; Kiesler & Sproull, 1986; Joinson, 2005). Researchers have also noted that because of this perceived anonymity, people tend to disclose more intimate details about themselves (Bargh, McKenna, & Fitzsimons, 2002). Added to the tendencies of humans to disclose more about themselves online, as well as the tendency of some to become more aggressive online, we must add the human tendency to want to shut down speech we find offensive to the mix, and, unfortunately, social media platforms can galvanize this tendency by allowing students to identify speech they don't like or encouraging groups of people to work together to shut down particular viewpoints (Johnson, 2016).

The creation of assignments based in social media must, by definition, deny the ability for students to be completely anonymous to faculty. The cost and risk of social sanctions may seem reduced to students (Bargh, McKenna, & Fitzsimons, 2002); however, the lack of face-to-face communication in online communication can encourage more assertive, and even aggressive, communication in users. Despite the heralding of social media usage as a means of making large lecture classes more communicative (Dyson, Vickers, Turner, Cowan & Tassone, 2015; Elavsky, Mislan, & Elavsky, 2011; Tyma, 2011), issues associated with perceived anonymity would seem to be even more likely in large lecture classes where students are not likely to know each other. Thus, faculty must be aware of these tendencies with regard to managing possible online conflict between two students who may feel emboldened to say things online that they would not say to a classmate face-to-face. Moreover, trollers who are not students, but who may choose to engage with students in these public forums, can have tendencies towards sadism and other anti-social behaviors (Buckels, Trapnell, & Paulhus, 2014), which puts a different kind of burden on students who may or may not be equipped to effectively manage such conflict and communication. Gagnon (2015) briefly notes a possible concern with issues such as Internet trolling, but there is no sustained attention to that concern in the essay. Even when social media platforms are not a part of the equation, "the world of the classroom is not a false world, but rather a microcosm of all the worlds we know, intersecting an interlocking in metronymic relationship to one another" and that world always already includes the violence, tension, social justice, and change that is part of the outside world (Fassett & Warren, 2007, p. 62). Thus, when we invite that outside world into our classrooms in very real ways using social media platforms as a pedagogical tool, faculty choosing to use those tools have an affirmative obligation to train students in effective online communication, as well as in strategies for the management of online conflict. Failure to do so could cause students to post things they later regret and/or cause students unintended stress associated with online microaggressions, bullying, and plain abuse. Moreover, and contrary to the goals of critical communication pedagogy, these unintended consequences are likely to fall disproportionately on to students who already deal with significant amounts of bullying and other forms of abuse.

Linked to the possible behaviors associated with perceived anonymity and its consequences, faculty must also consider *misconceptions of the First Amendment* that encourage students to believe that their speech is protected. A common retort to people in positions of power seeking to constrain or even stop the expression of citizens, in and out of the classroom, is that such restrictions infringe upon their "freedom of speech." There are four primary ways that this retort is problematic. First, such a response ignores the fact that the First Amendment protects us against governmental infringement on our speech, not against personal or corporate limits on our speech. In addition, though students do not "shed their constitutional rights to freedom of speech or expression at the schoolhouse gate" (*Tinker v. Des Moines*, 393 US 503 [1969], p.13), university speech codes exist and are enforced; thus faculty must be prepared to teach students about not only their free speech rights, but also the responsibilities of free speech as defined by their school's speech codes. Because of the public nature of social media, these concerns become even more important than if we were just talking about discussions inside the walls of the classroom.

Second, when students make mistakes in online communication, there is a common belief that one can just "delete" that mistake, but that is simply not true for two reasons. First of all, one of the principles of communication is that it is irreversible (Wood, 2010). The concept, of course, makes perfect sense when one thinks about it, but it is still an abstract concept that students may need additional help understanding. Students need to understand that we can apologize, take back, and try to mitigate the consequences of our communication, but that we are without power to make those changes in the minds of those who read our online communication. Under any circumstances, this principle of communication is vital to understand, but the need to understand that the irreversible nature of communication is amplified in online climates where perceived anonymity and misperceptions of freedom of expression by students can encourage harsh commentary or language that students may later regret.

Next, the First Amendment does not just protect speech. It also protects the right not to speak. In other words, it protects silence (*West Virginia State Board of Education v. Barnette* [1943] and *Wooley v. Maynard* [1977]). Indeed, the U.S. Supreme Court recognizes the right to silence as equal to the right to speak. And yet, as Hao (2011) recognizes, the assumption of Western classrooms is that silence equals disengagement when it may be a decision based in culture or political decision, for example. Hao astutely points out that critical communication pedagogy, with its uncritical focus on agency and dialogue, privileges speech over silence. This is an argument worth paying serious attention to and it becomes even more salient, perhaps, in classrooms that require students to engage publicly on social media platforms as a means of earning points. What are the ethics of forcing speech? Especially speech that is accessible to people all over the world? When we force speech are we living up to the principles of critical communication pedagogy or are we hypocritically punishing people for not enacting a very Western conception of learning and engagement? Practitioners of critical communication pedagogy need to have answers to these questions, especially before they begin requiring students to engage on social media.

Finally, students need to understand that online communication is never really deleted. Others can take screen captures of any communication and save or share it. In addition, data storage has become so cheap that groups and companies are attempting to store everything that has been shared online. Is it likely that someone will dig into the cache files of the Internet and unearth a post from two years prior that could hurt the reputation of the student that posted it? Probably not. Is it possible? Absolutely. Thus while faculty may communicate to students that they should assume that anything they post online is essentially the same as posting it on a public billboard, faculty must also make sure students understand that nothing is ever truly deleted from the Internet and to consider even more carefully before they post.

External Concerns

The impacts of the internal concerns discussed above can have very real *external* consequences for students that we have to consider. In a study of more than 300 college students, Clipson, Wilson, and DuFrene (2011) found that one in five students reported experiencing a lost or damaged relationship because of social media miscommunication. Given the risks associated with damaging our interpersonal relationships via social media, what consequences for student relationships outside their immediate interpersonal ones should we consider? First of all, we have to remember that future employers and/or internship supervisors may use data from social media when considering our students for positions. As Peterson (2014) notes, employers often use social media for recruitment purposes. Employers also use these platforms to help screen candidates (Ollington, Gibb, & Harcourt, 2013; Paik et al., 2014; Peluchette & Karl, 2010, Society for Human Resource Management, 2012). Furthermore, the Society for Human Resource Management found that 77 percent of human resource professionals accessed and considered social media websites for recruitment purposes with one in five using social media to learn more about applicants (Waldman, 2011). Employers hope to glean information about a person's levels of responsibility, common sense, and self-awareness (Hood, Robels, & Hopkins, 2014) from their social media posts and thus we must consider the future impact of student posts on social media.

The multitude of real-life examples of social media posts and their very negative implications on the lives of the poster should have faculty seriously considering the possibility of our students making devastating mistakes on social media and the possible impacts on students' lives. For example, in 2013 Justine Sacco tweeted to her paltry 170 Twitter followers this message: "Going to Africa. Hope I don't get AIDS. Just kidding! I'm white!" In between the time she tweeted that message, 30 minutes before boarding a plane in London, and landing in Africa eleven hours later, her life was turned upside-down. Her employer and fellow employees had already publicly commented on her tweet and thousands of people monitored Twitter alone and with groups in bars while she flew in hopes of seeing her life implode in real time once she landed (Ronson, 2015). Sacco lost her job—really, her career. She is also now forever linked to that very unfortunate tweet, so that anyone meeting her can easily discover that story with one simple Google search of her name. This example is undoubtedly extreme, but there is no way of knowing how likely it is for another person to have the same experience after one unfortunate tweet, as such odds depend on where that tweet is shared and if someone with an extensive social media following decides to repost the offending message. These odds are simply too high for me as a professor who regularly deals with issues of race, sex, sexuality, gender, class, and the like. One mindless tweet or one poorly worded tweet that is misconstrued by the audience, can do untold damage to a student's life and career aspirations. There is no amount of "student engagement" or "finding voice" that, for me, makes the chances of student embarrassment and even temporary ruin worth the risk, and thus suggestions that faculty should consider social media as a place for students to interrogate and comment on issues such as racism and race-related groups (Moody, 2010) strike me as dangerously ill-considered.

Another external concern is *privacy* and the micro and macro data collection that takes place on social media sites. In terms of micro-data collection, simply requiring a student to sign up for a Twitter or other social media account means that you have forced them to position themselves on "the grid." Students have the right to keep their names, thoughts, and personalities off of the Internet and thus requiring the use of such systems can be very problematic, especially when there is evidence that some students do not wish to integrate their personal social media usage with their academic work (Hewitt & Forte, 2006; Hew, 2011). Additionally, contrary to popular and academic belief, social media accounts are never "free" even though they cost no money to enjoy (Tyma, 2011). As Chang and Gray (2013) note, we exchange enormous amounts of data about ourselves and our habits in exchange for our Facebook and Twitter accounts. And even though research shows that only 20 percent of Millennials are worried about their privacy a good deal or most of the time, while 46 percent are only worried a little, and 34 percent do not worry at all (American Press Institute, 2015), faculty should think hard about whether or not *we're okay* with handing our students, their data, and their "user-generated content" over to for-profit corporations serving a multitude of marketers worldwide. These questions become even more salient as we begin to understand the role of social media in the aforementioned Facebook/Cambridge Analytica scandal and its impact on the U.S. presidential election. In this era of seemingly nonstop movement towards the privatization and corporatization of education at all levels, is this a trade we are willing to make for what seems to be relatively minimal gain?

Especially when we add the possible negative consequences discussed above to the equation?

In part to deal with issues linked to public messages and student privacy, some universities and colleges have purchased programs such as Yammer, which mimics the utility of Facebook, but serves only those linked to the organization via a specific e-mail. But these in-house platforms do not solve the problems of review by unintended audiences and privacy concerns. Student communication is still not safe from exposure using something like Yammer because while our students' mistakes initially may not be in the Twittersphere or amongst the YikYak herd, they are a mere screen capture and anonymous post away from being placed there for all to see. Issues of privacy are, in my view, even more concerning. Yammer has the ability to allow administrators/managers to monitor the use of certain words or phrases throughout the system and report back to them all uses of marked words or phrases. It also allows for a variety of big data analytics on its users. Thus, faculty using these systems in hopes of forgoing the problems associated with Twitter, Facebook, and the like should take a serious look at what data is being collected on themselves and their students using programs such as Yammer.

A final external concern deals with the utility of social media platforms when dealing with questions of communication, especially as they relate to incredibly complex issues of social justice and critical communication pedagogy. Thinking broadly, how can 280 characters effectively reflect the context surrounding what's being communicated in those 280 characters? How can one 280-character tweet about the Black Lives Matter movement account for the multitude of contexts with which people layer the issue of police brutality? Can it be done? Maybe. Is it done well the majority of the time? Probably not. Does an attempt to engage students in a discussion of Black Lives Matter via Twitter really illuminate this incredibly complex and important movement? Or does it, instead, allow for the further silo-ing of opinions and information on social media? Does it do some of both? How would we know? Regarding issues of such dire importance, where significant communication must occur to understand context, as well as people's *perceptions* of context, to move toward understanding, I have a difficult time holding out much hope for Twitter's role in this process. The platform can be useful in terms of encouraging awareness of certain issues. The recent #MeToo movement, for example, was amplified on social media. But we must wonder how many people suffered negative material, emotional, or physical consequences as a result of their #MeToo post. Thus, when we consider the fact that communication is always messy, rife with all of the complications of our identities as they relate to communication, as well as the abstract nature of language, and the multitude of contexts for interpersonal communication—psychological, physiological, relational, situational, social, environmental, perceptual, sociorelational, temporal, and cultural (Jackson, 2014)—how can 280 characters account for all of that? What do we have to choose to leave out? What gets left out in the mind of the reader that we intended to include? Whether I am teaching public speaking, interpersonal communication, gender and communication, conflict management, the rhetoric of American horror films, political communication, social movements, women's public address, or issues in freedom of expression, context always matters. And it does not *just* matter; it is *essential* to comprehending all we try to understand about communication. Thus, I am hard-pressed to grant 280 characters, or frankly, even a 5,000-word blog, the assumption that something meaningful about communication's context will be conveyed in a way that enlightens rather than obfuscates the important concepts I want my students to interrogate.

WHAT DOES ALL OF THIS MEAN FOR CRITICAL COMMUNICATION PEDAGOGY?

Students make mistakes in thinking and speech in class, but faculty are there to help navigate those mistakes and misunderstandings so that they don't do damage to the student or other students. That responsibility is important in all disciplines, of course, but in communication courses generally, and especially amongst faculty who want to "situate their inquiry in relation to larger, macro socio-cultural, socioeconomic structures, to explore the ways in which racism, sexism, classism, homophobia, and other forms of oppression permeate classrooms and research on classrooms, teachers, and students" (Fassett & Warren, 2007, p. 27), the importance of a faculty member's role in helping students navigate difficult conversations about complex and demanding topics that tend to emerge in communication courses cannot be overstated.

As Fassett and Warren (2007) suggest, critical communication educators understand identity as relational and relating to ideological contexts and power. Perhaps in an effort to expose and create "generative spaces to work with one another" and to name "our social, material circumstances" (Fassett & Warren, 2007, p. 55) so that we can act together to change them, some faculty have moved to social media platforms as a means of extending conversations outside the parameters of the classroom into "the real world." But as I have already noted (and as Fassett and Warren [2007] also note), the classroom is already very real, with its students and faculty always already imbued with the "violence, tension, social justice, and change that is part of the outside world" (Fassett & Warren, 2007, p. 62). Given this fact, do we really need social media platforms to engage students with issues important to the communication classroom? Do the benefits outweigh the risks?

As more classrooms move from buildings to cyberspace, do the ends of engaging students in the important issues made prominent in critical communication pedagogy justify the possible serious consequences of the means? At this point, I contend that they do not. The move to more online classes may have serious consequences for the goals of critical communication pedagogy. Given that even discussion posts can be posted as screen shots, how safe is it to have these crucial, yet sometimes very sensitive, conversations via a means that can be captured and communicated to the whole world and for eternity? What damage is possible in the name of addressing damage that already exists? These are questions that practitioners of critical communication pedagogy must consider and address as faculty.

Fassett and Warren (2007) argue that a "commitment to critical communication pedagogy is predicated on the significance of human communication as constitutive, as the means to produce, maintain, and interpret our worlds" (p. 56) and that the classroom has consequences, including the fact that both students and teachers leave lasting fingerprints on each other that can last a lifetime. It may or may not be the case that when they wrote these words they were considering the possible impacts of the inclusion of social media platforms in courses, such as assignments that can leave students unemployed and (for the immediate future) unemployable because of a careless "joke" posted online or online bullying that introduces a student to deep psychological pain or leads another student to severe reaction, such as harming oneself. But those particular fingerprints are not just possible; they can also be intensely palpable.

We should appreciate and encourage faculty who do not see the classroom as a place for the mere transmission of information, but rather, who work toward a critical communication pedagogy that views the classroom as a process of knowledge construction and a place to theorize about the social, cultural, and economic relationships of the classroom (Fassett & Warren, 2007). But we should also be mindful of Anyanwu's (2003) warning that the use of online communication in classrooms as an addition to, or replacement for, face-to-face communication should be thoroughly investigated before jumping onto the "bandwagon of technophiles" because it is important for both the students and faculty "to be properly informed of the operatives and consequences of new media technology in the definition of our sociocultural persona as well as the pedagogical outcome of teaching and learning" (p. 391). While arguments about the utility of extending writing "beyond and around the single path from student to teacher" (Yancey, 2004, p. 310), about the value of participatory cultures in education that offer "opportunities for peer-to-peer sharing, a changed attitude toward intellectual property, the diversification of cultural expression, the development of skills valued in the modern workplace, and a more empowered conception of citizenship" (Jenkins, Purushotma, Robison, & Weigel, 2006, p. 3), and about platforms such as Twitter that are "free to use" as tools that can "construct an environment where students must be on-task and to the point in their communication," which serves as a means of giving students a voice in large lecture environments (Tyma, 2011), are worthy goals, there are serious and impactful consequences to the use of social media to attempt to achieve those goals.

We must also consider whether or not these goals more likely to be achieved in face-to-face or in mediated communication? Bargh, McKenna, and Fitzsimons (2002) note two differences they found when comparing Internet and face-to-face communication. First they note that, "by its very nature, it facilitates the expression and effective communication of one's true self to new acquaintances outside of one's established social network, which leads to forming relationships with them" and second, "that once those relationships are formed, features of Internet interaction facilitate the projection onto the partner of idealized qualities," which previous research has deemed critical in the formation of close, intimate relationships (p. 45). Citing Derlega, Metts, Petronio, & Margulis (1993) and Murray, Holmes, and Griffin (1996), they supplement this finding by suggesting that Internet communication enables self-disclosure because of its relatively anonymous nature and because it fosters idealization of the other in the absence of information to the contrary. While these findings can be recognized, we must also consider the consequences of connections made outside of one's established network that are also based in the relatively anonymous nature of the Internet, but do not lead to positive relationship formation. In other words, we cannot just consider the possible positive outcomes of including social media in our teaching. We must also consider and weigh the possible negative outcomes. For example, Parcha (2014a) argues for the use of Twitter in classrooms using communication accommodation theory (Giles, Mulac, Bradac, & Johnson, 1987), which includes the concepts of convergence (emphasizing similarities to promote identification with another) and divergence (emphasizing differences between counterparts). Parcha utilizes Twitter in the classroom/the study to bring convergence to improve student-to-student connectedness, which it is argued will encourage students to engage in course material. The Twitter account is required to be public and students must tweet one "non-academic" tweet that "enhances rather than distracts from their classroom-appropriate image" (p. 231). The positive possibilities of such use of Twitter are foregrounded in the essay, but the possible negative consequences of the use of Twitter are only acknowledged with the brief pronouncement that one non-academic tweet must "enhance" rather than "distract from" a "classroom appropriate image."

In addition, Parcha (2014b) notes that "a 140-character tweet is non-threatening—offering students a chance to interact with one another without worrying about fellow students evaluating their writing or argumentation skills." The unstated problems that underlie the brief mention of "distracting" posts and "classroom appropriate image" are profound and deserve more than that brief mention. If Donald Trump has taught us nothing else, he taught us that Twitter is a fantastic place to make really bad arguments. He exemplifies some of the worst tendencies of social media—bullying, the promotion of patently false information, and even the endorsement of arguments and conspiracy theories that can cause material harm to others. I worry that the promotion of the latest technology in the classroom, even though it has been done with the best of intentions, has been conducted without much concern about the issues I have addressed in this chapter and can do our students and even our country harm.

Fassett and Warren (2007) deserve extensive quotation here.

> If the classroom is a microcosm of worlds, a metonym of the cultures we'll encounter throughout our lives, then it is also a site of social change. It is a meaningful environment for engaging difference, for creating community, and for envisioning the kinds of social organization we want for ourselves. We don't forget the ideological lessons we learn in school, and if we presume that, in the classroom, we cannot build a more just society, then we have already abdicated our own agency; we have lost ourselves to a series of false worlds by never knowing how to make them real. (p. 63)

Indeed, our classrooms are microcosms of the world and can be sites of social change and meaningful environments for engaging difference, creating community, and envisioning better social organizations. And frankly, that is the primary reason I wanted this job. I want to help teach, mentor, and guide students the way that my faculty taught, mentored, and guided me. But along with my desire to challenge students "to seek a newer world" (Kennedy, 1967) comes the responsibility of protecting them as best as I can as they engage that very thorny proposition and its processes. Keeping our discussions and debates of the "wicked problems" (Marar, 2013) of our world so part and parcel to my courses out of the public domain is one means of protection. We can create classrooms that engage these wicked problems, but we should work to limit the profoundly unproductive and sometimes even harmful ways that the rest of the world sometimes engages in these discussions.

Faculty who engage in critical communication pedagogy have indeed taken it upon themselves to consider the classroom a space of immense agency, a place where we can work together to build a more just society. But we must be careful with that power and that agency. Anyanwu (2003) warns that a nation that "empowers its citizens with the tools of technology but fails to train them to use those tools stands the risk of being used either by the tools or by those able to use the tools, who then marginalize the rest of society" (p. 391). Similarly, a faculty member who attempts to craft a generative space of immense agency that recognizes the constitutive power of communication and its role in creating the kind of identification with others required to bring about large-scale, meaningful changes in our world but does so, in part, through the use of social media platforms with little or no regard for their darker inclinations, runs the risk of further marginalizing a student at the hands of others using those same tools for very different means.

I am not arguing that there is not a place in the world for social media or that social media isn't an effective means of igniting change. It can, of course, be a very powerful tool for change. As previously mentioned, the #MeToo movement is a good example of that possibility. But these tools have limits in terms of democratization and they have significant drawbacks in terms of unintended consequences. And when faculty fail to recognize and consider the limits and drawbacks, we may work against the very important purposes we contend are at the heart of our pedagogy. The risk of our students being *used by those tools* or having others use those tools *to marginalize them* is significant, in my view. The possible costs for my students (and me as I bear some responsibility for what happens to them in the course of my class) are greater than any rewards I can imagine. So, I will teach students how social media platforms function, as well as how they are used in everything from politics to their own job searches after graduation, but I will not require that they engage these tools as part of my class. Well before social media came along, I was able to craft assignments and projects that allowed students to express as much or as little as they wanted to express publicly with regard to the wicked problems of the world and I will continue to do so. But social media posts will not be a required part of that education.

Students are adults, not children. And thus, I do not mean to imply that they do not have their own agency with regard to making decisions about their participation in social media platforms—they absolutely do. And perhaps the vast majority of time, our students will use those platforms as intended—to create identification and consubstantiality for the betterment of our world. But they are often actually *young* adults and I think that matters. It is certainly the case that older adults make terrible mistakes on social media and in life. But I am not charged with guiding and teaching those older adults. The vast majority of my students are traditional-aged students and despite my progressive political agency and action when I was in college, I know for certain that some of my thoughts were challenged and made better by faculty and other students. I want to guide my students the way that my faculty and fellow students helped guide me. I simply cannot do that effectively in a tweet.

Stern's (2011) thoughtful essay about the complexities of crossroads of pedagogy and life in the digital age encourages the use of blogs, Facebook, and Twitter, formally and informally, to reach students and does so in more careful ways than most essays arguing for the same ends. She argues that if the web allows social space for students who may need to talk or need role models to reach out to faculty in a tweet or Facebook message, then she is not sure why more academics have not "embraced the technology for that means" (p. 260). I hope that this chapter has pointed to some of the reasons why many academics have chosen another path in their classrooms. Connecting with students via non-traditional means of communication seems useful to critical communication pedagogy in a number of ways, but as I hope I have shown here, we have to balance the different goals of critical communication pedagogy—crafting particular relationships with students that recognize our situatedness versus encouraging critical engagement with course materials. These are worthy goals, but in our efforts to engage students in issues of social justice via the use of critical communication pedagogy, we have to decide if that type of critical engagement encourages the kinds of critical mistakes we want to make sure our students avoid.

NOTE

1. Questions about whether we should meet students "where they are" instead of teaching them that in certain contexts, such as learning environments, social media and technology use is not acceptable, is another discussion entirely.

REFERENCES

American Press Institute (2015). Digital lives of Millennials. Retrieved October 16, 2016 at https://www.americanpressinstitute.org/publications/reports/survey-research/digital-lives-of-millennials/.

Anyanwu, C. (2003). Myth and realities of new media technology: Virtual classroom education premise. *Television and New Media*, 4.4, pp. 389–409.

Aragon, A., AlDoubi, S., Kaminski, K., Anderson, S. K., & Isaacs, N. (2014). Social networking: Boundaries and limits, part 1: Ethics. TechTrends, 58.2, pp. 25–31.

Bargh, J. A., McKenna, K. Y. A., & Fitzsimons, G. M. (2002). Can you see the real me? Activation and expression of the "true self" on the Internet. *Journal of Social Issues*, 58.1, pp. 33–48.

Buckels, E. E., Trapnell, P. D., & Paulhus, D. L. (2014). Trolls just want to have fun. *Personality and Individual Differences*, 67, pp. 97–102.

Caplan, S. E. (2007), "Relations among loneliness, social anxiety and problematic internet use", *CyberPsychology and Behavior*, 10, pp. 234–42.

Chang, R. L. & Gray, K. (2013). Ethics of research into learning and teaching with Web 2.0: Reflections on eight case studies. *Journal of Computing in Higher Education*, 25, pp. 147–65.

Clipson, T., Wilson, A., & DuFrene, D. (2011), March. An examination of gender differences in reported experiences with online social networking. Paper presented at the annual conference of the Association for Business Communication, Southwest United States, Houston, Texas.

Dalgren, P. (2014). Social media and political participation. In C. Fuches & M. Sandoval (Eds.), *Critique, social media, and the information society* (191–202). New York: Routledge.

Dayter, D. (2011). Twitter as a means of class participation: Making student reading visible. *Journal of Applied Linguistics and Professional Practice*, 8.1, pp. 1–21.

Derlega, V. L., Metts, S., Petronio, S., & Margulis, S. T. (1993). *Self-disclosure*. London: Sage.
Dyson, B., Vickers, K., Turtle, J., Cowan, S., & Tassone, A. (2015). Evaluating the use of Facebook to increase student engagement and understanding in lecture-based classes. *Higher Education*, 69, pp. 303–13.
Elavsky, M, Mislan, C., & Elvasky, S. (2011). When talking less is more: Exploring outcomes of Twitter usage in the large-lecture hall. *Learning, Media, and Technology*, 36.3, pp. 215–33.
Fassett, D. L. & Warren, J. T. (2007). *Critical communication pedagogy*. Thousand Oaks, CA: Sage.
Foucault, M. (1975). *Discipline and punish: The birth of the prison*. New York, NY: Vintage.
Freire, P. (1968). *Pedagogy of the oppressed*. New York, NY: Seabury.
Gagnon, K. (2015). Using Twitter in health professional education. *Journal of Allied Health*, 44.1, pp. 25–33.
Giles, H., Mulac, A., Bradac, J. J., & Johnson, P. (1987). Speech accommodation theory: The first decade and beyond. In M. McLaughlin (Ed.), *Communication Yearbook*, 10 (pp. 13–48). New York: Routledge.
Gray, K. (2008). Educational technology practitioner-research ethics. In M. Quigley (Ed.), *Encyclopedia of information ethics and security* (pp. 164–69). Hershey, PA: Idea Group, Inc.
Hao, R. N. (2011). Rethinking critical pedagogy: Implications on silence and silent bodies. *Text and Performance Quarterly*, 31.3, pp. 267–84.
Hew, K. F. (2011). Students' and teachers' use of Facebook. *Computers in Human Behavior*, 27, pp. 662–76.
Hewitt, A. & Forte, A. (2006). Crossing boundaries: Identity management and student/faculty relationships on the Facebook. Paper presented at Computer Supported Cooperative Work conference, November, 4-8. Banff, Alberta, Canada
Hood, K. M., Robels, M. & Hopkins, C. D. (2014). Personal branding and social media for students in today's competitive job market. *The Journal of Research in Business Education*, 56(2) (pp. 33–47).
Hundley, H. & Shyles, L. (2010), "US teenagers' perceptions and awareness of digital technology: A focus group approach", *New Media & Society*, 12. 3, pp. 417–33.
Jackson, J. (2014). *Introducing language and intercultural communication*. New York, NY: Routledge.
Jenkins, H., Clinton, K., Purushotma, R., Robison, A., & Weigel, M. (2006). Confronting the challenges of participatory culture: Media education for the 21st century. Retrieved on October 11, 2016 at http://wheatoncollege.edu/president/files/2012/03/Confronting-Challenges-of-Participatory-Culture.pdf.
Johnson, B. G. (2016). Network communication and the reprise of tolerance theory: Civic education for extreme speech and private online governance. *First Amendment Studies*, 50.1, pp. 14–31.
Joinson, A. N. (2005). Internet behaviour and the design of virtual methods. In C. Hine (Ed.), *Virtual methods*. New York: Berg
Jouneau-Sion, C. & Sanchez, E. (2013). Preparing school to accommodate the challenge of Web 2.0 technologies. Education and Information Technologies, 18.2, pp. 265–70.
Junco, R., Heibergert, G, & Loken, E. (2010). The effect of Twitter on college student engagement and grades. *Journal of Computer Assisted Learning*, 27, pp. 119–32.
Junco, R., & Chickering, A. W. (2010). Civil discourse in the age of social media. *About campus*, 15(A), pp. 12–18. Accessed at http://blog.reyjunco.com/pdf/Junco%20&%20Chickering%20-%20Civil%20Discourse%20in%20the%20Age%20of%20Social%20Media.pdf.
Junco, R., Elavsky, C. M., & Heiberger, G. (2013). Putting Twitter to the test: Assessing outcomes for student collaboration, engagement, and success. *British Journal of Educational Technology*, 44.2, pp. 273–87.
Keen, A. (2007). *The cult of the amateur: How today's Internet is killing our culture*. New York: Currency.
Kennedy, R. F. (1967). *To Seek a Newer World*. New York, NY: Doubleday.

Kiesler, S., Siegel, J., & Mcguire, T. W. (1984). Social psychological aspects of computer-mediated communication. *American Psychologist*, 39.10, pp. 1123–34.
Kiesler, S. & Sproull, L. S. (1986). Response effects in the electronic survey. *Public Opinion Quarterly*, 50.3, pp. 402–13.
Kuznekoff, J. H., Munz, S., & Titsworth, S. (2015). Mobile phones in the classroom: Examining the effects of texting, Twitter, and message content on student learning. *Communication Education*, 64.3, pp. 344–65.
Lewis, J. & West, A. (2009), "'Friending': London-based undergraduates' experience of Facebook", *New Media & Society*, 11. 7, pp. 1209–29.
Lowry, P. B., Zhang, J., Wang, C., & Siponen, M. (2016). Why do adults engage in cyber bullying on social media? An integration of online disinhibition and deindividuation effects with the social structure and social learning model. *Information Systems Research*, 27.4, pp. 962–86.
Marar, Zayad. 2013. "Why does social science have such a hard job explaining itself?" *The Guardian*, Apr. 8, 2013. https://www.theguardian.com/higher-education-network/blog/2013/apr/08/social-science-funding-us-senate.
Moody, M. (2010). Teaching Twitter and beyond: Tips for incorporating social media in traditional courses. *Journal of Magazine and New Media Research*, 11.2, pp. 1–9.
Moran, M., Seaman, J., & Tinti-Kane, H. (2011, April). Teaching, learning, and sharing: How today's higher eduction faculty use social media. Pearson Learning Solutions. Retrieved October 15, 2016 from http://files.eric.ed.gov/fulltext/ED535130.pdf.
Murray, S. L., Holmes, J. G., & Griffin, D. W. (1996). The self-fulfilling nature of positive illusions in romantic relationships: Love is blind, but prescient. *Journal of Personality and Social Psychology*, 71, pp. 1155–1180.
Ollington, N., Gibb, J., & Harcourt, M. (2013). Online social networks: An emergent recruiter tool for attracting and screening. *Personnel Review*, 42(3), 248–65.
Paik, L. S., Shahani-Denning, C., & Griffeth, R. W. (2014). An examination of attractiveness biases in the context of hiring through social networking sites. *Journal of Organizational Psychology*, 14(1), 52–66. Retrieved October 14, 2016 from http://www.nabusinesspress.com/JOP/PaikLS_Web14_1_.pdf.
Parcha, J. M. (2014). Accommodating Twitter: Communication accommodation theory and classroom interactions. *Communication Teacher*, 28.4, pp. 229–35.
Parcha, J. M. (2014a). #whoreallycaresabouthashtags: Using Twitter's hashtag to foster an interactive environment. *Communication Currents* 9.5. Retrieved October 20, 2016 from https://www.natcom.org/CommCurrentsArticle.aspx?id=5369.
Peluchette, J., & Karl, K. (2010). Examining students' intended image on Facebook: 'What were they thinking?!,' *Journal of Education for Business*, 85(1), 30–37.
Peterson, E. A. (2014). Business strategies for managing the legal risks of social media. *Journal of Management and Sustainability*, 4.3, pp. 96–101.
Reed, P. (2013). Hashtags and retweets: Using Twitter to aid community, communication, and casual (informal) learning. *Research in Learning Technology*, 21, pp. 1–21.
Ronson, J. (2015). How one stupid tweet blew up Justine Sacco's life. *New York Times Magazine*. Retrieved October 15, 2016 at http://www.nytimes.com/2015/02/15/magazine/how-one-stupid-tweet-ruined-justine-saccos-life.html?_r=0.
Skoric, M. D., Ying, D. & Ng, Y. (2009), "Bowling online, not alone: Online social capital and political participation in Singapore", *Journal of Computer-Mediated Communication*, 14.2, pp. 414–33.
Society for Human Resource Management. (2012). HR discipline of technology and communications. Managing and Leveraging Workplace Use of Social Media. Retrieved October 11, 2016 from http://www.shrm.org/templatestools/toolkits/pages/managingsocialmedia.aspx.
Stern, D. M. (2011). You had me at Foucault: Living pedagogically in the Digital Age. *Text and Performance Quarterly*, 31.3, pp. 249–66.
Suit, L., Winkler, P., Campbell, L., Pennington, K., Szutenbach, M. P., Haight, R., Roybal, D., & McCollum, M. (2015). A correlation study of social network usage among health care students. *Journal of Nursing Education*, 54.4, pp. 207–13.
Tinker v. Des Moines, 393 U.S. 503, (1969).

Tyma, A. (2011). Connecting with What Is Out There!: Using Twitter in the large lecture. *Communication Education*, 25.3, pp. 175–81.
Waldman, J. (2011). *Job searching with social media for dummies*. Hoboken, NJ: John Wiley and Sons.
West Virginia State Board of Education v. Barnette. 319 U.S. 624 (1943).
Walther, J. B. (1996). Computer-mediated communication: Impersonal, interpersonal, and hyperpersonal interaction. *Communication Research* 23.1, pp. 3–43.
Wood, J. T. (2010). *Interpersonal communication: Everyday encounters*. Boston, MA: Wadsworth.
Wooley v. Maynard. 430 U.S. 705 (1977).
Yancey, K. (2004). Made not only in words: Composition in a new key. *College Composition and Communication*, 56.2, pp. 297–328.

Chapter Seven

Applying Critical Communication Pedagogy through Online Discussions on Stereotypes and Prejudicial Speech

Tabitha Hart

In January 2015, as the spring semester was just beginning, my university community was still reeling from an incident of stereotyping and prejudicial speech that had occurred the previous year. During a philanthropy board meeting, a key donor had explained her contribution to the university by stating that Latina students did not have it in their DNA to succeed (O'Connor, 2014; Roberts, 2014). Two distinct aspects of this incident caused upset. First, there was the expression of a negative stereotype about community members, i.e. a simplistic, pre-formed belief about people and/or their cultural group, both their characteristics as well as (potentially) their "social roles [and] the degree to which members of the group share[d] specific qualities" (Dovidio, Hewstone, Glick, & Esses, 2010, p. 7). Second, no refutations of the donor's prejudicial speech were offered during the meeting, and because the donor's remarks went initially unchallenged, community members felt doubly hurt ("SJSU students protest alleged racist comment made by donor," 2014). Indeed, previous research validates the perils of allowing stereotyping and prejudicial speech to go unchallenged, not least because beliefs about out-groups are heavily influenced by the opinions expressed by in-group members (Sechrist & Stangor, 2001; Sinclair, Lowery, Hardin, & Colangelo, 2005; Stangor, Sechrist, & Jost, 2001). When in-group members express a stereotype, fellow members are more likely to adopt or condone that stereotype (Blanchard, Crandall, Brigham, & Vaughn, 1994; Sechrist & Stangor, 2001; Sinclair et al., 2005; Stangor et al., 2001), and when a stereotype is seen as widely shared by one's group, its durability increases (Sechrist & Stangor, 2001; Sinclair et al., 2005; Stangor et al.,

2001). Silence, in this case, is not golden; rather, it suggests that the views being expressed are acceptable (Blanchard et al., 1994; Bolgatz, 2005; Carey & Hoffman, 2016).

On the other hand, speaking out—even mildly—against stereotypes and prejudicial speech can make a positive impact (Aboud & Fenwick, 1999; Harper, 2015; Lun, Sinclair, Whitchurch, & Glenn, 2007; Sinclair et al., 2005), especially when this is done with one's in-group (Sechrist & Stangor, 2001; Smith & Postmes, 2011). This is because the processes by which we harbor, make, and also challenge stereotypical assumptions are effectively *social* (Lun et al., 2007; Smith & Postmes, 2011). When people hear in-group members condemning racist or stereotypical views, they become more likely to condemn those views as well. Anti-prejudicial responses also model tolerance and empathy (Guerin, 2003). What's more, when stereotypes are challenged or invalidated, targeted group members are also less likely to conform to them (Smith & Postmes, 2011). In this way, simply challenging stereotypes and prejudicial speech, especially with members of one's in-group, can potentially be a highly effective method for mitigating their negative effects, raising awareness, and even changing hearts and minds.

All of this was on my mind as I prepared to teach my newest hybrid (partially online, partially in person) course on intercultural communication, the overarching goal of which was to explore communication as cultural act, one that both constitutes and challenges cultural identities. Developing a heightened awareness of stereotypes and engaging in self-reflection—which are important in fighting stereotyping (Houghton, Furumura, Lebedko, & Li, 2013; McKee & Schor, 1999)—were already included in the syllabus. However, as the donor incident clearly illustrated, awareness and reflection alone are not enough. Like so many activities that are the focus of communication studies courses (preparing and delivering presentations, negotiating, persuasion, conflict resolution, etc.), speaking out against stereotypes and other prejudicial speech is a learned skill. For these reasons, it was necessary to include a practical skill-building component. Out of this need, I implemented a semester-long online discussion activity into my course. This activity, "Challenging Stereotypes," was structured to help students develop and practice communication skills for pushing back against stereotyping and prejudicial speech.

In this chapter, I describe the Challenging Stereotypes activity and analyze the student-led dialogues that arose from it. As I do so, I illustrate how this online activity fostered critical communication pedagogy mores and methods in my hybrid class. The chapter concludes with reflections on the strengths and weaknesses of using an online discussion forum for critical communication pedagogy purposes and, more generally, for social justice-oriented instruction.

CRITICAL COMMUNICATION PEDAGOGY

A classroom is a political space, where "students and teachers do not check their histories at the door when they enter it. Rather, the classroom reflects the inequalities in the world around us . . . there are no blank slates or level playing fields for any of us" (Kandaswamy, 2008, p. 7; cf. Lebedko, 2013). Instead of avoiding this inevitability, a critical communication pedagogy (CCP) perspective addresses it head-on. Through sustained analysis of the apparatuses of oppression in teaching and learning spaces, CCP calls direct attention to social injustices, with the aim of redressing them (Fassett & Warren, 2007; Warren & Fassett, 2010). Specifically, CCP mandates that scholar-practitioners critically examine how power operates in teaching/learning spaces, and how in/equality is produced and reproduced there through teaching/learning discourses (Allen, 2011; Fassett & Warren, 2007; Kahl, 2013). Beyond raising awareness, CCP also has an interventionist function, being designed to directly empower people to challenge and resist social injustices from the starting point of educational spaces (Cooks, 2010; Fassett & Rudick, 2016; Fassett & Warren, 2007; Kahl, 2013; Rudick & Golsan, 2016).

Following the CCP perspective, speaking out against stereotypes and prejudicial speech is potentially an act of social justice, one that could enable a student to take immediate action "beyond textbooks and lesson plans and into communities beyond the institution" (Cooks, 2010, p. 302). To this end, the CCP framework offers at least five communicative tools for analyzing how stereotypes and prejudicial speech arise, and for directly challenging and resisting them. To begin with, CCP tells us that we must apprehend how we—whether collectively or individually—are implicated in social injustices. Whether intentionally or not, we "create the phenomena we observe, through our assumptions, values, past experiences, language choices, and so on" (Fassett & Warren, 2007, p. 50). We are therefore obligated to include ourselves in the systems of oppression that we analyze. Next, CCP encourages us to actively imagine potential futures, prompting us to ask, "In what kind of world do we want to live?" (Simpson, 2010, p. 362). By imagining and articulating our ideal societies, we are better prepared to realize them. Third, CCP tells us that we must communicate mindfully. While it is through communication that systems of oppression are created and maintained, it is equally true that communication is our surest means of resistance (Cooks, 2010; Simpson, 2010; Warren & Fassett, 2010). By strategically selecting equitable and just communication practices (whether names, key terms, norms, rules, etc.), speech becomes a tool for transforming the world (Fassett & Warren, 2007; Simpson, 2010). Fourth, we must accept that no talk is inconsequential. Even "mundane," quotidian speech is important, because it constitutes identities, realities, and the larger systems (social, political, historical, economic) within which we operate (Fassett & Rudick, 2016; Fassett & Warren, 2007). Indeed, such "everyday" talk must be the "primary site of intervention" (Fassett & Rudick, 2016, p. 19). Finally, CCP suggests that we support democratic communication, i.e. the types of dialogic exchanges in which all participants have a voice and can air their viewpoints and experiences (Fassett & Warren, 2007; Simpson, 2010).

THE PEDAGOGICAL VALUE OF ONLINE DISCUSSIONS

Discussions are a popular pedagogical approach in communication classes because they can synthesize and integrate course materials, allow students to share their perspectives and experiences, build community, and help students advance their critical thinking skills (Brookfield & Preskill, 2005). For these same reasons, *online discussions* have become a common feature of online and hybrid (i.e., partially online, partially traditional) courses, too. When done well, online discussions give learners a forum to meaningfully engage with one another, co-create knowledge, and develop valuable skills (deNoyelles, Zydney, & Chen, 2014; MacKnight, 2000; Mandernach, 2006). From a practical standpoint as well, online discussions are advantageous. Whereas in-class discussions are necessarily limited in duration, asynchronous online discussions can be set up to last whatever length of time is desired, from hours to days or even weeks. This allows participants ample time to engage with the material and share their thoughts at their chosen pace. Online discussions also give students an alternate or additional space to interact. Those who might be disinclined to speak out in class may find it easier to post online, and students who like responding with greater frequency can do so—everyone gets to talk. The extended time period possible with online discussions also removes pressure, allowing participants time to compose their thoughts, which may be especially helpful when discussing controversial topics. What's more, composing one's thoughts in writing rather than in speech requires more time, more work, and arguably more thought. Threaded discussions, in which participants can reply to other replies, keep participants focused on responding to their peers, rather than directing their messages to the instructor (often a pitfall in face-to-face classroom discussions). In this way, online discussions can encourage greater peer-to-peer communication. Finally, online discussions make participants' thinking, reasoning, and knowledge construction visible and also create a durable record of communication. This helps everyone (instructor, participants) easily follow contributions (Deal, 2009); can assist with giving and getting qualitative feedback, potentially increasing critical reflection (Bolgatz, 2005); and is beneficial for assessment purposes, whether self-assessment or instructor assessment of students' learning.

METHODS

Stemming as it did from the donor incident, my primary intention for the Challenging Stereotypes (CS) activity was to help students develop and utilize the types of "discursive resources" that are required to respond to stereotypes and other types of prejudicial speech (Guerin, 2003; cf. Paluck, 2011). The textbook that I had selected for my course, Kurylo's *Inter/Cultural Communication* (2013), contained examples of stereotypical and prejudicial speech at the end of each chapter (the "Say What" sections), and it was this material that I drew on. Specifically, I asked students to select a Say What snippet, imagine that they were observers present on the scene, and compose responses including what they would say and do. At the beginning of the semester, I shared four potential strategies outlined by the Teaching Tolerance program as an optional starting point: interrupt, question, educate, and echo (Willoughby, 2012). In their second and final post, I asked students to give one another feedback.

I conducted the Challenging Stereotypes online discussion activity over two semesters in two separate iterations of an upper-division undergraduate course on intercultural communication. The first iteration was taught in Spring 2015, with 28 students enrolled, and the second was taught in Spring 2016, with 25 students enrolled. In both cases the course was *hybrid*, meaning that it included in-class, face-to-face meetings as well as online components. For the online portion of the course, the learning management system used was Canvas, which offers various functionalities, including online discussions. In both cases, the course shells were password-protected and viewable only to enrolled students. Each weekly online discussion thread remained open for one week, during which time students could read and compose posts anytime. Each post was automatically identified by the author's name and a thumbnail of the image associated with their account—both of which each individual user had the ability to edit—as well as the date and time of the post. (Note that, in presenting data excerpts here, all such identifying information has been removed, and pseudonyms have been applied to all individuals in order to protect their privacy.) Once the weekly deadline had passed, the thread closed to further additions, though students could still view the threads while the semester was in progress. At the end of the semester, however, the shells closed and access was blocked off to anyone other than the instructor. A total of 26 discussion threads were created across the two courses: 14 threads in one, with 28 students participating, and 12 threads in the other, with 25 students participating. Together these 26 threads comprised approximately 1,200 separate posts.

To process the data, I saved the threads as pdf files, converted them to rtf, and imported them into TAMS Analyzer (Weinstein, 2002–2012), a free, open-source qualitative data analysis (QDA) software program written for

Mac OS. Like other QDA programs, TAMS is a useful tool for methodically scrutinizing, tagging, sorting through, and retrieving excerpted data (Hart & Achterman, 2017). For this project I used TAMS to closely analyze students' communicative strategies, experiences, and learning outcomes as presented in the data. From this process, the following findings emerged.

FINDINGS

A key point in the students' discussions throughout the semester was navigating what tone to strike as they composed their responses, particularly when communicating with in-group members such as friends, family, colleagues, etc. In general, the students felt that their responses should not cause any (additional) offense, and that they should avoid furthering or heightening any confrontation. In their posts, they maintained that responders should neither "lash out" nor go "overboard," and they expressed disapproval of talk that was "rude," "harsh," "defensive," "angry," or "aggressive." Instead, students indicated that it was important to be "calm," "professional," "non-confrontational," and "polite," even though this could be very difficult, especially if one felt offended. Nevertheless, the students believed that it was important to maintain one's composure and often praised one another for doing so in their imagined conversations.

In analyzing why students valued a polite tone in responding to stereotypes and prejudicial speech, particularly (but not only) with in-group members, two key reasons emerged. The first reason had to do with the students' characterization of some stereotypes and prejudicial speech as arising from a lack of knowledge. Specifically, students felt that maintaining a polite tone with their conversational partners would enable them to present thoughtful, well-reasoned, and information-based refutations. By crafting their responses in this way, students felt, they could educate others into changing their stereotyped and/or biased views. This positionality is illustrated in Excerpt 1. Here, a student, Lawrence, responds to a stereotype about feminism. Lawrence writes that he would explain the definition of feminism as well as its importance. With his next strategy of "ask[ing] them if they could relate to being treated unfairly," Lawrence effectively seeks to build empathy between his conversational partner and the target of that partner's words (feminists). Lawrence concludes by identifying himself as a feminist, again using information (on the gender wage gap) to explain and educate. Two of Lawrence's classmates, Isabel and Leah, respond with praise for the way he explains and justifies his position without "lash[ing] out in a disrespectful way." Leah further speculates that such stereotypes arise out of a lack of education or information ("people . . . are simply not informed"). The consensus is that by politely offering counterinformation, the students can help the conversational partner to "understand why his statement and belief is wrong."

Excerpt 1

Inequality like that is the reason that I am a feminist.

> Lawrence
> Say What? "I asked him if he considered himself to be a feminist. He looked at me with a disgusted look and said, 'No, do I look like a lesbian to you?'"
>
> Response: I would politely inform them that the idea that feminists were lesbians was incorrect. I would make sure to note that feminists were people who believed in equal rights between men and women. I would then go onto to explain why there was a need for people to support feminism. For example, it is currently unfair that women and men can perform the same job, yet women will be more likely to make 70% of what the man was making. I would ask them if they could relate to being treated unfairly, and then inform them that inequality like that is the reason that I am a feminist.
>
> Isabel
> Hi Lawrence,
> I think you did a really good job of immediately taking the time to address the important piece of clarifying what feminism is. In addition I really like that you explained WHY there is a need for feminism. . . . I think you did a good job of explaining feminism in a short and concise way.
>
> Leah
> Hi Lawrence!
> I really like that you don't lash out in a disrespectful way at all. Instead you make an effort to better inform him so that he can understand why his statement and belief is wrong. I like that you provide an example and explain that even as a man you are also a feminist. I think you did a great job. A lot of the reason these statements are made by people is because they are simply not informed.

The second reason why students valued a polite tone in responding to stereotypes and prejudicial speech related to their desire for dialogue, i.e. a side-by-side communication process (talking with others, rather than to or at them) that uses conversation to share and explore how others see and experiences the world, and why. As one of my students wrote, "I [am] more interested in knowing WHY someone would say something like that, rather than just telling them not to." Overall, the students expressed the belief that dialogue was a way to engage in mutual understanding, build and sustain empathy, encourage reflection, and change hearts and minds. In fact, engaging others in dialogue is a proven strategy for responding to prejudicial speech (Pedersen, Walker, & Wise, 2005). In particular, dialogue that leads participants to self-disclose, share personal examples, and explore perspectives from others' vantage points has been shown to result in pronounced, durable mitigation of prejudicial views (Broockman & Kalla, 2016). Asking the other person why they are making prejudicial assumptions can lead them to reflect upon and possibly investigate their beliefs (Harper, 2015). Ideally, it is best for conversational partners to enter into deeper dialogue and to share their personal views and experiences, "[so] they can reflect on their own ideas and biases and identify where stereotypes have been imposed on them" (Heenan, 2005, p. 509, see also Broockman & Kalla, 2016). Interestingly, dialogue is also a major component of the CCP approach, which explicitly advocates for it as a "discursive form" (Cooks, 2010, p. 295). To engage in dialogue in the spirit of CCP does not presume a right or wrong way of seeing and being in the world, nor does it require agreement *per se* (Fassett & Warren, 2007; cf. Pedersen et al., 2005). Rather, CCP characterizes dialogue as a way to collaboratively "(de)construct ideologies, identities, and cultures" (Fassett & Warren, 2007, p. 55).

The ways in which my students composed conversational moves to facilitate dialogue were illustrated in Excerpt 1, in which Lawrence made an information-based bid to inspire a sense of connection between his conversational partner and the targeted group. These dialogic moves are further illustrated in Excerpt 2, where students respond to stereotypes about femininity and sexuality. In this excerpt, a student, Daniela, states her intention to avoid shaming or arguing, preferring instead to engage in "dialogue with people about their thoughts and attitudes toward different cultural groups." This type of "open communication," she says, is a way to advocate for targeted groups (here LGBTQ+). Another student, Annie, posts a response in which she self-discloses about being on the receiving end of this stereotype as a female student athlete. Based on her own experiences, Annie writes, she would "ask [the conversational partner] why she feels that [way]" and would then "share [her] own experiences," i.e. Annie also would choose a dialogic interaction. What Excerpt 2 neatly illustrates is how students used the discussion forum to reflect on dialogue's potential for sharing and exploring one another's perspectives. What's more, they also used it to actively engage in their own dialogic exchanges with one another.

Excerpt 2

I would share my own experiences with her and try to change her views.

Daniela
Say What? My roommate Kris came up with the comment, "Most students must think I'm a lesbian because I'm always in my sweats and I never do my hair and makeup when I go to class. . . ."

Response: My aim with this conversation would be to not make Kris feel bad and lead into an argument because I disagree with her comment. I want to be in dialogue with people about their thoughts and attitudes toward different cultural groups (LGBT) because open communication is the best way to advocate for marginalized groups. . . .

Annie
Personally, for this [example], I actually felt like I have more real life experience with this situation. . . . At my community college, I was a student athlete. I was one of those girls that wore sweatpants every day to class and never really tried to do my hair or makeup. I consider myself to be heterosexual, and I always wore sweats because I knew after I was done with class I was going to go to practice or workouts, therefore there was no reason to dress up. Even now, no longer being a student athlete, I come to class in workout gear most of the time because I go workout after class. Because I dress a certain way for class does not define my sexuality. Because I have had experience with this situation personally (common stereotype of softball players being lesbian), I consider myself to be an advocate for diminishing that stereotype. Women who don't dress "feminine" all the time doesn't make them a lesbian.

As far as responding to her comment, I would probably ask her why she feels that dressing a certain way defines her sexuality. Then I would share my own experiences with her and try to change her views on what being lesbian "looks like."

Just as Annie shared her experience of being stereotyped as a female athlete, so too did other students share theirs. For example, a male student of color posted that "depending on where I am walking . . . people grip their belongings, watch me from their peripherals, [and] show a bit a fear all because of my appearance." A female student posted that "someone asked me my ethnicity and [when] I said I was Palestinian, they [responded] 'Oh, then why aren't you wearing the hijab, aren't all Arabs Muslim?'" Another student reported that "in high school, my best friend had an older brother [who] would tell her to get tutored by me because I'm a 'smart Asian.'" As with Excerpt 2, these stories, as shared in the online discussion forum, illustrated students' efforts to engage in the same kind of dialogic perspective exploration that they worked towards in their imagined responses to stereotypes and prejudicial speech. They also confirmed how students themselves experienced bias in what Fassett and Warren (2007) termed the "mundane and (un)intentional (in)actions" (p. 51) of daily life. In other words, oppression is created and sustained in part through unspectacular, everyday communicative acts.

Herein lies another important aspect of dialogue in the CCP framework: namely, that dialogue is a means of both excavating and challenging the ideologies that undergird communication, as well as the identities, cultures, thoughts, and/or behaviors that those ideologies shape. There was evidence that my students used our online discussion forum to engage in the complex work of investigating and thinking critically about normative assumptions (their own included) and how those assumptions worked on and through them. This is illustrated in Excerpt 3, where two students respond to the stereotypical belief that children are better off treated by female rather than male doctors. The original responder, David, posts that he would tell the receptionist that they were being "sexist," and that gender roles are increasingly irrelevant. Another student, Lynne, responds to David by reflecting on the inescapability of assumptions about gender, writing that "men and women have grown up seeing gender roles being reinforced constantly—it's an ingrained, unconscious mindset that can be difficult to educate oneself out of." Lynne's observations get at the question of where stereotyping and prejudicial beliefs come from: they come from us, and the cultural/communicative landscapes that we inhabit. The way forward, as CCP tells us (and as illustrated by David and Lynne's exchange), is to analyze how beliefs and assumptions arise from and are inextricably woven into our everyday lives.

Excerpt 3

It's an ingrained, unconscious mindset that can be difficult to educate oneself out of.

> David
> Say What? I [telephoned] to make a dermatologist appointment for my son. I asked whether the doctor whom I had used before would be willing to have an infant as a patient. . . . The receptionist . . . responded, "Yeah. I guess. But you may be better off seeing, well, we have a female doctor. She may work out better. . . ."
>
> Response: First off, I would definitely take my business elsewhere. Second, I will tell the man that he is being completely sexist. . . . It's a new time in American history, grow up man. Embrace the fact that gender roles are fading away.
>
> Lynne
> Both men and women have grown up seeing gender roles being reinforced constantly— it's an ingrained, unconscious mindset that can be difficult to educate oneself out of. I think it's good to point out the problem with what the receptionist said, but it would be more effective to ask her why she thinks a woman doctor would be better. Doing so would make her reflect on her thought process and maybe help her become aware of why her words were

flawed. It may also help to nudge her in the right direction with a question like "Don't you think men can handle infants too?"

Following the CCP framework, using communication to identify oppression is only a step (albeit an important one) towards the end goals of resistance and, ultimately, transformation (Cooks, 2010; Fassett & Warren, 2007; Simpson, 2010). Just as oppression occurs through "seemingly innocuous communicative acts" (Fassett & Rudick, 2016, p. 20; cf. Fassett & Warren, 2007; Warren & Fassett, 2010), so too does change happen gradually and incrementally in our daily interactions (Fassett & Warren, 2007; Warren & Fassett, 2010). At the end of each semester, I invited my students to compose posts reflecting on the potential for changing stereotypes and prejudicial speech, as well as what they had learned by engaging in the online discussions. In response, students wrote at length about feeling increased motivation to speak out against stereotyping and prejudicial speech, as well as enhanced confidence in doing so. Even more striking, however, were students' posts reflecting on how stereotyping and prejudicial speech arose from subconscious assumptions, including their own. As one student put it,

> After taking this course, I realized that I actually stereotype more than I thought. I have assumed that couples aren't couples because they are of different races, I have assumed that people don't have good jobs because of their skin color, and I have assumed that people from certain countries would act a certain way. I hate to admit it, but I do stereotype people quite regularly. This class has opened my eyes to a new way of thinking.

In this post, and those like it, students expressed not only a willingness to engage in reflective dialogue, but even a preference for it as a method of raising awareness:

> One thing that always pops in my head outside of class is how to confront people who are stereotyping. The "Say What?" assignments really made me see how much stereotyping happens on a regular basis and knowing how to respond in situations like that has helped me. I think that before this class, I would have hesitated to correct someone, or shed some light on their ignorance. However, doing the assignments has desensitized that hesitation to a point where I don't think about it. I can let people know to be more conscious of their biased opinions/stereotypes. They may only be words, but those kinds of words can cause a lot of damage.

Finally, students communicated belief in the potential for change, as well as increased confidence in themselves as change agents:

> With the standing up against stereotypes I personally feel like I was able to see real life examples of how groups can be marginalized or shown in a bad light

and how I can choose to deal with situations. This was one example of how this class allowed me to help me define and become more culturally aware and make a change about things that don't sit well with my personal beliefs (as well as develop new [beliefs]).

While they acknowledged that the process of creating change was long and imperfect they still felt motivated by the prospect of what could be. As one student wrote, "Situations such as these demand a conversation to be struck up and the ideologies displayed must be discussed, especially if these problems have any hope of completely disappearing!"

DISCUSSION

In this chapter, I described the Challenging Stereotypes activity, which required students enrolled in my hybrid intercultural communication course to compose responses to stereotypes and prejudicial speech via an online discussion forum. As they did so, students used their online discussions to engage in non-hypothetical discussions about their own experiences, identities, and communicative practices. Simultaneously, students adopted a dialogic approach, which enabled them to excavate some of the ideologies undergirding the speech that they were responding too. Additionally, students used the forum to reflect on how ideologies arise from and are maintained through communication. At the end of the semester, the students' reflections indicated that participating in these online discussions had had a transformative effect on them, inspiring them to speak out, to be (more) reflective, and to engage in (more) dialogue with others.

Taken as a whole, the online discussion forum, ostensibly just a sandbox for experimenting with communicative interventions, also proved to be an effective means for incorporating CCP mores and methods into this class environment. This occurred in four significant ways. First, CCP scholar-practitioners "promote critical thinking by engaging their students in society by acting as problem-posing educators" (Kahl, 2013, p. 2616). The CS activity presented students with a problem (snippets of stereotypes and prejudicial speech) and engaged them as critically minded devisors of potential solutions (how to respond). Second, CCP uses "dialogue as both metaphor and method for [understanding] our relationships with others" (Fassett & Warren, 2007, p. 54). That is, the process of coming to understand oneself in relation to others is collaborative (accomplished together with others), dialogic (accomplished by both sharing with others and listening to what others share), and mutual (accomplished by understanding one's own self/positionality as well as those of one's partners in dialogue). As illustrated in this chapter, the students used the CS activity to foster a (virtual) space in which they could engage in this type of dialogue. Third, the CCP framework requires that we (develop) reflexivity and self-knowledge, including how identities (whether our own or others') are created and sustained through communicative practices. This is related to another aspect of CCP, which is the importance of grasping cultural communication at a systemic level, including how power and oppression work through our communicative practices (Fassett & Rudick, 2016; Fassett & Warren, 2007). As illustrated in the findings section, students used the CS activity to make forays into this complex excavation process, exploring how language practices shaped their thoughts, assumptions, identities, and behaviors, for better and for worse. Fourth, CCP is intended to empower people to take action against oppression, whether by "generating knowledge that is counter to dominant, oppressive ideologies" (Fassett & Rudick, 2016, p. 29; cf. Kahl, 2013) and/or by mindfully using communication to "imagin[e], creat[e], and [maintain] a world in which justice is desired, possible, and (if only partially) realized" (Simpson, 2010, p. 381). As demonstrated in this chapter, at its most fundamental level, participating in the online CS activity gave students a forum to devise, try out, revise, and improve potential responses to stereotypes and prejudicial speech. More importantly, it offered a space in which they could deeply explore how such speech arises from—and can be resisted through—daily communicative practices. In all these respects, the online discussion forum proved to be both useful and effective for applying both theoretical and methodological aspects of the CCP framework into my (hybrid) class.

Importantly, simply introducing an online discussion component into a course is not what matters—it's how such tools are used that really counts. As with any learning activity, online discussions must be effectively planned and run (Lander, 2014). Ideally, they should be structured to give students maximum opportunity to express their views and experiences in dialogue with their peers (Bolgatz, 2005). Put differently, the students, not the instructor, should be encouraged to do most—if not all—of the talking (McKee & Schor, 1999). The instructor, on the other hand, is responsible for moderating and managing the communication (MacKnight, 2000). As with all learning environments, an online discussion forum will have and/or develop its own procedural protocols, whether technical (how to compose, edit, delete posts, or do a threaded reply) or relational (norms and rules for communicative competence). Students should not be expected to know these intuitively (deNoyelles et al., 2014). Instead, the instructor must explain and model expectations, or engage the class in collaborative efforts to determine them. Because interpersonal and relational communication and the "enact[ment of] personal and social relationships with others" (MacKnight, 2000, p. 40) are a key part of online discussions, participants must be attentive to interpersonal communication expectations as well as knowledge construction (Lander, 2014, p. 43). This, combined with the necessary technical knowledge (e.g. knowing how to use the platform), makes discussion forums complex teaching/learning spaces. CCP scholar/practitioners could contribute by expanding their work into online and technology-mediated learning environments. They are uniquely positioned to critically investigate what makes online environments conducive (or not) to CCP-inspired dialogue, and/or how identities and ideologies are produced and sustained via technology-mediated teaching/learning environments.

On a similar note, while online discussions are amenable to almost any topic, simply presenting social justice subject matter is no guarantee that participants will think critically, engage in dialogue, or reflect deeply. In all forums, whether online or offline, effective social justice–oriented teaching and learning depends on a thoughtfully chosen focus as well as careful planning and preparation. In online discussions, topics must be meaningful, and students must have the resources required for responding in a significant way (Wang, Woo, & Zhao, 2009). Prompts should be carefully composed to suit the medium, and formulated to encourage sustained group discussion (MacKnight, 2000; Mandernach, 2006). The online discussion environment must be safe, open, and conducive to open communication, allowing participants to be honest and take risks in sharing their perspectives (McKee & Schor, 1999), and shared ground rules are important (Bolgatz, 2005). Here too, with their strong roots in instruction and pedagogy, CCP scholars/practitioners could make both theoretical and applied contributions. For example, a CCP framework would be a powerful tool for exploring processes of creating and maintaining safe and inviting online environments, offering guidance on bringing social justice topics into technology-mediated teaching/learning spaces, and/or further promoting the study and practice of social justice in online and hybrid environments.

CONCLUSION

The donor incident that inspired the CS activity in January 2016 has paled in comparison to the openly stereotypical and prejudicial speech that now occurs in the public forum, where our highest-ranking national and international officials openly engage in racist, sexist, homophobic, and ableist speech. The urgency to speak out is greater than ever, and CCP scholar/practitioners have renewed the call for "concrete and actionable" work (Fassett & Rudick, 2018), particularly "teaching and learning (and researching about either) with a social justice agenda" (Fassett & Rudick, 2018). As described in this chapter, there is potential for carrying out CCP-grounded work and social justice–oriented instruction via technology-mediated channels such as online discussion forums. It is my sincere hope that readers will feel encouraged to replicate and extend this work.

REFERENCES

Aboud, F. E., & Fenwick, V. (1999). Exploring and evaluating school-based interventions to reduce prejudice. *Journal of Social Issues, 55*(4), 767–86.
Allen, B. J. (2011). Critical communication pedagogy as a framework for teaching difference and organizing. In D. K. Mumby (Ed.), *Reframing difference in organizational communication studies: Research, pedagogy, practice* (pp. 103–25). Thousand Oaks, CA: Sage.
Blanchard, F. A., Crandall, C. S., Brigham, J. C., & Vaughn, L. A. (1994). Condemning and condoning racism: A social context approach to interracial settings. *Journal of Applied Psychology, 79*(6), 993–97.
Bolgatz, J. (2005). Teachers initiating conversations about race and racism in a high school class. *Multicultural Perspectives, 7*(3), 28–35.
Broockman, D., & Kalla, J. (2016). Durably reducing transphobia: A field experiment on door-to-door canvassing. *Science, 352*(6282), 220–24.
Brookfield, S. D., & Preskill, S. (2005). *Discussion as a way of teaching: Tools and techniques for democratic classrooms* (2nd ed.). San Francisco, CA: Jossey-Bass.
Carey, B., & Hoffman, J. (2016, October 12). Lessons in the delicate art of confronting offensive speech. *New York Times*.
Cooks, L. (2010). The (critical) pedagogy of communication and the (critical) communication of pedagogy. In D. L. Fassett & J. T. Warren (Eds.), *The Sage handbook of communication and instruction* (pp. 293–314). Los Angeles, CA: Sage.
Deal, A. (2009). *Collaboration tools: A teaching with technology white paper*. Retrieved from http://www.cmu.edu/teaching/technology/whitepapers/CollaborationTools_Jan09.pdf.
deNoyelles, A., Zydney, J. M., & Chen, B. (2014). Strategies for creating a community of inquiry through online asynchronous discussions. *MERLOT Journal of Online Learning and Teaching, 10*(1), 153–65.
Dovidio, J. F., Hewstone, M., Glick, P., & Esses, V. M. (2010). Prejudice, stereotyping and discrimination: Theoretical and empirical overview. In J. F. Dovidio, M. Hewstone, P. Glick, & V. M. Esses (Eds.), *The SAGE handbook of prejudice, stereotyping and discrimination* (pp. 3–28). London, UK: Sage.
Fassett, D. L., & Rudick, C. K. (2016). Critical communication pedagogy. In P. L. Witt (Ed.), *Handbooks of communication science: Communication and learning* (Vol. 16, pp. 573–98). Berlin, Germany: DeGruyter Mouton.
Fassett, D. L., & Rudick, C. K. (2018). Critical communication pedagogy. In D. Cloud (Ed.), *Oxford encyclopedia of communication and critical studies*. New York: Oxford University Press.
Fassett, D. L., & Warren, J. T. (2007). *Critical communication pedagogy*. Thousand Oaks, CA: Sage.
Guerin, B. (2003). Combating prejudice and racism: New interventions from a functional analysis of racist language. *Journal of Community & Applied Social Psychology, 13*, 29–45.
Harper, S. R. (2015). Black male college achievers and resistant responses to racist stereotypes at predominantly white colleges and universities. *Harvard Educational Review, 85*(4), 646–74.
Hart, T., & Achterman, P. (2017). Qualitative analysis software (ATLAS.ti/Ethnograph/MAXQDA/NVivo). In J. Matthes (Ed.), *International Encyclopedia of Communication Research Methods*. Hoboken, NJ: John Wiley & Sons, Inc.
Heenan, D. (2005). Challenging stereotypes surrounding disability and promoting anti-oppressive practice: Some reflections on teaching social work students in Northern Ireland. *Social Work Education, 24*(5), 495–510.
Houghton, S. A., Furumura, Y., Lebedko, M., & Li, S. (Eds.). (2013). *Critical cultural awareness: Managing stereotypes through intercultural communication*. Newcastle upon Tyne: Cambridge Scholars Publishing.
Kahl, D. H. (2013). Critical communication pedagogy and assessment: Reconciling two seemingly incongruous ideas. *International Journal of Communication, 7*, 2610–30.
Kandaswamy, P. (2008). Beyond colorblindness and multiculturalism: Rethinking anti-racist pedagogy in the university classroom. *Radical Teacher, 80*, 6–11.

Kurylo, A. (Ed.) (2013). *Inter/cultural communication*. Thousand Oaks, CA: Sage.
Lander, J. (2014). Conversations or virtual IREs? Unpacking asynchronous online discussions using exchange structure analysis. *Linguistics and Education, 28*, 41–53.
Lebedko, M. (2013). Theory and practice of stereotypes in intercultural communication. In S. A. Houghton, Y. Furumura, M. Lebedko, & S. Li (Eds.), *Critical cultural awareness: Managing stereotypes through intercultural communication* (pp. 4–23). Newcastle upon Tyne: Cambridge Scholars Publishing.
Lun, J., Sinclair, S., Whitchurch, E. R., & Glenn, C. (2007). (Why) do I think what you think? Epistemic social tuning and implicit prejudice. *Journal of Personality & Social Psychology, 93*(6), 957–72.
MacKnight, C. B. (2000). Teaching critical thinking through online discussions. *Educause Quarterly, 4*, 38–41.
Mandernach, B. J. (2006). Thinking critically about critical thinking: Integrating online tools to promote critical thinking. *InSight: A Collection of Faculty Scholarship, 1*, 41–50.
McKee, A., & Schor, S. (1999). Confronting prejudice and stereotypes: A teaching model. *Performance Improvement Quarterly, 12*(1), 181–99.
O'Connor, L. (2014). University officials step down after anti-Latina comments. *Huffington Post*.
Paluck, E. L. (2011). Peer pressure against prejudice: A high school field experiment examining social network change. *Journal of Experimental Social Psychology, 47*, 350–58.
Pedersen, A., Walker, I., & Wise, M. (2005). "Talk does not cook rice": Beyond anti-racism rhetoric to strategies for social action. *Australian Psychologist, 40*(1), 20–30.
Roberts, M. (2014, November 10). San Jose State University students denounce board member's alleged racist statement. *NBC Bay Area*.
Rudick, C. K., & Golsan, K. B. (2016). Difference, accountability, and social justice: Three challenges for instructional communication scholarship. *Communication Education, 65*(1), 105–7.
Sechrist, G. B., & Stangor, C. (2001). Perceived consensus influences intergroup behavior and stereotype accessibility. *Journal of Personality & Social Psychology, 80*(4) 645–54.
Simpson, J. S. (2010). Critical race theory and cricial communication pedagogy. In D. L. Fassett & J. T. Warren (Eds.), *The Sage handbook of communication and instruction* (pp. 361–84). Los Angeles, CA: Sage.
Sinclair, S., Lowery, B. S., Hardin, C. D., & Colangelo, A. (2005). Social tuning of automatic racial attitudes: The role of affiliative motivation. *Journal of Personality & Social Psychology, 89*(4), 583–92.
SJSU students protest alleged racist comment made by donor. (2014, November 10). Retrieved from https://abc7news.com/education/sjsu-students-protest-alleged-racist-comment-made-by-donor/389631/.
Smith, L. G. E., & Postmes, T. (2011). Shaping stereotypical behaviour through the discussion of social stereotypes. *British Journal of Social Psychology, 50*, 74–98.
Stangor, C., Sechrist, G. B., & Jost, J. T. (2001). Changing racial beliefs by providing consensus information. *Personality and Social Psychology Bulletin, 27*(4), 486–96.
Wang, Q., Woo, H. L., & Zhao, J. (2009). Investigating critical thinking and knowledge construction in an interactive learning environment. *Interactive Learning Environments, 17*(1), 95–104.
Warren, J. T., & Fassett, D. L. (2010). Critical communication pedagogy: Reframing the field. In D. L. Fassett & J. T. Warren (Eds.), *The Sage handbook of communication and instruction* (pp. 283–291). Los Angeles, CA: Sage.
Weinstein, M. (2002–2012). T.A.M.S. Text analysis markup system: An open source qualitative analysis system. http://tamsys.sourceforge.net/.
Willoughby, B. (2012). Basic strategies. *Speak up at school*. Retrieved from http://www.tolerance.org/publication/basic-strategies

Chapter Eight

Beyond the Classroom Walls

The Intersection of Critical Communication Pedagogy and Public Pedagogy as Evidenced in "Let's Plays"

Jeremy M. Omori

Fassett and Warren (2007) reclaim the classroom as a meaningful space for activism and for practicing and performing interpersonal justice. What we teach and learn in a classroom ultimately extends out of its four walls; it is also true that someone who practices Critical Communication Pedagogy (CCP) is able to do so beyond the classroom setting. Yet CCP scholars have not explicitly discussed how CCP extends outside of their classroom. In this chapter, I intend to show how reflexivity and dialogue are utilized pedagogically through the gaming and commentary of Let's Plays (LPs) in order to express the importance of developing and practicing CCP outside of a classroom space.

Until the beginning of my doctoral program, I did not have a classroom space (either physical or digital) in which to practice CCP, but I did what I could to practice it in my everyday teaching as both a tutor and a healthcare trainer. Through my observations and engagement with spaces of learning and teaching outside of a classroom, I came to realize that there were other means to practice and embody CCP through Public Pedagogy (PP). PP focuses on the teaching and learning that happens beyond schooling (Sandlin, Schultz, & Burdick, 2010) through everyday and informal pedagogy. LPs provide one such example. LPs are videos of a video game being played by a gamer who provides commentary while playing the game. This commentary can be about the game itself as it is progressing, about the game in general, or unrelated to the game; it can be for informational or entertainment purposes.

Whereas CCP brings in change and reflexivity within the classroom, PP focuses on how teaching and learning happens outside of the classroom. While CCP acknowledges that engagement with social issues is not precluded in the classroom, these conversations are missing or exist as secondary thoughts that stop at the end of the academic's pen. PP offers CCP scholars and practitioners another perspective to look at teaching and learning in their daily lives, whether within the four walls of a classroom or in an online class space. While PP literature offers a large breadth of critical approaches in pedagogical topics, CCP literature acknowledges that reflexivity and dialogue are at the forefront of teaching. LPs have the potential to showcase this relationship in their capacity to become a space for both dialogue and reflexivity.

LPs, similar to curriculum planning, require a balance of informative and engaging commentary, along with practice and preparation to perform the skills needed to play through the game via recording or livestream. Just as course materials become personal to the teacher in preparing/presenting them and to the student learning them in a classroom, an LP is also personal to the LPer producing it and to the audience viewing it. An LPer creates an LP and posts it onto their YouTube channel where it is watched and evaluated by viewers who create comments providing support or criticism of playing strategies or of topics brought up by the LPer. The LPer reads comments and discusses them in following videos as they progress through the LP series. LPs, through this process, become a space of community where people regularly watch and interact with each other as an LP series progresses (with subsequent videos throughout a span of time varied by the length of the game being presented in the series). The LPer and viewer parallel the teacher and student, respectively. Within a CCP framework, listening and reading feedback and critiques are utilizations of reflexivity and dialogue, while interacting with viewers on how to proceed through the game provides an engaging space. Similar to a CCP classroom, LPs also provide a space to discuss social issues, whether derived from the game itself or through unrelated commentary.

DEFINING PUBLIC PEDAGOGY

Public Pedagogy (PP) has only recently seen a surge of popularity as a term and concept within the past couple decades in education literature (Sandlin, O'Malley, & Burdick, 2011; Burdick & Sandlin, 2013), including the recent launch of the peer-reviewed journal, *Journal of Public Pedagogies* in 2016. PP looks at the "spaces, sites, and languages of education and learning that exist outside of the walls of the institutions of schools" (Sandlin, Schultz, & Burdick, 2010, p. 1). However, more recent critiques in defining and using

PP tackle the vastness and oftentimes superficial use of the term "public pedagogy" in research. As Savage (2010) notes, in his critique of the idea of *public pedagogy*, breaking down "public" to its rawest form,

> The utility of "public pedagogy" as a conceptual frame began to blur and weaken when I started thinking about what constitutes the "public" in the term. I began to wonder: In our rapidly globalizing and corporatizing era, what exactly are *public* knowledges, *public* spaces and *public* educative influences? In other words: why I am calling this "thing," this term, *public*? (p. 104, emphasis original)

Even in analyzing the idea and word of "pedagogy," Savage importantly questions,

> What makes something educative or pedagogic in nature? Isn't *everything* educative? Or is it? And most importantly: What distinguishes the 'pedagogy' in public pedagogy from traditional accounts of socialization or interpellation and the old saying that '*ideology is everywhere*' thus all ideology is educative? (p. 107, emphasis original)

As much as PP can be all encompassing, this can also become a problem when not taking into consideration the accessibility that a text or topic has to offer to an audience. PP scholars must take special care and consideration of their audience and the relevancy in teaching and learning their text has to said audience. As Burdick, Sandlin and O'Malley (2014) demonstrate with their anthology, *Problematizing Public Pedagogy,* we must rethink the field in the ways that PP can substantially contribute to both academic and social justice research and practice. PP can provide ways of framing, studying, and enacting pedagogy that, while not intended to be definitive, rather point out different approaches and ideas of PP while still providing further clarity.

I approach PP through CCP. I was introduced to PP through an interdisciplinary approach—beyond just focusing on communication and education, but also analyzing the ways in which gender studies, justice studies, and transborder studies (to name a few) also apply and speak to one another. I am also a gamer who, as a master's student with only a part-time job, could not afford to play games. Instead, I turned to watching LPs as a way to enjoy watching a story and game unfold without having to pay for the game. However, watching LPs—both games I have and have not played—made me interested in the LPers' approach to their videos, and the communities they created. As someone who practices CCP, I began to see pieces of reflexive thought and dialogue between LPer and their audience through different social media platforms. I began thinking about how LPs as PP can help bridge the conversation with CCP—especially as a public forum to talk about and observe nuances of power.

PUBLIC PEDAGOGY INTERSECTING WITH CRITICAL COMMUNICATION PEDAGOGY

Both PP and CCP play out through the learning and teaching communities. Both are concerned with change and justice at a personal, communal, and macro level. Both CCP and PP recognize mundane moments to be spots for teachable moments that happen organically. Where CCP and PP intersect then is a space for dialogue and reflexivity in formal and informal teaching, within and outside of the classroom walls, while being cognizant of how identity and culture play a part in these spaces and moments. I will portray this in several key ways, first in expanding the classroom, and through dialogue and self-reflexivity.

Ellsworth and the Expansion of the Classroom

As Fassett and Warren (2007) note:

> Critical communication educators look to postmodern and poststructural understandings of human identity, to senses of students and teachers as relational selves produced in collusion and collision, to theories and methodologies that help them account for identities as produced in cultural—and therefore inherently ideological—contexts. (p. 40)

Further:

> Critical communication educators, interested in how best to engage the classroom (and research on the intersections between communication and classrooms) as a space for social justice and change, this shift in thinking about identity is not simply a change in language. (p. 40)

The classroom, viewed as either a physical or digital space of learning, is important in what we say and do within, but we can also learn outside of this space. Ellsworth (2004) notes with the self and other, in relation to the architecture of the space of learning:

> Our experiences of a building arise not only out of our cognitive interpretations to historical or aesthetic meanings but also out of the corporeality of the body's time/space as it exists in relation to the building. (p. 4)

Furthermore:

> Like media and architecture, pedagogy involves us in experiences of the corporeality of the body's time and space. Bodies have affective somatic responses as they inhabit a pedagogy's time and space. Specific to pedagogy is the experience of the corporeality of the body's time and space when it is in

the midst of learning. Because this experience arises out of an assemblage of mind/brain/body with the time and space of pedagogy, we must approach an investigation into the learning experience of the learning self through that assemblage. (pp. 4–5)

Ellsworth gives us language to describe and reconsider what a classroom is. The body's response to pedagogy's time and space encourages us to engage and unpack the learning experience within that moment. While we are constantly unpacking the relationship between teacher and student within the setting of a classroom, it is also worth investigating how this learning relationship with the self and other works in other spaces and time. We can likewise broaden the idea of a "classroom" to a greater public that houses different bodies. While Ellsworth focuses her attention to other physical spaces of learning, I expand this definition to also look at digital spaces as sites of learning. While this is obvious when we look at an online or hybrid class—a very clear educational space—online media has been utilized as a tool for learning outside of traditional definitions of a classroom. In looking at online media as a forum for learning and teaching, we expand our ideas of how we can address social issues and identity in different ways. Online media encompasses numerous platforms for learning and information gathering and sharing. As Atay (2018) notes, "Due to the digitalization of our everyday realities, including teaching and learning, we often encounter individuals from other cultures in online platforms perhaps more frequently than in our face-to-face interactions" (p. 180). LPs as a digital platform create a space for a wide and diverse audience to communicate with one another. As such, LPers and their LPs provide "multiple ways for people from all over the world to communicate and have called upon numerous pedagogical techniques and approaches to unpack mediated representations and make sense of digitalized and globalized cultural experiences" (p. 182). In this sense, an LP can be viewed as a classroom between teacher (LPer) and student (viewer).

Dialogue and Self-Reflexivity at Play

Toyosaki and Atay (2018) discuss the importance of reflexivity and dialogue within Critical Intercultural Communication Pedagogy (CICP). Both are not only important in theory but also in practice. In similar language with PP, CICP aims to blur pedagogy within and outside of the classroom walls. Though CICP is different from PP, both Toyosaki and Atay (2018) provide a framework of CICP that helps to bridge together CCP and PP.

Dialogue is important where we can have open and important conversations about content, and the ways in which power impacts our everyday lives (Atay, 2018). Furthermore, dialogue is organic where there is mutual trust and "recognition of interdependence rather than dependence and control" (González & Cramer, 2018, p. 220). LPers who look to be interactive in how they produce their LPs create opportunities to generate dialogue with their audience. To some extent, this also includes critiques by viewers on the LPer's playstyle and skill with the particular game—whether the critical feedback was desired or not—and LPers often try to address pertinent critiques.

Self-reflexivity is from within; it takes into consideration the self in relation to others and their intersectional identities (Toyosaki & Chuang, 2018). While LP audiences include a broad and often global audience, identities can become muted behind a username so that, even with statistics and numbers that list demographics such as age and gender, the process and relation of identity between audience and LPer must be further considered. Toyosaki and Chuang (2018) discuss intersectional reflexivity as a "relational commitment to one another" (p. 230). Intersectional reflexivity acknowledges the relationship between people and their intersecting identities, leading to uncomfortable positions of self-implications (Jones, 2010). Further, "reflexivity got to hurt. Reflexivity is laborious" (p. 124). For LPers, feedback and engagement from their audience is important. Similar with handling negativity from students (and teacher) in the classroom, LPers are tasked with handling the labor of going through negative and sometimes destructive comments from viewers. In regards to "blind" Let's Plays—games that the LPer has not played before—the interactions between the LPer and their audience become opportunities for teaching and learning, requiring the LPer to be comfortable with being vulnerable while failing and asking for help from viewers.

"LET'S PLAYS" AS PUBLIC PEDAGOGY

In order to frame LPs as sites of PP, I look at Biesta's (2014) pedagogies of the public, for the public, and in the interest of publicness. He describes a "pedagogy *for* [and therefore, aimed at] the public" (p. 21, emphasis original), as well as a "pedagogy *of* [therefore, done by] the public" (p. 22, emphasis original), and finally, outlining a way to "move beyond such a regime so that public pedagogy can work at the *intersection* of education and politics" (p. 23, emphasis original). The approach Biesta takes is defining "public pedagogy as a specific 'form' of pedagogy, a specific form of doing educational 'work,' in which pedagogy 'operates' in a public way . . . in which such a public mode of pedagogical operation might be understood" (p. 16). In framing the pedagogy of, with, and in the public interest, Biesta (2014) attempts to "(re)connect the educational and political and locates both firmly in the public sphere" (p. 16). While the three are distinct, they also work together simultaneously. LPs exemplify the simultaneous nature of working *for* (the video is produced for a public audience), while allowing for the opportunity for an LP to become a collaboration between LPer and audience (*of* the public), and finally, the interest in publicness here looks at the ways in which many LPers do LPs as not just for money, but for personal enjoyment and to share their passion with others.

What makes LPs an important site of pedagogy is the relationship between player and viewer, which can be paralleled with Freire's (1970/2003) idea of students working together to create what is taught and discussed while the teacher directs and monitors knowledge construction that is relevant for and with the students. While LPs exist in different forms, I am specifically interested in "blind" LP's in which the LPer has little to no experience in the game they have selected to play and depends on viewers to help them. While the LPer may invite their viewers to play along with them, often the collaboration between LPer and viewers is through viewer feedback and responses to requests by the LPer for help. LPs may also serve as not only a visual but also an audial guide for gamers from the commentary that LPers provide. Furthermore, LPs serve as a narrative journey for those who may not be able to afford the game or due to physical or visual impairments. While the former two are given a way to experience the game visually, the latter is provided a space to experience what is happening in the game through the LPer's commentary and descriptions of the game's story and mechanics.

LPs are large enough to be considered their own genre, ranging not only from YouTube but through numerous forums, as well as live streaming video platforms such as Twitch. Some of the most notable LPers include Markiplier, Chuggaaconroy, and PewDiePie, with the latter grossing one of the largest followings of subscribers and viewers worldwide (Mandle, 2015). For this chapter, I will be discussing Stephenplays and Lucahjin's works for their approach in presenting their materials. They are significant because of the particular ways they involve their viewers in their LPs to create community within their content, and how they take the time to dialogue with their viewers, using viewer feedback to help proceed in their videos.

Stephen Georg first gained YouTube recognition from his video blog (vlog), Stephenvlog (Georg, 2009). However, shortly after the creation of his side channel, Stephenplays, he has since focused more on LPs while continuing to vlog on the side. While Georg had a few YouTube channels before, both Stephenplays and Stephenvlog are his most popular channels. Georg states he chose the title "Stephenplays" as a way of differentiating how Let's Plays were typically presented without much or any input from the audience, and to "bring back the 'let's play [together]' in Let's Plays" (M. Georg, 2011). Alongside Stephen is his wife, Mallory (Mal) Georg, who joins him in some of his LPs; she would eventually go on to create her own channel, MalMakes, and published her first video in January 2016 (Georg, 2016). What makes Georg interesting is his approach to creating dialogue with his viewers. While he seldom talks about social issues, he invites his viewers' choices on games to play and how to play certain parts of the more open-ended games, providing viewers a voice on what they want to see (González & Cramer, 2018).

Reese Dressler, also known as Lucahjin, plays mostly indie dating simulator games, often "blind," and is characterized by her use of lewd phrasing and sexual innuendos. She is aware of the frustrations she causes viewers with her mistakes and recontextualizes them as forms of entertainment. She has noted in several of the endings of her LPs that she is grateful for the advice and support her viewers give her, describing her hope that her videos give viewers the space to act like she is a big sister to them, and expresses that they are helping her to complete a game (Dressler, 2014b). She is inclusive of her viewers throughout the journey of her LPs and tries to finds ways to interact with her viewers.

Both Georg and Dressler are interesting in their approach to LPs from a PP/CCP standpoint. On a more macro level of analysis, their work can be observed reflexively on the ways we consume media (Atay, 2018)—especially when we take into consideration the amount of viewer involvement they allow in their work. What is also interesting with both Georg and Dressler is the way they approach dialogue on the micro/personal level as a way to bring up issues in identity. While Mal or Stephen have not explicitly mentioned gender performance within gaming, Dressler acknowledges herself as a female gamer in her LPs, showing how identity is still performed and embodied within a digital platform (Cheong & Gray, 2011). With CCP, identity is shown to still be at the forefront here in how one performs and is received by others (Fassett & Warren, 2007).

Blind Let's Plays as a Site of the Public

Both Stephenplays and Lucahjin have presented several blind LPs on their channels. While they are both gamers and have done LPs of games they were knowledgeable of, blind LPs give viewers the opportunity to be more involved and help the LPer decide on what steps or quests they should do next. If they are unable to progress in the game, they reach out to the viewers for advice on where to go or what they need to do to progress. To provide more context of how Stephenplays and Lucahjin approach their audience with their LPs, I will discuss some of the highlights from their more popular and recent blind LPs, then discuss in the following section how this relates to building a shared space of learning and community.

Stephenplays Skyrim *and* Fallout 4

Skyrim is Georg's longest running LP and is one of the few, if not only, LPs of *Skyrim* in which the entire game is completed, including all possible side quests. His finale video for this LP series was his first to receive over one million views (S. Georg, 2016). Georg's later LP, *Fallout 4*, was created by the same developer as *Skyrim* and has similar gaming mechanics and structures. As part of Georg's general process for his videos, he went through all the viewer comments for feedback, hints, and suggestions on how to proceed. *Skyrim* and *Fallout 4* are open world games where choices made by the player change the outcome of the game. This, along with the games not having a linear story path, make the gameplay and LP more open for exploration and allow for greater interactions between LPer and viewers. Georg and his viewers provided narrative for the avatar, a silent protagonist, projecting these constructed avatar and cast's identities into the narrative of the game's storyline (Georg, 2014a; Georg, 2014b).

In a similar vein, *Fallout 4*, Georg's latest large project, is an attempt to follow a lot of the same approaches he took in his *Skyrim* LP, with subtle changes that create more community involvement with his viewers. Georg is currently playing through the game without any knowledge of the game while having his viewers help him as they did in his *Skyrim* LP (Georg, 2015). Along with helping him in his *Skyrim* LP, viewers also submitted fanart, which so impressed him that he began to request viewers submit fanart to be displayed at the end of every video (Georg, 2015). As Georg continues playing through *Fallout 4*, he tries to be inclusive both for himself and for his viewers in the sense that he lets his viewers have a say in what he does, as well as provides feedback to his viewers on the comments that they make.

Lucahjin Plays Pokemon HeartGold *and* Legend of Zelda: Ocarina of Time

Similar to Georg, Dressler has a strong community fanbase. She incorporates sexual humor while retaining a sister-like image in her videos (Dressler, 2014b). She is not afraid to make mistakes and is well aware of the fact that this can aggravate her viewers (Dressler, 2013). Dressler presents her failures in a way that can be seen as productive in her LPs. Dressler allows for growth in her failures, in the way that Jones (2010) describes self-reflexivity. This form of self-reflexivity is "relational and dialogical" (Toyosaki & Chuang, 2018, p. 230) and is often painful and difficult in the sense that one must be open to see and hear through one's beliefs, no matter how well-intended one with power may be (Delpit, 1995, as cited in Toyosaki & Chuang, 2018, p. 230). In her characteristically lewd manner, Dressler renames the protagonist in her LP of *Legend of Zelda: Ocarina of Time* "Fuck me" (Dressler, 2013) and the rival character in her LP of *Pokemon HeartGold* "My butt" (Dressler, 2015b), creating humorous situations when the particular character is referred to within the game's dialogue. Like Georg, Dressler received fan art, which she used at the start of her *Pokemon HeartGold* videos; she also took in song requests that she would sing during the games.

Dressler had many problems in her *Legend of Zelda: Ocarina of Time* LP and depended greatly on feedback from her viewers. She also had help from other LPers, though while it was interesting to see the collaboration and guidance she received from other LPers, viewers still commented on her having trouble with playing in the game's major plot areas. She knew and acknowledged this throughout her LP, yet viewers were still entertained by the dialogue between LPers and the conflicts they had. Specifically, a fan created an animation of a lewd dialogue between characters (Dressler, 2014a). In this sense, Dressler attempts to make up for her mistakes through humor; despite being an otherwise good gamer, she is often apologetic for her "poor playing." While part of her LP persona as a big sister, the use of apologies is interesting in the sense that she is cognizant of her failures and shows her devotion to continue trying—when she tells her viewers tongue-in-cheek that they will just have to deal with her mistakes.

Shared Experience in Creating Community

Both Stephenplays and Lucahjin provide many opportunities for fans to connect with them and with each other. While they display some of the more common ways of communication through social media or the comments sections of their videos, they both approach community building in different ways. In this section, I will go over some of the different ways they have directly and indirectly approached and interacted with their communities on social issues—specifically, when approaching their viewers on the topic of LGBTQ+ issues. Similar to how one approaches a classroom differently depending on the group dynamic and the teacher themself, both Stephenplays and Lucahjin have their own target audiences and their own ways of dealing with social issues in their communities that are both productive and problematic.

The "Stephenites": Expansion, Growth, and Involvement.

The Stephenplays community, who are also known as the "Stephenites," is a supportive community that was built through the content Stephen and Mal Georg have created over the years. Georg has provided a number of ways for fans to be involved such as helping out with content, assisting with the Stephenplays Wiki, and donating to support him and Mal, as well as holding a monthly session to answer questions and respond to fanmail. Likewise, they host two charity events where they stream live and play games for donations to contribute to a local hospital in their area.

Georg's fans are able to connect with him and Mal more personally perhaps in part due to his vlog channel, on which he posts videos of his and

Mal's daily lives. He describes things that occur in their days as well as gives opinions on certain products or issues. While the vlogs attempt to be politically neutral, there are times when Georg mentions his and Mal's support for certain social issues—namely LGBTQ+ issues (Georg, 2012; Georg, 2013a). This instance struck up controversial conversations among viewers (Georg, 2013a), ultimately forcing Georg to moderate and delete comments, before disabling comments altogether. He later released a statement of what happened and the reasons for his actions (Georg, 2013b); in doing this, the peace was kept within the community. This was a moment where Georg acted as a more active facilitator for his viewers, before making the executive decision to move on to other topics. While on the one hand, Georg moderated and shut down conversation on a debated issue to maintain peace in his community, it is also important to note that he did his best to moderate and omit attacks against opposing views (Georg, 2013b). In CCP, while, it is important to facilitate and be open with dialogue (Fassett & Warren, 2007; Atay, 2018; González & Cramer, 2018), we must also be aware of and be mindful of positions that may attack one another, which leads to arguing rather than dialogue.

Lucahjin: Gender and Sexuality Embodied and Performed

Similar to Georg, there were times where Dressler stated her personal position on social issues. For example, the day that gay marriage was legalized in the United States, she presented a dating simulation game in which Wario and Bowser, two masculine male antagonists in the *Super Mario* universe become romantically involved (Dressler, 2015a). Likewise, on an earlier video with a guest LPer, she censored and scolded him for using homophobic language to describe a character in the game (Dressler, 2014c). It is here in these moments that Dressler used her position as an LPer and entertainer to provide a moment of reflexivity for her viewers and guest on social issues.

Similar to Stephenplays, her fanbase sends her fan mail and gifts. Likewise, when she streams on Twitch, viewers have the option to provide monetary donations. In her live streams, she has a more intimate and immediate space to interact directly with her viewers, which she uses to talk about their lives, interests, and questions that they might have. While her live streams are of her playing games, the conversations she has have created a space for viewers to relax and enjoy, while also providing memorable moments. In one of her Twitch streams, she disclosed that she was a fan of the children's cartoon, *Steven Universe*, which has many progressive themes on strong female leads, gay romantic relationships, and blurring the lines of gender. She said her favorite character was Jasper, a large, masculine, and brutish female antagonist. She would later ask on Twitter if she was the only one who liked Jasper, receiving a large positive response (Lucahjin, 2015). Due to her viewers' responses, Dressler began to incorporate Jasper into her LPs, such as renaming a Pokémon that looked like a boulder "Jasper" in her *Pokemon HeartGold* LP, placing Jasper from an antagonist in *Steven Universe* into a protagonist role in her LP.

THE PERSONAL BECOMING PUBLIC AND REALITY

I wish to conclude this chapter with my experiences and my interactions as both a pedagogue and a fan of both Stephenplays and Lucahjin. They both gave me countless hours of entertainment, as well as many moments of reflection in how their content was meaningful for me. As a critical communication pedagogue who studies public pedagogy, I believe it is important to embody the practices we hold on to not only within our teacher/student personas, but as our personal personas as well. This is difficult and designed for us to fail. Yet, in failure, we are able to be reflexive in our own limitations and grow to be more inclusive in our teaching and ways of being. I provide two experiences where I was touched and interacted with Stephenplays and Lucahjin, and the ways I dialogued and was reflexive in my failures.

Change of Careers

I remember watching an episode of Stephenvlog about Mal's resignation as a teacher (S. Georg, 2016). Her story hit me in a very personal way as she and Stephen were explaining the reasons for her resignation and the challenges they were facing. When I returned to graduate school, five years after receiving my bachelor's degree, I started to remember the joys of being back in academia. I was miserable where I worked. I remember many nights I would talk to friends about dreading the next day, wishing it would end, and how I could not take working at a company I had no passion for, while going to school and working on the side towards a career I would much prefer to be in. Stephen and Mal described similar issues, with cruel students and even crueler parents making Mal's daily work miserable, along with working long hours for no apparent gratitude. Yet, perhaps what hurt most about her resignation was that she would not see the students she did form positive bonds and relationships with the following school year. I wrote to her, describing my similar situation of being unhappy with my career, and while it was an uneasy and awkward message, she received it gratefully and described her current plans to continue to teach while hoping that she might one day return to teach in a class.

Forgetting Privilege and Context

I cannot explain why, but Jasper, from the cartoon show, *Steven Universe*, has become a unique and cherished character for me, despite her characterization as a physically and mentally abusive individual. I remember a passing comment Lucahjin made in a live stream, casually mentioning that Jasper was one of her favorite characters. Her viewers went crazy, fetishizing Jasper and claiming that "the Jasper love is real!" I must have been caught up in that when I twisted a friend's arm to create a twerking Jasper GIF for me while half-jokingly telling him that he should also advertise it to Lucahjin. He ended up making it for me as a birthday gift; I was ecstatic. I shared the picture with Lucahjin with his blessing in the hopes that she would share it with others, but she only liked the picture. For all the craze and hype she made, it was admittedly disappointing.

These experiences I had with Mal Georg and Reese Dressler provided me with reflexive moments that made me think of my position and approach, as well as where I was and how I came to be where I am now. Reflexivity through our failures is how we grow not only as pedagogues, but as individuals (Warren, 2011; Toyosaki, 2013). In both instances, I had conversations with both LPers and have gotten to know them outside of the LP role. The dialogue I had with Mal became something that resonated with me on a personal and emotional level, where I was compelled to say something. I also questioned my attempt to show Dressler the GIF of Jasper twerking and began thinking about how my position as a cis man might come off as sexualizing and fetishizing a female-identified character. Both conversations make me think how we are always thinking about issues of social justice and identity in relation with others (Fassett & Warren, 2007). Despite having different outcomes, these experiences portray the roles of LPer/viewer as similar to the roles of teacher/student that Freire (1970/2003) makes sure to specify are distinct from one another. However, at the same time, there is indeed much that can be learned from one another, and that should not be discounted either.

As much as Stephenplays (both Stephen and Mal Georg) and Lucahjin are entertainers and gamers, the community that has been built around them and their work is supportive and provides a space for much dialogue whether about a video game or about important real-world issues. Similar to LPs, teaching is personal, and one cannot entirely disassociate from one's position and what they carry into the classroom (Warren, 2011). While LPers may look at LPs as a form of income, it is the conversations and communities that are created with and among viewers that make the experience more personal. A colleague once mentioned to me that while the theories and course concepts are important for students to know, the most memorable classes are the ones where she remembers the conversations had with her instructors. For

LPers to share a bit of their life, both the good and bad, the connections created become heart work (Dannels, 2015) for and with the viewers.

LPs give pedagogues an opportunity to analyze how social issues are informally discussed and how dialogue and self-reflexivity happen outside of the classroom. As a pedagogue who does both CCP and PP, I see the value that LPs have to branch these fields together. Whereas CCP research is limited by how it impacts students in a classroom beyond the classroom walls, PP can become cumbersome in determining the value of the pedagogical text because of its too-broad scope. By taking both CCP and PP into consideration, with their common goals, we allow for a self-reflexive and dialogical framework that works towards social issues that work inside and outside of the classroom. While time and energy are put into each video recording, the rapport LPers establish with viewers is organic, in the sense that relationships are created through dialogue with their viewers (Fassett & Warren, 2007); their genuine identities and positions are always with them in their videos. This relationship between LPers and their viewers can show how people are informally teaching and learning through self-reflexivity and dialogue, and the power that is associated within the self and the other. CCP is the active work and relationship between teacher and student through self-reflexivity and dialogue (Dannels, 2015; Toyosaki & Atay, 2018). The work that is created within this learning space is relational, much in the same way that LPers and their viewers create the LP experience together.

REFERENCES

Atay, A. (2018). Mediated critical intercultural communication. In A. Atay & S. Toyosaki (Eds.), *Critical intercultural communication pedagogy* (pp. 179–94). Lanham, MD: Lexington Books.

Biesta, G. (2014). Making pedagogy public: For the public, of the public, or in the interest of publicness? In J. Burdick, J. A. Sandlin, & M. P. O'Malley (Eds.), *Problematizing public pedagogy* (pp. 15–25). New York: Routledge.

Burdick, J. & Sandlin, J. A. (2013). Learning, becoming, and the unknowable: Conceptualizations, mechanisms, and the process in public pedagogy literature. *Curriculum Inquiry, 43*(1), 142–77.

Burdick, J. Sandlin, J. A., & O'Malley, M. P. (2014). Breaking without fixing: Inhabiting aporia. In J. Burdick, J. A. Sandlin, & M. P. O'Malley (Eds.), *Problematizing public pedagogy* (pp. 1–11). New York: Routledge.

Cheong, P. H. & Gray, K. (2011). Mediated intercultural dialects: Identity perceptions and performances in the virtual worlds, *Journal of International and Intercultural Communication, 4*(4), 265–71.

Dannels, D. P. (2015). *8 essential questions teachers ask: A guidebook for communicating with students.* New York, NY: Oxford University Press.

Dressler, R. (2013, July 13). Ocarina of Time [Blind]—1—WHY IS EVERYONE HUMPING SOMETHING? [Video file]. Retrieved from https://www.youtube.com/watch?v=TXhPvNkJ3_A.

Dressler, R. (2014a, July 23). Lucahjin Animated | NABOORU'S TINY HOLE. [Video file]. Retrieved from https://www.youtube.com/watch?v=fdnpkH1kuJA.

Dressler, R. (2014b, August 20). Super Paper Mario (Blind) -69- GRAND FINALE. [Video file]. Retrieved from https://www.youtube.com/watch?v=fZANrgdZpXQ.
Dressler, R. (2014c, December 3). Putt Putt Goes to the Moon -2- DENIED. [Video file]. Retrieved from https://www.youtube.com/watch?v=hfe83_aAFsY.
Dressler, R. (2015a, June 27). WTS Saturday—WARIO DATING AGAIN! [Video file]. Retrieved from https://www.youtube.com/watch?v=RclyIKnFl3o.
Dressler, R. (2015b, September 21). Pokemon HeartGold (Blind) -3- My Rival. [Video file]. Retrieved from https://www.youtube.com/watch?v=QICQOvJsp3s.
Ellsworth, E. (2004). *Places of learning: Media, architecture, pedagogy*. New York, NY: Taylor & Francis Group.
Fassett, D. L. & Warren, J. T. (2007). *Critical communication pedagogy*. Thousand Oaks, CA: Sage.
Freire, P. (1970/2003). *Pedagogy of the oppressed*. New York, NY: The Continuum International Publishing Group Inc.
Georg, M. (2016, January 16). Zelda: Wind Waker—Time Lapse Painting. [Video file]. Retrieved from https://www.youtube.com/watch?v=ryqyVNW1Dic.
Georg, S. (2009, November 24). Day Zero (Day 0—11/24/09). [Video file]. Retrieved from https://www.youtube.com/watch?v=fUFyRAjUIhI.
Georg, S. (2011, April 20). Stephen Plays: Minecraft—Ep. 1. [Video file]. Retrieved from https://www.youtube.com/watch?v=BwWGQ3535dE.
Georg, S. (2012, June 29). Clarinet (Day 945—6/26/12). [Video file]. Retrieved from https://www.youtube.com/watch?v=JpB2Dp98EYM.
Georg, S. (2013a, May 8). We Support the Gays! (Day 1251—4/28/13). [Video file]. Retrieved from https://www.youtube.com/watch?v=39UR9bIXkH8.
Georg, S. (2013b). The Gays™. Retrieved from http://stephengeorg.tumblr.com/post/49968985709/the-gays.
Georg, S. (2014a, May 19). Stephen Plays: Skyrim #282. [Video file]. Retrieved from https://www.youtube.com/watch?v=gwmwEY5L_CA.
Georg, S. (2014b, May 22). THE END OF SKYRIM (#283). [Video file]. Retrieved from https://www.youtube.com/watch?v=RD5xmXbywfM.
Georg, S. (2015, November 11). Fallout 4 #1—"War Never Changes". [Video file]. Retrieved from https://www.youtube.com/watch?v=N0WFIhn2mR8.
Georg, S. (2016, September 7). Mal Resigned—8.17.16. [Video file]. Retrieved from https://www.youtube.com/watch?v=sM1PvlsPvZc.
González, A., & Cramer, L. (2018). Dialogue and intercultural communication pedagogy. In A. Atay & S. Toyosaki (Eds.), *Critical intercultural communication pedagogy* (pp. 217–26). Lanham, MD: Lexington Books.
Jones, R. G., Jr. (2010). Putting privilege into practice through "intersectional reflexivity:" Ruminations, interventions, and possibilities. *Reflections: Narratives of Professional Helping*, *16*(1), 122–25.
Lucahjin. (2015, August 5). Am I the only one that likes Jasper [Web log comment]. Retrieved from https://twitter.com/lucahjin/status/628038017320681472.
Mandle, C. (2015, July 5). YouTuber PewDiePie opens up about his $7.3 million earning from playing video games. Retrieved from https://www.independent.co.uk/news/people/youtuber-pewdiepie-opens-up-about-his-73-million-earnings-from-playing-video-games-10374402.html.
Sandlin, J. A., O'Malley, M. P., & Burdick, J. (2011). Mapping the complexity of public pedagogy scholarship: 1894–2010. *Review of Education Research*, *81*(3), 338–75.
Sandlin, J. A., Schultz, B. D., & Burdick, J. (2010). Understanding, mapping, and exploring the terrain of public pedagogy. In J. A. Sandlin, B. D. Schultz, & J. Burdick (Eds.) *Handbook of public pedagogy* (pp. 1–6). New York: Routledge.
Savage, G. C. (2010), Problematizing "public pedagogy" in educational research. In J. A. Sandlin, B. D. Schultz, & J. Burdick (Eds.) *Handbook of public pedagogy* (pp. 103–15). New York: Routledge.
Toyosaki, S. (2013). Pedagogical love as critical labor: Relational pedagogy as whiteness. *Qualitative Communication Research*, *2*(4), 411–33.

Toyosaki, S., & Atay, A. (2018). Introduction: Critical intercultural communication pedagogy. In A. Atay & S. Toyosaki (Eds.), *Critical intercultural communication pedagogy* (pp. vii–xvi). Lanham, MD: Lexington Books.

Toyosaki, S., & Chuang, H-Y. S. (2018). Critical intercultural communication pedagogy from within: Textualizing intercultural and intersectional self-reflexivity. In A. Atay & S. Toyosaki (Eds.), *Critical intercultural communication pedagogy* (pp. 227–47). Lanham, MD: Lexington Books.

Warren, J. T. (2011). Reflexive teaching: Toward critical autoethnographic practices of/in/on pedagogy. *Cultural Studies ⇔ Critical Methodologies, 11*(2), 139–44.

Chapter Nine

Expanding Mediated Communication for Inclusivity

Allison Brenneise

Many of us who teach in higher education have few opportunities to think about and develop our abilities surrounding accessibility. Therefore, the goal of this essay is to raise awareness of the need for more inclusive instruction and instructional methods. Doing so requires critical communication pedagogues to recognize that students with challenging disabilities are coming to college (or are there already) and to broaden their understanding of media and mediated communication, to include the high and low technologies that students with disabilities bring to mediated environments. To do this, I share scenarios (with permission and marked by italics) that are representative experiences of what lead up to and were my son Tyler's foray into higher education. I unpack meanings and provide insights into how the scenario could play out more inclusively. Then I provide recommendations for creating a more inclusive classroom environment using simple mediated accommodations that will meet the needs of many students in the classroom, not just those with disabilities.

AN UNEXPECTED INVITATION

In the summer just prior to his scheduled orientation to visit his dream school, my youngest son Tyler received a postcard from the university inviting him to participate in an innovative program. Designed to reignite a love of learning in first-year students, the invitation highlighted how participants would work toward meeting the required general curriculum while earning college credits through college seminars taken together with a cohort of other first-year students. Students would read "real books" which could be purchased in regular bookstores and focus their engagement with faculty and staff on a semester-long theme. That theme would carry discussions across disciplines and content areas as students learned to think critically and deeply, thus (re)invigorating a love of learning. For Tyler, a student with an autism spectrum diagnosis (ASD), learning disabilities, and prosopagnosia (an inability to recognize people by their faces), this opportunity had the potential to meet many needs. Since social interactions for people with face blindness are uncertain (people with face blindness cannot tell who they are communicating with by remembering a familiar face), a cohort of the same peers could reduce the number of disclosures that Tyler would have to make. In a small group of familiar peers, Tyler might only have to share his accommodative request for peers to identify themselves when they approach him a few times before they began to understand that he really couldn't recognize them by their faces. It would decrease the extra cognitive load that comes with face blindness, figuring out the identity of the stranger who is speaking. When Tyler did not recognize them, they would understand that he was not being rude and both parties could experience relief from the negative feelings that can sometimes arise when people violate social expectations. A network of familiar peers might see Tyler as human, like themselves, and develop an affinity for him. If friendship were too lofty a goal because the social and communicative challenges associated with an ASD can cause misunderstandings and discomfort for people who have not experienced young adults with a significant disability, sharing a classroom where all voices are present may nurture an appreciation of the richness and diversity that inclusion of all types can offer (Smart, 2009).

Previously, Tyler had been successful as the football manager at his high school. Once the players got to know him, they involved him in their activities, sat with him at lunch, and looked out for him in the hallways. Friendships developed; Tyler belonged and reflects on those experiences as some of the best in his lifetime. Strange and Banning (2001) suggest that without a sense of belonging to the institution of higher education, it is much more difficult for students to persist to degree. English (1993) describes the tendency for students with disabilities to experience social barriers and to be "socially disengaged" (as quoted in Nichols & Quaye, 2009, p. 48). O'Brien and Shedd (2001) linked student social involvement with other students and faculty on campus to an increased probability of student persistence. The invitation to experience his first year in this smaller setting offered the potential for Tyler to have a meaningful college experience which he envisioned as having academic and social success.

Moreover, the opportunity to read books other than traditional textbooks in college would be a boon for Tyler's independence. In addition to autism and face blindness, Tyler has multiple learning differences. He has slow cognitive processing; his speech and response times can be slow because the way his brain processes auditory and visual information works differently. These challenges are often experienced by people with an autism spectrum diagnosis (Medwetsky, 2006; Minshew & Williams, 2007; Prizant & Wetherby, 2005; Williams & Minshew, 2010). For Tyler, reading is quite difficult. Adding to Tyler's learning challenges are significant fine motor issues, which make writing a slow and arduous process for him. Writing is not fluid or automatic; he appears to draw each letter, like an artist. The amount of effort it takes for him to write is immense. Fortunately, he benefits greatly from assistive technology in the form of text-to-voice and voice-to-text software; he is adept in using them to read and write. Instead of having to enlist the support of the office supporting students with disabilities and wade through the institutionalized process of textbook conversion for reading at a later date, off-the-shelf (or mainstream) books are typically available via online subscription services for people with print disabilities, such as Learning Ally and Bookshare. These services offer the user the opportunity to select from a bevy of popular books and some textbooks, and a few mouse clicks provide them with the immediate enjoyment of reading. Just like his peers, Tyler could go to his "bookstore" and select the books he needed, without needing to involve an office full of disability support staff and text conversion bureaucracy (Fassett & Morella, 2008; Pensoneau-Conway & Cosenza, 2016).

After a thoughtful discussion together, Tyler made the decision that he would enroll in the program at orientation when he would choose his classes. As the time to meet with his advisor got closer, Tyler's anxiety was palpable. Having to meet with an authority figure with administrative power to choose whether or not he got the classes he wanted was difficult enough without the repeated announcements that parents were not to accompany their student to advising. To ease his nervousness, I handed Tyler a note to give to the advisor should he lose his voice and be unable to communicate, which sometimes occurs when Tyler interacts with authority figures. Tyler's overworked sensory system did not fare well amongst the noise and visual clutter present in the carpet-less auditorium wherein 30 advisors simultaneously met with 30 students. There was no accommodation for this advising session. Within approximately 10 minutes, Tyler was out and inviting me to join him with the advisor. My role was small: provide verbal prompts that assured him the safety he needed to communicate his wants and needs. Tyler did the rest and left orientation enrolled in the program.

A week prior to move-in day for first-year students, we were in contact with the advisor who wanted to arrange a meeting with Tyler and the program's director. Tyler prepared a legal document for me to be able to accompany him to the meeting and to be his voice if he could not speak. Two days before the semester began, we met with the director, the advisor, and the disability services representative, whose purpose for attending was to facilitate discussion surrounding the accommodations Tyler required. The director agreed to let me stay, but claimed she could not speak to me directly, even though she had Tyler's express written permission. She demanded to know (among other things) how Tyler would be able to engage in the course, a course and activities he had never experienced in a setting that was also unfamiliar. This would be a challenge for any student, especially for a student whose diagnosis impedes the development of Theory of Mind (Baron-Cohen, Leslie, & Frith, 1985). Theory of Mind (TOM) is the ability to "read" the social expectations of others. With impaired TOM, generalizing or transferring skills learned in one environment to another is especially difficult. Specifically, the director wanted to know how Tyler would participate in activities such as "quick writes" (University Writing Council, 2011). A "quick write," she explained, was an activity where students individually respond to a writing prompt (quickly) and then exchange their writing with a peer for their written comment. Because Tyler was speechless, I explained to the director how that pedagogical activity could take place in real time in the class. The director, unable to conceive how the program would run with a person like Tyler in it, said, "Tyler would be a good match for [their] program, but the program was not a good match for him," and then recommended to Tyler that he disenroll from the program. The person from disability services sat there silently throughout the meeting even as Tyler's rights to reasonable accommodations for communication in the meeting and accessibility in the program were trampled. Still in this audience of "professionals," I informed Tyler that he did not legally have to disenroll, but grades in college matter. If the director and advisor were forecasting their unwillingness to accommodate him before the program started, they were unlikely to change. And because instructor prophecy can influence student outcomes (Rosenthal & Jacobson, 2003), the risk would be great.

The situation Tyler faced is necessarily complex. The director's unwillingness to accommodate Tyler's communication needs, which would allow him to participate in a program offered to all first-year students, appeared to be based on her own ignorance in working with someone with Tyler's challenges. She may have wondered how he managed to be admitted. How could he learn? Would he bring down the intellectual and academic rigor of the program? Could she teach him? What would the other students think? What does this mean for the future of the academy?

In U.S.-American society, people without disabilities tend to fear and avoid interactions with people with disabilities (Garland-Thomson, 1997; Smart, 2009). Garland-Thomson (1997) suggests that when people without disabilities merely look at and see people with physical disabilities, they become anxious and feel vulnerable, as one typically does not focus on one's own body. Seeing how people with learning disabilities navigate academic spaces differently may cause some instructors without disabilities to feel uncertain, and vulnerable, and creates a situation wherein they can no longer take their own bodies "for granted" (p. 6). If people without disabilities are already uncomfortable and unsure, it makes sense that they will not want to continue the interaction. It is much more likely that the director may have wanted the discomfort to end and did whatever she could to make it so at a significant cost to herself, to Tyler, and to the students in her program.

Alternatively, some faculty in higher education tend to believe that they are better positioned to determine who should and should not receive disability accommodations (or college educations) than the committees who grant admission based on criteria that does not require disclosure of disability. Cultures of disbelief (Fassett & Morella, 2008) fester when it is assumed that all college students share a minimum level of ability (and communication) and lead to the inaccurate beliefs about students who request disability-related accommodations, especially graduate students. Those inaccuracies lead to questions of belonging and suggest students who require disability accommodations are either incapable of learning without accommodation or, worse yet, depict them as dishonest (Fassett & Morella, 2008; Fraser, 2007).

Tyler's story above is not just an instance of marginalization; it reveals broader patterns of disadvantage masquerading as individual agency. In a nuanced way, by positioning herself as being unwilling to speak to the advocate Tyler brought to the meeting, the director attempted to silence Tyler's voice in the meeting. By claiming that she was legally unable to speak with me, even though Tyler provided her with a notarized legal document (Power of Attorney) selecting me to act on his behalf in the meeting and even after waiving his rights under the Family Educational Rights and Privacy Act (FERPA), the director sent a message to Tyler (and to others present) that his communication was not valid or to be trusted. It had the effect of negating the supposed agency he was supposed to have in the situation and erased his agentic voice. As Tyler came in to the program, he thought he had agency to make choices from a full menu of options, but instead found structures within the institution (gatekeepers) effectively blocking access.

In these ways, the student is at a disadvantage because they lack the agency of voice and independence they thought that they possessed or had been encouraged to believe they possessed. The student without an ASD (or other disability) registers for classes without disclosing any personal information, takes the class, and when, or if, they struggle, they may suffer the natural consequences of failure or poor grades. Students with disabilities are required to disclose their disability status to (maybe) get accommodations but the effect of those disclosures may cause faculty to view them suspiciously, as in the case presented here. Moreover, the use of unfamiliar technology may also work against the student.

Beyond technology's ability to convert text into readable material for some users, technology provides an exceptional opportunity for people who do not communicate verbally to communicate expressively with those of us who were previously unable to, for lack of a better phrase, hear them. Augmentative and alternative communication (AAC) is a broad term which describes a variety of methods which supplement or replace speaking and/or writing for people whose disability impacts their ability to produce or comprehend oral or written communication. AAC devices can be high tech (voice-output devices), low tech (letter boards), and anywhere in between. They are selected and personalized to meet the individual need of the user. For example, for thirteen years of her life, Sue Rubin (2014) could not communicate that she was comprehending receptive communication because she could not express herself orally or in writing. Ultimately, digital keyboarding and facilitated communication were technological tools that allowed Rubin (2014) to communicate with people who, thinking her autism was too profound, had never expected her to be able to communicate with them.

Facilitated communication is controversial as some people "doubt" (Biklen, 1990, p. 297) this method of communication that recognizes the inherent movement and sensory differences associated with autism (Ayres, 1965; Phagava et al., 2008; Segawa, 2010; Teitelbaum, Teitelbaum, Nye, Fryman, & Maurer, 1998; Wolpert, 2006) and provides the individual with the necessary physical supports that they need to be able to interact, learn, and in the end, communicate. Because most people with severe autism are not presumed to be intellectually competent, there is disbelief that the person can communicate at all. People who do not presume competence believe that the facilitator is guiding the person's hands or typing for them and, thus, question the authenticity of the method and the communication.

Technology allowed Rubin to transcend the physical limitations of her voice. Rubin spent years marginalized by those who were unable to dialogue with her before digital technology allowed her to share her thoughts with the world. Rubin (2014) reports that even before she had the technology which allowed her to share her thoughts, she always had the conscious ability to put together her thoughts and intentions. However, most people who met Rubin would not have known that Rubin was thinking critically but was without a way to express the thoughts. Additionally, Rubin is limited by the multiple inabilities of people without disability to envision communication in another way than the one that seems natural to them (ableism). While Rubin was unable to communicate expressively before technology, people without disabilities were unable to communicate with her receptively—they clearly couldn't get to her thoughts and intentions on their own, and they made assumptions about her abilities based on their views and experiences in the world.

Like Rubin, Tyler is slow in oral and written communication. However, had the Director been open to his use of technology in class, she (and his peers) may have had an opportunity to be enriched. Hearing from neurodivergent people brings richness to society, providing access to opportunities to learn from *and collaborate with* people to form a more inclusive community. Because folks like Rubin and Tyler communicate differently, they see the world differently; their versions of reality are shaped by their experiences as outsiders in an insider's world (Brenneise, 2018; Smart, 2009). Because they experience the world differently, they have unique insights to provide that able-bodied people cannot. This alone is worth our time to change the way we think about accessibility and our responsibility to change our pedagogies to those that are more inclusive.

As instructors who may not have much exposure to interacting with and/ or teaching students with disabilities, some of the accommodations that we are asked to make can feel downright frightening. Students who have those accommodations are an excellent resource to tap. The technical assistance manual that accompanies the Americans with Disabilities Act Amendments Act of 2008 directs public entities to give "primary consideration" (United States Department of Justice, 1996, II-7.1100) to the choice of communication accommodation expressed by the individual making the request. The United Department of Justice (1996) text clarifies that this means that the person's preferred communication accommodation must be honored unless the entity can "demonstrate that another equally effective means of communication is available, or that use of the means chosen would result in a fundamental alteration in the service, program, or activity or in undue financial and administrative burdens" (II-7.1100). Requiring institutions to honor the choice of the individual focuses on the individual's right to and responsibility for personal agency and allows for dialogue between instructors and students.

RECOMMENDATIONS/ACCOMMODATIONS FOR A RICH, INCLUSIVE MEDIATED CLASSROOM

The mundane commentary that surrounds accessibility and modeling it for students in their day-to-day experience in the classroom presents students without disabilities with language and behaviors that they can use when they are in positions to make decisions on behalf of others who may be less fortunate. For students with disabilities in the class, these actions destigmatize and normalize disability accommodations. In my experience when both people with and without disabilities feel supported, their uncertainty decreases, and it just might be in your classroom where students are able to see each other as human, and friendships have the opportunity to take hold. Here are five simple accommodations that would have made college more accessible for Tyler. Critical communication pedagogues can add these to their course design to be more inclusive for everyone, not just students with disabilities. They include providing accessible open and ongoing dialogue, reading materials for all, notetaking support, captioning/microphone use, and alternate solutions for classroom response.

OPEN AND ONGOING DIALOGUE

Asking students how they use technology to do what you require or asking how they see scarier accommodations such as flexible attendance or flexible assignments is a step toward the agency students are promised in higher education. When I first encountered flexible accommodations for assignments or attendance, I did not know what to do and so I asked the students how these accommodations work when they use them. In opening the lines of communication, the students and I were able to work out individual ways to integrate these accommodations. The students e-mail me when they know they cannot attend as a result of their disability. Most of the time this is before the absence. Each day in my classes, students can earn participation points, and since the flexible attendance accommodation is an excused absence, I send the student the activity and ask them to complete it or I create a simple assignment that allows them to partake and benefit from what occurred in class. When students have a need for flexibility with assignments, they also communicate the need before the due date. Some students only ask for a class period extension; others ask for a full week. As long as the accommodation request does not fundamentally alter the course learning outcomes, I can be flexible with attendance or assignments. However, when the requested flexibility interferes with critical learning objectives for the course, I might not be able to allow for flexibility. For instance, in my public speaking classes, when students are giving speeches, all students are required to attend even when they are not speaking because public speakers need an audience, audience members give speakers feedback, and there are a limited number of days available to give speeches. On those days it is not feasible to provide flexibility with attendance or with last-minute requests for flexible due dates. However, I can provide flexibility with other attendance days or other assignments, such as outlines, in those classes.

In situations where students use technology with which the instructor might be unfamiliar, for example, asking the student how it may work requires some vulnerability on behalf of the instructor but again provides the students with agency and provides them practice in the types of advocacy they will need to do throughout their lives. Asking how a quick write might look when a person uses a laptop or other AAC could be much like other situations that occur in a classroom. As an instructor, I often ask students to print a piece of writing to receive peer feedback. Inevitably, some forget to bring those materials to class. Often the solution is the substitution of a screen in lieu of the paper. Sometimes the peer who is asked to look at the screen will write their responses on paper; other times that peer types the response. It depends on the peer's preference. This is how I saw quick writes working with Tyler. He may have to speak into his device to encode his message using voice-to-text. If it was too distracting for him to speak aloud in a quiet room, he could easily step out into a hallway and speak his content. Then, he would give his device to his peer, who would read and comment as he read the peer's response to the best of his ability. Finally, he would speak a message back to the peer that could be shared real time or sent via e-mail. It may take a few minutes longer and is potentially inconvenient, but it would not derail a class to allow someone to get their thoughts on paper in a non-traditional way. I have visually impaired students in my classroom who talk to their access assistants or otherwise have someone audibly speaking to them (to describe images or content) while I speak; it is only a big deal if one makes it so.

Although the instructor may feel vulnerable when asking students how to implement their accommodations and the initial ask might feel awkward, it gets better. Inviting the student to office hours to discuss their accommodations is a first step. Next, ask how the student has used the accommodation in the past. What did that look like? How does the student propose to implement the accommodation in this class? How will the instructor be notified that the student needs to invoke the accommodation? How will the student make up participation for the time they miss? How long will assignment deadlines be extended?

I often discuss my concern that with too much assignment deadline extension, the student may become overwhelmed with accumulating future due dates, but I have not seen students run into that problem. After the student and I have discussed all of their accommodations, and I ask if there are other things I can do to support their learning, I memorialize the conversation by sending an e-mail to the student detailing our agreements. This step is invaluable because I do it immediately after we meet, and if there is ever a question regarding our agreements, I have a record of our discussion that is easy to find.

MAKE READING MATERIALS ACCESSIBLE TO EVERYONE, ALL THE TIME

Instructors can reduce the bureaucracy for students who have print access issues experience by downloading print articles (PDFs) that have optical character recognition (OCR) for accessibility turned on and posting them to their learning management system (LMS). One way to tell if the article is accessible for text-to-voice users is to electronically search the document. If one can search the text electronically, the text is ready for an optical character reader. If the text is not searchable, a full version of Adobe Acrobat can convert scanned text or downloaded text in moments after checking the proper box. Otherwise, search the Internet for free OCR software or web-based conversion sites, download it, and use it to turn on OCR accessibility.

I recognize that posting print materials with OCR recognition turned on can have some unintended effects. First, because text is now searchable, students who do not have the same print access needs will be able to search the text for key words. I have overheard my students describe how they use the search function to find answers for online reading quizzes. I know this means that some students may not be benefitting from reading what I have assigned. While this is unfortunate, I think making the reading materials accessible to any person who has access to my course materials reduces some of the runaround that students with disabilities experience in higher education. As a mother who has had to remind her son how to maneuver the disability accommodation runaround on college campuses, it is worth it to me to decrease that experience for others. Moreover, it normalizes the use of assistive technology, and when the teacher talks about it, it raises the awareness of students who have never had to think twice about their privilege to access text without technological intervention.

Second, some pedagogues are moving away from posting primary research articles on their LMS, in order to assist academic authors in tracking usage data. However, for students with print disabilities, the less time they have to wait for accessible reading materials, the more time they can spend reading. Students who have print disabilities often read every word of a reading. This can take a long time, especially if they have auditory or visual processing challenges which impede their ability to visually scan and comprehend texts. Additionally, voice-to-text is becoming an example of an "electronic curb cut" (Jacobs, 1999) since voice-to-text and text-to-voice is available to almost everybody with a computer, smartphone, and/or other electronic device.

NOTE TAKING

Proponents of Universal Design for Learning recommend instructors post their lecture notes online for students to access. Doing so would assist any student who misses class including athletes and students with mental health challenges. Additionally, the instructor's notes or slide script can assist international students in learning English and can support students with processing, comprehension, and learning challenges. Moreover, when instructors provide their lecture notes, students with any needs for effective communication benefit greatly. When students who need note takers have to rely on classmates to take notes for them, students do not get a say in what notes they receive. Their classmates take notes for themselves based on what they need to know, which might not be the same content that is needed by the student who requires the note taker. The instructor does take the risk that students who skip class will be advantaged by this practice. However, students who stand in the way of their own learning by choosing not to come are paying for the course and may still benefit from the course if they have access to these notes.

Another note-taking solution is to make it a graded consciousness-raising participation activity. This assignment has several functions, including the creation of a class record in case anyone needs to know what happened in class or wants to jog their memory. It offers each participant practice in providing accommodations for individuals who require them for effective communication in classrooms. Depending on the size of the class, the number of times each student would perform the role and the number of points would be up to the instructor. On their assigned day, the student would be responsible to memorialize the class content and discussions by taking good notes. The student would not be expected to take verbatim notes, but it is the student's responsibility to record the main points to the best of the student's ability. The student would then be expected to upload the notes to the learning management system the following day. Of course, students who require an accommodation for this activity could receive one.

Finally, a word on closed-captioning; it is not just for Deaf and Hard-of-Hearing students anymore. Almost all viewable content on Youtube is closed captioned and using it is as easy as clicking a mouse. Students with expressive and/or receptive language difficulties are not the only students who benefit from closed-captioning. It provides paired auditory and visual information, which supports processing and comprehension. Use it wherever possible; require students to use it when making presentations.

MICROPHONES AND CLOSED CAPTIONING

This semester I had the opportunity to teach 130 students in a large lecture course. The room was wide but not very deep. I thought I spoke at a good volume and that everyone could hear me. At the four-week mark, I checked in with the students to see what was working in the class and what could be improved. A number of students requested that I wear a microphone because contrary to my belief, they were having difficulty hearing. I mustered the courage to wear the microphone that sat in the drawer beside me the next time I met with them. Imagine my surprise when students in the front of the class marveled at how much better they could hear me!

Even though there were no students who received hearing-related disability accommodations in that class, many students do have hearing needs. Some students like my son Tyler have auditory processing issues that are reported by the office for students with disabilities under a generic term such as "learning disability" and the only accommodations might be extra time on tests or possibly there is a request for use of an FM system. FM systems require speakers to use a microphone and listeners to wear a headset. The amplification from the speaker's microphone goes directly to the listener with the receiving headset. In the classroom, students present with undiagnosed hearing needs. One student told me that she played in the drumline throughout high school, and while she doesn't have an official hearing loss, when I wore the microphone, she was able to hear much more of the course content. Another student admitted to not wearing hearing protection at concerts and listening to very loud music in earbuds; as a result this student struggles to hear. For students with attentional issues and distractibility, the microphone provided a cue to listen. It may feel odd to wear a microphone in small classroom settings, but I have begun to wear one in my smaller (30-student) classroom environments. I also require students who are giving presentations to the class to use the microphone, as well. Requiring students to use the microphone provides an opportunity to talk about accommodations and allows for the teacher to destigmatize disability. Those of us who assume that everyone can hear us because we have loud teacher voices neglect to address the needs of people who have hearing difficulties, and whether those difficulties rise to the level of a disability should not be the concern. Rather, we should work to meet the needs of all present in our classrooms, and the microphone is technology that can assist us in that quest. Requiring our students to do the same decreases their uncertainty about using technology and raises their awareness of real issues in human communication.

ALTERNATE SOLUTIONS FOR CLASSROOM RESPONSE

What other ways can a student respond to your learning prompt? When I think of the quick-write scenario we faced, I'm reminded of an opportunity I had to hear a colleague discuss how they used audience response software technology in a large-lecture course. My colleague told a story about a student with a visual impairment disability who was interacting successfully with the software to keep up with the content until the screens changed and required students to respond. In those moments, the entire class would hear, "Shit! Shit! Shit!" as the student scrambled to enter a response within the time allotted, and the instructor would offer the student reassurance that all would be okay. As I heard the story, the voice inside me said, "Shit! Shit! Shit!" I felt for the student who was excluded from participation because the response window was too short. I felt for that student whose disability was on display each time the response window closed too quickly. I felt anger as I wondered why this went on for a semester without a solution or workaround. I vowed to do better. I certainly could provide the student with a list of engagement questions prior to class that could be turned in later in the day. I could even leave the window for answers open longer. Engagement software can be useful for many students. As with all things that we use, we bear the burden of reflecting on how they worked for us. Is it okay if one student is excluded each time we do a quick write or each week when we use an inaccessible classroom response system? It is important to have support from others who are thinking about accommodations. I am available to be a sounding board in challenging moments. Please feel free to connect with me.

CONCLUSION

As educators concerned with social justice and access to quality education for all students, we need to think about what all our students will need after they have obtained their degrees. Thinking proactively about what students need after they have obtained their degrees allows pedagogues to develop courses with those future objectives in mind, engage and collaborate with others, advocate for policies that are equitable and maximize learning for all, and resist institutionalized creation of barriers that impede inclusive access to higher education. In this chapter, I provided concrete ways we can make our face-to-face or otherwise mediated classrooms more accessible and inclusive for all learners.

When in the academy, it becomes our responsibility to ensure that we make accommodations (per the ADAAA of 2008) for people who identify themselves as needing access to effective communication (or other accommodation), using the proper channels to do so on their campus, such as an office for student services. When we are outside of our responsibilities in the academy, we may not have to be concerned with a legal responsibility to provide effective communication for people with communication challenges. Regardless of the situation, it is my hope that practitioners concerned with teaching and studying communication are sensitive and responsive to human beings who face barriers in this regard.

Many offices that serve students with disabilities in higher education may have institutionalized what will be provided to students with disabilities, and it may appear that accommodations are standardized and limited to the same small list. In a study to identify the career development and service provision issues of students with disabilities in higher education, one participant cautioned, "When things get institutionalized, they don't meet the needs at all of someone with a disability. I just don't fit the mold" (Aune & Kroeger, 1997, p. 349). Reasonable accommodations are driven by individual need, not precedent (Americans with Disabilities Act Amendments Acts of 2008, 2011). The name of the accommodation can remain the same but mean something different for each individual student. Accommodations are not one-size-fits-all. A student with an ASD may need social supports another student with an ASD may not. Many of the recommendations I have made already will address the needs of many students with disabilities such as those experienced by people with an ASD, learning disability, or other invisible disability. My goal is that the reader will consider in which ways the recommendations here may be appropriate for the people they are thinking about regardless of their ability. No matter the specific disability, if students seek and receive specific accommodation using the procedures for disability accommodations set forth by their institutions, instructors have the responsibility to provide those accommodations in most cases, with the exception of those that create an excessive financial or administrative burden on the institution, or those that change the nature of academic requirements (ADAAA of 2008, 2011, §12182 [b][2][ii]). One should always check with the office that provides support to students with disabilities when questions of exception arise.

The ADAAA of 2008 is intended by Congress to ensure access to society for people who have disabilities, as well as to ensure the provision of accommodations needed for access. For persons who have physical disabilities, the law specifically articulates the need to overcome barriers produced by architecture and transportation. The ADAAA of 2008 (2011) describes the barriers in these two domains and articulates specific measures to be taken to ensure access in both of these arenas. It also addresses communication and highlights some barriers to communication, specifically those barriers impacting access due to deafness, hearing loss, inability to speak, or blindness. Communication deficits can also be a manifestation of other disabling conditions. For more conceptualized communication deficits resulting from sensory processing disorders, such as those seen in an ASD, the law does not list specific examples of auxiliary aids and services or accommodations to be utilized to support communication access for these individuals. Critical communication pedagogues interested in becoming more inclusive will have to develop ways to accommodate students because the law does not list what is necessary to serve them. A good place to start is to focus on the credibility of the person with the disability to have knowledge regarding the support or service that is effective for herself or himself to ensure personal effective communication, as well as requiring institutions to give "primary consideration" to the choice of the person with the disability, focusing on the individual's right to and responsibility for personal agency.

The language of the ADAAA itself creates a barrier by using the word "disabled" or "disabilities." The prefix "dis" comes from Latin and indicates negation, lack, or deprivation; the root "ability" refers to power or capacity to do or act physically, mentally, legally, morally, financially, etc. Disability, then, infers incompetence, and the acceptance of that inference remains boldly intact in the psyche of many of our citizens. While the goal of legislation is protection and access for persons with disabilities, the prescribed process of attaining needed accommodations positions persons with disabilities in a subordinate position in that they must self-disclose, verify they are disabled, and request support, all in the face of the deeply held notions of incompetence, and thus, low expectations.

These attitudes are present in today's institutions of higher education and it was surprising to see them at work when Tyler first went to college. I wish the outcome had been different for him with the director because it is possible that year would have been transformative for us all: the director, instructors, Tyler and his classmates, and me. Instead he disenrolled from that program, and we scrambled to find acceptable courses that had openings two days before the start of the semester. Today, Tyler has graduated, *cum laude*, from an institution which valued the perspectives he offered. His struggle to find employment spurs me on to work toward creating inclusion in institutions of higher education. The leaders of tomorrow are in its classrooms and can learn to be more inclusive as it is modeled for them.

REFERENCES

Americans with Disabilities Act Amendments Acts (ADAAA) of 2008, 42 U.S.C. §§12101 et seq. (2011).
Aune, B., & Kroeger, S. A. (1997). Career development of college students with disabilities: An interactional approach to defining the issues. *Journal of College Student Development, 38*(4), 344–56.
Ayres, A. J. (1965). Patterns of perceptual-motor dysfunction in children: A factor analytic study. *Perceptual and Motor Skills*, 335–68. doi:10.2466/pms.1965.20.2.335
Baron-Cohen, S., Leslie, A., & Frith, U. (1985). Does the autistic child have a "theory of mind"? *Cognition, 21*, 37-46. doi:10.1016/0010-0277(85)90022-8

Behrmann, M., & Minshew, N. (2015). Sensory processing in autism. In M. Leboyer, & P. Chaste (Eds.), *Autism spectrum disorders: Phenotypes, mechanisms, and treatments*. (Key Issues in Mental Health ed., Vol. 180). Basel, Switzerland: Karger. doi:10.1159/000363586

Biklen, D. (1990). Communication unbound: Autism and praxis. *Harvard Educational Review, 60*(3), 291–314.

Brenneise, A. D. (2018). Social experiences of young adults with an autism spectrum disorder: Toward an understanding of communication (dissertation). Southern Illinois University, Carbondale, IL: ProQuest Dissertations & Theses A & I (Order No. 10751431). Retrieved from https://search-proquest-com.proxy.lib.siu.edu/docview/2081020386?accountid=13864.

Fassett, D., & Morella, D. (2008). Remaking (the) discipline: Marking the performative accomplishment of (dis)ability. *Text and Performance Quarterly, 28*(1–2), 139–56. doi:10.1080/10462930701754390

Fraser, M. (2007). A literate dyslexic (LD). *Hastings Women's Law Journal, 18*(2), 223–228.

Garland-Thomson, R. (1997). *Extraordinary bodies: Figuring physical disibility in American culture and literature*. New York: Columbia University Press.

Jacobs, S. I. (1999). *Electronic Curb Cuts*. Retrieved from Accessibility Society: http://www.accessiblesociety.org/topics/technology/eleccurbcut.htm.

Medwetsky, L. (2006, June 13). Spoken language processing: A convergent approach to conceptualizing (central) auditory processing. *The ASHA Leader*. doi:10.1044/leader.FTR2.11082006.6

Minshew, N., & Williams, D. (2007). The new neurobiology of autism: Cortex, connectivity and neuronal organization. *Archives of Neurology, 64*(7), 945–50. doi:10.1001/archneur.64.7.945

Nichols, A. H., & Quaye, S. J. (2009) Beyond accommodation: Removing barriers to academic and social engagement for students with disabilities. In S. R. Harper & S. J. Quaye (Eds.) *Student engagement in higher education: Theoretical perspectives and practical approaches for diverse populations* (pp. 39–60). New York: Routledge.

O'Brien, C., & Shedd, J. (2001). *Getting through college: Voices of low-income and minority students in New England*. Washington, DC: Institute for Higher Education Policy.

Pensoneau-Conway, S., & Cosenza, J. (2016). Disability subjectivity in educational contexts. In A. Atay, & M. Z. Ashlock (Eds.), *The discourse of disability in communication education: Narrative-based research for social change* (pp. 57–73). New York: Peter Lang.

Phagava, H., Muratori, F., Einspieler, C., Maestro, S., Apicella, F., Guzzetta, A., . . . Cioni, G. (2008). General movements in infants with autism spectrum disorders. *Georgian Medical News*, 100–105.

Prizant, B., & Wetherby, A. M. (2005). Critical considerations in enhancing communication abilities for persons with autism spectrum disorders. In F. R. Volkmar, R. Paul, A. Klin, & D. Cohen (Eds.), *Handbook of autism and pervasive developmental disorders* (3rd ed.). Hoboken, NJ: John Wiley and Sons.

Rosenthal, R., & Jacobson, L. (2003). *Pygmalion in the classroom: Teacher expectation and pupils' intellectual development*. Norwalk, CT: Crown House Publishing Company.

Rubin, S. M. (2014). *About me*. Retrieved from Sue Rubin: http://sue-rubin.org/about-me/

Segawa, M. (2010). Walking abnormalities in children. *Brain and Nerve, 62*(11), 1211–20. doi:doi.org/10.11477/mf.1416100787

Smart, J. (2009). *Disability, society, and the individual* (Second ed.). Austin, TX: Pro-Ed: An International Publisher.

Strange, C. C., & Banning, J. H. (2001). *Educating by design: Creating campus learning environments that work*. San Francisco: Jossey-Bass Inc.

Teitelbaum, P., Teitelbaum, O., Nye, J., Fryman, J., & Maurer, R. (1998). Movement analysis in infancy may be useful for early diagnosis of autism. *Proceedings of the National Academy of Sciences in the United States of America, 95*(23), 13982–87. doi:10.1073/pnas.95.23.13982

United States Department of Justice. (1996). *The Americans with Disabilities Act: Title II technical assistance manual: Covering state and local government programs and services*. Washington, D.C.: United States Department of Justice, Civil Rights Division, Disability

Rights Section: [Supt. of Docs., U.S.G.P.O., distributor, 1996]. Retrieved from Americans with Disabilities Act: https://www.ada.gov/taman2.html.

University Writing Council, UPEI. (2011). The Quickwrite: A Brief Introduction. Retrieved August 27, 2018, from http://www.upei.ca/uwc/wac/strategies/quickwrite.html

Williams, D., & Minshew, N. (2010, April 27). How the brain thinks in autism: Implications for language intervention. *The ASHA Leader*, pp. 8–11. doi:10.1044/leader.FTR1.1505 2010.8

Wolpert, L. (2006). *Malignant sadness: The anatomy of depression.* London, UK: Faber & Faber.

Chapter Ten

Building Critical Feminist Media Literacy with *Hot Girls Wanted*

Discussing Gender, Sexuality, and Labor in the Age of Internet Pornography

Giuliana Sorce

With roughly 18 billion dollars, the porn industry is one of the largest grossing economic markets in the U.S. This number includes revenues generated through media (e.g., pay-per-view videos, online clips, magazines), merchandise (e.g., novelties, fan memorabilia, body products), and venues (e.g., exotic dance clubs). Data from the 2018 report of Covenant Eyes[1] reveals that over 30,000 users watch porn every second with 90 percent viewing free content on online streaming sites and 57 percent of teens searching for porn at least once a month. With genres ranging from BDSM to Hentai,[2] producers now cater to fetishes and niche audiences more than ever.

Arguably, digital technology has proliferated the market in many ways. Production costs are lowering, more amateur content is entering the market, and this reflects in porn consumption rates. In their study on trends of wireless behavior, Kamvar and Baluja (2007) found that one in five searches on the leading online search engine Google involve pornography. Ogasa and Gaddam (2011) further note that the most popular category of porn searches was "youth" and that porn viewers preferred realistic, amateur productions, while particularly enjoying content with female actors who looked like they could be underage. Carlo Scalisi, owner of "21st Sexury Video," explains that "[a]mateurs come across better on screen. Our customers feel that. Especially by women you can see it. They still feel strong pain" (Covenant Eyes, 2016).

The prevalence of porn in our media culture is uncontestable. As one of the most profitable genres in our contemporary media market, the porn industry produces high numbers of media texts sought out by large audiences. In the form of media texts, pornographic images distribute cultural messages about bodies, gender, sexuality, and pleasure. Since viewers receive those messages and can internalize them in various ways, it is important that critical media scholarship and pedagogical practices address this phenomenon. The proliferation of the industry and its production scale has also made porn the focus of media critics, who investigate, with different foci, the relationships between mediated messages and cultural assumptions about sexuality and intimacy.

Over the past 30 years, directors from all over the world have produced an array of documentaries that focus on the industry. Productions range from critical films on the porn industry to documentaries of ex-porn stars to postfeminist independent films that display porn as a tool for women's sexual liberations. A series of documentaries focus on the lives of people in the industry: *The Dark Side of Porn*, a U.K. documentary television series, examines the social issues that women in porn face (Channel 4, 2005), and in *Not a Love Story*, the director and a stripper set out to explore sex shops and learn more from actors involved in the porn industry (Sherr Klein, 1981). For *9 to 5 Days in Porn*, the producer interviewed over 70 persons involved in California's porn industry (Hoffmann, 2008), and in *Aroused*, the viewers can "sit down" with some of the most famous porn actresses of our time (Anderson, 2013). While these documentaries focus on the people (working) in porn, there are also several documentaries that scrutinize the industry itself.

For instance, *I'm a Pornstar* (David, 2014) details the insatiable demand for male amateur talent in gay porn, revealing the importance of "fresh faces" in this billion-dollar industry. In line with industry critiques and cultural influences, Dines and Jhally's (2014) documentary *Pornland* critically examines the patriarchal system of the porn industry, pointing to how the existing hegemonic structures mass "produce" sexual imageries that are often harmful to women. Clothier and Glenn (2003) critically investigate the case of Thomas Reedy, the man who ran the first internet pay-per-view child pornography site, and the aftermath of the porn industry is the focus of *After Porn Ends* (Wagoner, 2012).

Other documentaries aim to contextualize pornography in contemporary culture by providing insights into individual consumer experiences. In the premium network documentary *Sexy Baby: A Documentary about Sexiness and the Cyberage,* Showtime producers Bauer, Gradus, and Huckabee (2012) illustrate the effects of porn consumption and sexualized imagery by sharing the experiences of young girls and ex-porn stars alike to problematize the mediation of what "sexy bodies" are in the digital era. An earlier documentary by Ed Venner (2007) follows the lives of four British teenage boys as they struggle with porn addiction.

As these examples of documentary films illustrate, there is no shortage of film material on the subject of porn or the industry at large. However, as the porn industry adapts to digitalization, ever evolving consumer bases, and new niche markets, the problems and social issues change alongside it. While many of the aforementioned documentaries are solidly produced and make compelling arguments, there is a more recent documentary that reflects the current porn landscape through a timelier lens: *Hot Girls Wanted* (hereafter *HGW*).

HGW (2015) allows a very current view into the porn industry by focusing on the fast-growing "professional amateur" market.[3] Next to a glimpse into the changing lives of new talent, the documentary also reveals online recruitment strategies by producers. In chronicling the fast-paced nature of the industry, *HGW* reveals the quick turnover of talent, while discussing the pivotal role of social media in establishing new faces (and keeping them relevant). As such, the documentary critically taps into the extremely popular fetish of "teen porn,"[4] one of the most sought-after categories by porn consumers (Ogasa & Gaddam, 2011).

Drawing on critical communication pedagogy and critical feminist pedagogy, I hope to make visible how instructors can utilize *HGW* in a range of media and communication coursework to build critical feminist media literacy. Throughout this chapter, I argue that *HGW*'s contemporary view of the industry provides opportunity for critical discussions about (online) porn and its relationships to gender, sexuality, and labor in topic areas that engage a wide variety of our coursework. These include courses with a predisposed interpretive or critical lean—such as (critical) rhetoric and persuasion, critical/cultural studies, or gender and diversity in media—as well as courses that are not typically denoted as critical or "feminist"—such as health communication, international/intercultural communication, or (broadcast) journalism.

Accompanied by scholarly literature (I include specific suggestions below), *HGW* can aid students' understandings of porn in relationship to dominant gender representations, mediated accounts of sexuality and intimacy, as well as the changing dynamics of our digitizing mediascape around media production and labor. Educators across our discipline can harness *HGW*'s critical discussion potential to highlight contemporary social issues around the porn controversy from a variety of pedagogical angles. Thus, I argue, there are clear pedagogical merits to employing *HGW* in the classroom.

This chapter proceeds with an overview of critical feminist communication pedagogy around media literacy, followed by a summary of *HGW* and suggestions of how to apply the documentary in various media and communication classrooms. This chapter closes with a discussion of potential backlashes instructors might face (from students, colleagues, or departments) and offers a set of critical discussion questions to help course preparation for different topic areas in common media and communication coursework.

CRITICAL FEMINIST MEDIA LITERACY IN THE MEDIA AND COMMUNICATION CLASSROOM

Critical communication pedagogy evaluates pedagogical choices, teaching practices, assignment structures, and content selection in communication and media studies. As a critical strand within instructional communication scholarship, critical communication pedagogy examines power in its various manifestations—how we treat our students, how we grade work, what readings we assign, or what activities we put in our lesson plans. As such, power exists not only in classroom structures and dynamics but also in the very selection of teaching materials, readings, and course topics.

With respect to course structures, course design and course leadership, Fassett and Warren (2007) note that critical communication pedagogy privileges non-hierarchical interactions (e.g., students as active discussion leaders) that illuminate, and sometimes destabilize, traditional power structures in the classroom. In shifting these dynamics, students are encouraged to think through the course materials on their own terms, which productively places the learning responsibility on them and raises the "critical thinking" profile of the course. In addition, Cooks (2010) explains that the critical classroom not only takes into account instructor-student dynamics but also makes available pedagogical materials that engage the epistemologies of the critical communication paradigm.

Critical communication pedagogues invite a focus on course content that engages socio-cultural perspectives. For instance, course contents in critical communication classrooms could engage concepts like ideology, cultural hegemony, capitalism, identity politics, or social marginalization, to name a few. Though the selection of course concepts lends itself to coursework that centers on critical approaches—such as critical/cultural communication theory or feminist media studies—it is also possible to integrate a critical perspective into courses that focus more on skills, e.g., public speaking. Critical pedagogy has different approaches: scholars can come at it from perspectives such as feminism or postcolonialism, and historically, work in this area has been done by scholars across critical traditions, such as gender studies or postcolonial theory. In facilitating critical discussions and asking students to push their own understandings of what is "natural" or "commonplace," critical communication pedagogues empower students to become critically engaged with the course materials, which has shown to build confidence and stimulate active learning (Bean, 2011; Kellner & Share, 2005).

Feminist communication scholars have long been doing the work of critical communication pedagogy. Kellner and Share (2005) reference the contributions made to communication pedagogy by feminist scholars such as Carmen Luke and Sandra Harding with respect to pedagogical standpoints and classroom values. Organizational and philosophical convictions about teaching and pedagogy have direct implications for the level of critical engagement in the classroom; thus, critical feminist communication pedagogues commit to incorporating multicultural perspectives, highlighting diversity, and unmasking marginalizing messages.

In their foundational text on critical feminist pedagogy, Luke and Gore (1992) articulate the goals of a feminist classroom: "Teachers who care about provoking students . . . demand critical examination of what lies below the surface" (p. x). This means endorsing a "relational, practice-centered, contextualized, open-ended" pedagogy that aligns with the goals of feminist axiology (p. xi). According to Luke and Gore, this framework may also facilitate an "adventure in self-reflection" where students may gain self-awareness and reflexivity that enable them to connect and situate themselves in the discussion. Enabled by critical pedagogical engagement, students may become conscientized (in the Freirean sense) to particular sets of social issues.

More recently, Aldridge Sanford and Martin Emami (2018) conceptualize critical feminist communication pedagogy as follows: "CFCP is defined as a teaching and learning paradigm in which intersectionality is valued while participants share power, connect curriculum to lived experiences, dialogue about intercultural differences, and seek solutions and understanding through communication" (p. 201). In this definition, critical communication pedagogy and critical feminist pedagogy merge under the shared goals to deconstruct power, open up dialogue, and make course concepts relevant to students' lives—they share an epistemological and axiological investment.

In communication and media studies, the curriculum often prompts instructors to integrate media literacy assignments. Media literacy assignments are ideally suited to facilitate critical discussions of social issues and power as they offer tangible ways to illustrate a critical idea. Scholars in the field often speak of "critical media literacy" as a way to connect to the critical pedagogical philosophy charted above (see also Lewis & Jhally, 1998; Kellner & Share, 2005). Critical media literacy shares epistemological investment with feminist pedagogy, as illustrated by Kellner and Share (2005): "Critical media literacy involves cultivating skills in analysing media codes and conventions, abilities to criticize stereotypes, dominant values, and ideologies, and competencies to interpret the multiple meanings and messages generated by media texts" (p. 372).

The critical analysis of media texts—their production, messages, and audience interactions—can form an ideal assignment to employ critical communication and feminist pedagogy in order to foster critical feminist media literacy. Critical feminist media literacy then denotes skill-building to help students unpack and understand identity-based codes, stereotypes, and meanings in media. Building on intersectionality as a pillar of critical feminist communication pedagogy (Aldridge Sanford & Martin Emami, 2018), critical feminist media literacy assignments can, for example, include discussion assignments based on visual material that prompts students to think about how media represent marginalization on the basis of gender, sexuality, race, ability, class or religion.

Research in media literacy has shown that audiovisual materials, such as documentaries or video clips, can help generate class discussion because they have the potential to visualize issues, offer opportunities to engage with course topics in a more stimulating manner, and aid retention (Goldfarb, 2002; Silverblatt et al., 2014). Additionally, documentaries provide a means to connect theory with a concrete example (Foss, 1983) and illustrate how media texts can form the base for scholarly analysis (Elsaesser & Buckland, 2002). Through their ability to visualize, media stimulate students with a variety of learning styles, which aids retention and students' long-term memory (see also Schweppe & Rummer, 2014). More recently, Marcus and Stoddard (2009) argued that documentary films enable students to explore multiple perspectives of a particular issue and help teachers to introduce controversial issues into coursework.

While research compellingly shows that documentaries help generate course discussions, controversial issues—such as porn—need careful facilitation. It is advisable to prepare for backlash while guiding students into the subject matter and introduce relevant scholarly literature that makes sense for the course. Literature on gendered labor, the political economy of media, but also dominant representations of gender and sexuality in media cultures can lay the groundwork for a successful introduction of *HGW* in the classroom (I discuss this in more detail below). In order to show the didactical merits of this particular documentary in the critical media and communication classroom, the following section proceeds with a summary of *Hot Girls Wanted*.

HOT GIRLS WANTED

Directed and produced by Jill Bauer and Ronna Gradus; written, edited, and produced by Brittany Huckabee; and produced by actress Rashida Jones, *HGW* is an 84-minute documentary that premiered at the 2015 Sundance Film Festival in Utah and was soon thereafter released on Netflix. *HGW* details the lives of young "professional amateur porn" actresses as they enter, work in, and exit the industry. *HGW* follows the lives of several female newcomers as they live and work with their talent agent Riley in Miami,

Florida. We learn that the porn industry in Florida is booming due to recent lawmaking that enforces condom use in California, the long-term "porn capital of the world." *HGW* provides critical insights into the changing nature of the porn industry in the age of the internet—it highlights the quick cycles of fame and desirability created through free or subscription-based online porn, the use of social media in making talent "celebrities," and statistics on the proliferation and consumption of porn on the internet.

HGW exposes the specific tactics of agents to acquire new talent, chronicles the daily routines of young amateur actors, and, thus, engages the audience on a very personal level by following the journey of several young women so closely. In the documentary, Riley assures that he will never run out of new talent as "every day a new girl turns 18, and every day a new girl wants to do porn." In one scene, Riley posts a new advertisement on Craigslist under the "Talent" tab. His advertisement reads "Free Flight to Miami" and he assures the documentary producer that he will have at least five responses by morning. In the next frame, the producer asks the women currently living and working with Riley how they had heard of the industry. They reply in unison: "Craigslist."

Riley is correct with his prediction; we see Michelle alias "Brooklyn" come join them in Riley's home and make her debut in the industry. Riley shares his excitement with the *HGW* production team: "She is 19 with double Ds and looks like she's 12." *HGW* makes one point very clear: Teen porn is what sells best. The "professional amateur" industry is driven by "fresh faces" and Riley's ideal newcomers are always young, always petite, and always inexperienced. Riley's staging choices in his productions feed into the fetish of "illegal" sex with young girls who could be underage—the women are made to wear pigtails or nerdy glasses in (remnants) of school uniforms or are paired to perform alongside much older counterparts. Ava, one of the young actresses, is visibly distraught at having to have sex with a man and shares this in front of the camera.

The filmmakers' cinematographic choices enable *HGW* to connect with the audience on multiple levels; it continuously reveals statistics on porn consumption (provided by Debby Herbernick and Bryant Paul of the Kinsey Institute), displays the role of social media in the industry, and switches between group shots and intimate camera moments. Perhaps most touching are the instances that invite viewers to experience the young women's moments of confusion and despair. Watching the documentary is very much comparable to a rollercoaster ride—as viewers, we are able to sympathize with the girls when they miss home or have difficult conversations about their job with their loved ones, and in the next frame, we become voyeurs of their profession.

HGW leaves its viewers torn between anger, sympathy, disgust, and sadness, and successfully engages the problematic reality of young women in today's "professional amateur" market. As viewers, we follow a new amateur actress named Tressa (alias "Stella May") to visit her parents' home, where she has to justify her decision to be a porn actress to her mother and boyfriend. It is through these more intimate, private snapshots that viewers build a particularly strong parasocial relationship with "Stella May"—*HGW* displays how she struggles with her internal dilemma of understanding her family's concern and the lure of quick money and "freedom" that porn gives her.

HGW is unique in the ways in which it provides a mirror of the porn industry in the age of the internet—an economy and trade that has expanded, shifted and created new spaces for production speeds and turnarounds that simply were not possible before. The documentary also deals with the quick turnover rate of talent in porn, which has arguably accelerated through digitalization. By the time the producers leave Riley's house, and return three months later, none of the young women the documentary has followed work for him anymore. The final frame of the documentary shows Riley's house filled with a dozen new women with similar stories as Tressa, Michelle, and the others that came before them. Through this timely viewpoint and ability to connect various social, cultural, and economic issues, *HGW* makes for a potentially fruitful pedagogical application. In the following, I chart the ways in which the documentary could invite critical engagements in a range of coursework within media and communication studies.

HOT GIRLS WANTED IN THE CLASSROOM

As educators, we oftentimes struggle to excite students about the course material. Think of those weeks where the coursework primarily involves theory—student participation and retention can drop significantly, and so we have to find ways to engage students and entice them to learn. Previously, I have offered a brief synopsis on the merits of critical feminist media literacy assignments, including the didactical affordances of audiovisual material. Documentaries that highlight controversial issues—such as *HGW*—can provide a tangible way to involve students in conversations about social problems, thereby building their critical consciousness. Within media and communication studies, instructors offer coursework ranging from general education requirements to special-topics courses, and many courses have room to integrate critical feminist media literacy assignments.

My goal here is to show how *HGW* can become of pedagogical value in a variety of critical courses within the field, including (critical) rhetoric and persuasion, critical/cultural studies, or gender and diversity in media. In addition, I will show how *HGW* can open the possibility for critical feminist media literacy in coursework not traditionally denoted as "feminist" or "critical," such as health communication, international/intercultural communication, or (broadcast) journalism. Before detailing the potential applications of *HGW* in media and communication studies, I begin by charting how instructors can prepare themselves and create a lesson around the documentary.

Instructor Preparation

Before the introduction of *HGW*, instructors should give careful consideration to academic scholarship that helps contextualize the issues that are portrayed in the documentary. This will, of course, vary on the focus of the course, but there are three major areas that instructors should have working knowledge of to facilitate meaningful discussions. Perhaps it is worthwhile to mention here that instructors with formal training in women's, gender, and sexuality studies will likely have a theoretical background and/or didactical experience to navigate sensitive discussions and facilitate a classroom climate that stimulates informed critical thinking. However, instructors hoping to embrace the critical communication pedagogy paradigm can still manage to create a critical feminist space for their students with some additional course preparation.

First, I suggest instructors interested in screening *HGW* view the documentary with their course "blinders" on; i.e., to engage in an initial, private viewing of the documentary with the pedagogical frame, main topics, and learning outcomes of their particular course in mind. This first viewing experience will help generate ideas about important scholarship to pair the documentary with, develop useful discussion questions or activities, but also flag potential questions students may have. Following this initial viewing, instructors should begin with their specific lesson preparation.

I suggest instructors then screen some of the foundational texts of the pro-porn and anti-porn literature, both historic and contemporary (Rich, 1983; Garlick, 2010; Boyle, 2011). This grounding is important as students will undoubtedly ask about why the topic has generated such passionate debate, and what specific discourses the debate has produced. Reviewing some of the literature on sexuality in porn (Fox & Bale, 2018), gender representations in porn (Morse, 2015) and racialized sexualization (hooks, 1992) will also be useful to both instructors and students. While doing course preparation for *HGW*, instructors might also benefit from McNair's (2009) account of teaching the subject of pornography over a time-span of 30 years and his exploration of how students' attitudes toward porn—and its reception in the classroom—have changed.

To facilitate critical feminist media literacy as a skill-building and reflexive exercise, instructors might benefit from developing a viewing guide for students. Such guides, usually distributed right before the screening, have many didactical benefits—they help focus students' attention and flag the elements of *HGW* that are relevant to the particular course. Viewing guides can offer anything ranging from generic prompts, specific topic areas, relevant theoretical perspectives, or specific questions to think about as students view *HGW*.

Preparing Students for *HGW*

Next, instructors should select one or two relevant scholarly readings for their students that are intended to accompany the screening of *HGW*. Students will view the documentary differently if they have had some sort of formal introduction to scholarly debates that deal with the issues portrayed. It is important to set the pedagogical tone for such a screening—a theoretical preparation sets an intentional frame so that students do not misunderstand the purpose of *HGW* (for instance, thinking of the screening as "an easy movie day"). In particular, I would recommend scholarship that introduces the porn industry (Smith, 2011; Jacob & Klesse, 2014) and studies that contextualize the effects of sex work and porn on women (Griffith et al., 2013). Other potential studies that contextualize *HGW* are scholarly treatments of sex labor (Parvez, 2006), porn consumption among various demographics (Attwood, 2005), and an introduction to post-feminist debates in media studies (McRobbie, 2004).

Next to this "scholarly" introduction, instructors might facilitate a less formalized class discussion. During this discussion, instructors should make explicit how the showing of *HGW* connects to the curriculum, prescribed topic areas, or course theories. Students might not see the pedagogical value in such a screening on their own terms. Instructors should make the decision if such a conversation is needed based on their knowledge of the students and class dynamics. In addition, instructors might wish to give students an opportunity to raise concerns; for instance, students might worry about breaking religious protocol or facing parental backlash. Keeping an open line of communication and constantly debriefing before, during, and after the screening can help mediate misunderstandings and critiques.

Implementing *HGW* in the Media and Communication Classroom

Media and communication curricula across the globe have developed courses alongside the rise of the interpretive and critical tradition. These kinds of courses often embrace a critical perspective in teaching and student learning and make explicit connections to critical or feminist pedagogy. Courses that are clearly marked as critical or feminist—such as (critical) rhetoric and persuasion, critical/cultural studies, or gender and diversity in media—are ideal formats to build critical feminist media literacy via *HGW*. The following details some potential assignment considerations for the aforementioned courses:

- A course on (critical) rhetoric and persuasion could, for instance, study the persuasive structures evident in *HGW*. In particular, students could spend time deconstructing the arguments of producers as they engage in talent acquisition or the persuasive arguments the women's families, partners, and friends bring forth (to talk them "out of" a career in the porn industry). Conversely, students could then analyze the arguments the women in *HGW* bring forth as to why they chose this particular career. Thinking back to the critical-feminist impetus for choosing a documentary such as *HGW*, a debriefing discussion following the screening could unveil the workings of power as represented in *HGW*. For instance, instructors could ask students to trace patriarchal structures that push women—more so than men—into sex labor. A critical rhetorical approach, then, could emphasize and help deconstruct the overall discourses of power (of gender, of sexuality, of labor) evident in *HGW*.
- A critical/cultural course in media and communication could employ *HGW* to build critical feminist media literacy via analysis of power dynamics of media. Specifically, instructors could prompt students to look at two areas comparatively, or split the class into two groups to take an in-depth look at each: First, the representational elements in *HGW*'s media content and imagery (representations of gender, sexuality, race, class, etc.) and *HGW*'s portrayals of the media industry (political economy of media in digital times, the impact of the porn industry, advertising and online porn, etc.) could be addressed. A twofold assignment like this builds critical feminist media literacy as it points students toward thinking about the interplay of structural and content-based power dynamics in media.
- A specific assignment for *HGW* in a gender and diversity (or even a feminist) media course, for example, could be a series of small-group presentations concerned with various aspects of the changing nature of the porn industry in the age of the Internet. Group work might also have the benefit that students feel more comfortable with the subject matter. Alternatively, instructors could ask students to live tweet (or course blog) as they are watching the documentary and then display the reactions for an in-class discussion. Instructors could also ask students to write a reaction paper on their existing knowledge of the porn industry (or porn consumption rates) and then ask them to re-write their assessment upon viewing of the documentary. Moreover, a critical feminist media literacy assignment could ask students to deconstruct the commodification of (female) pleasure as evident in *HGW*, for instance alongside postfeminist discourses (self-sexualization, sex labor as a personal choice, etc.).

In addition to these three course areas, *HGW* also opens up opportunity to build critical feminist media literacy in courses that are not traditionally understood as "feminist" or "critical." Instructors can still introduce *HGW* in a variety of contexts by making the documentary relevant to the learning objectives. To illustrate, the following section offers suggestions for assignments in health communication, international/intercultural communication, and (broadcast) journalism:

- *HGW* raises many points about health-related communication, such as mediations of contraception use and safe sex, the representation of consensual intimacy, or the interplay between emotion and well-being in audiovisual media. In particular, contemporary issues such as gendered sexualization on social media or the commercialization of sex labor dovetail well with the messages of the documentary. One exercise that could work well as an individual, partner, or group assignment is using *HGW* as a critical prompt to construct a health communication campaign. Instructors could thus task students to create a communication campaign using various media to explain the underlying health issues and how these relate to larger, systemic issues, such as sociocultural attitudes.
- Another use of the documentary could be in an international media or intercultural communication course to build critical feminist media literacy in a comparative sense. Students would watch *HGW* as a U.S-centric film (one that displays U.S.-American values about gender, sexuality, labor, pleasure, etc.) and then watch a foreign-produced documentary—such as *Teens Hooked on Porn* or *The Dark Side of Porn*—that focuses on the porn industry in other locations. There is much cultural information to be derived from how porn producers in different areas develop content, who they hire to appear, what fetishes they cater to, etc. In a specific assignment, instructors could split students into two groups: One group could be asked to interrogate the cultural values presented in the documentary; a second group could be asked to study how the foci of the documentaries provide cultural insights about the problems associated with porn culture.
- In courses on (broadcast) journalism, students seek to develop skills in media writing and content development. Instructors could task students with developing a critical evaluation of *HGW* for a radio or television segment on film. Here, students could write a mock media review of the documentary and integrate a set of authors discussed in the course. Alternatively, instructors could ask students to identify published reviews of *HGW* in mainstream media and write an analysis on how journalists discuss the documentary and the issues it raises.

As these suggestions illustrate, instructors can employ HGW in a variety of media and communication courses to develop course assignments with the overall goal to build critical feminist media literacy. Paired with the applicable theoretical frames, *HGW* can become a powerful visual tool to illustrate contemporary issues of the porn industry, ranging from gender representations to labor relations in the digitizing mediascape.

CONCLUSION

Pornographic content is available with one click, one push, one swipe on most devices that can access the internet. The porn industry is a pillar of the contemporary online marketplace with consumption rates that make commercial online giants such as Amazon look like small businesses. Pornographic images distribute cultural messages about sexuality and pleasure; as much as niche productions transgress normative associations of sexuality, porn often reinscribes patriarchal gender norms and divisions of labor. Audiovisual media productions, such as documentaries, have the potential to serve as intervention texts that interrogate commonplace practices, associations, behaviors, and perceptions of cultural norms.

Throughout this chapter, I have offered the documentary *HGW* as a tool to build critical feminist media literacy in the media and communication classroom around questions of gender, sexuality and labor in digitizing mediascapes. As instructors in the field, the critical analysis of media is often already a substantial part of our teaching—from media production and political economy analyses, to media content and messages evaluations, to assessing audience engagements with mediated texts. Fostering media literacy is a critical element of these course activities. Critical feminist media literacy captures skill-building efforts to help students unpack media stereotypes and understand potentially marginalizing, normative media messages. At the same time, fostering critical feminist media literacy can also create more nuanced understandings of our digitizing media industry around hegemonic practices, stakeholders, and structures.

HGW is a documentary that captures the culture of the present-day porn industry well—its quick talent turnover, its integration of social media, its expansion in the online space, and its exploitation of young women. In arguing that *HGW* can serve as a fruitful visual pedagogical instrument, I have offered potential introductions of the documentary across coursework in our discipline. These include courses with a transparent critical aim, such as (critical) rhetoric and persuasion, critical/cultural studies, or gender and diversity in media. In these types of courses, the documentary can illustrate concepts such as ideology, hegemony, cultural norms, or gender and sexuality. I have also offered potential uses of the documentary in courses that are not typically understood as very critical or even "feminist," but which nonetheless form staples of many media and communication programs, such as health communication, international/intercultural communication, or (broadcast) journalism. In these cases, *HGW* can still be applied to discuss overarching topic areas such as commercialization and digitalization, or be used for practical assignments, such as writing or production exercises.

Given its topic area and visual impact, I have argued that *HGW* is most successful if properly planned. This includes a grounding in relevant scholarly literature, proper instructor preparation, as well as solid introduction to relevant topic areas for students. While guiding students into the subject area of online porn culture, it is advisable for educators to prepare for critical responses—these can include adverse reactions from students themselves, parents/family, colleagues, or administrators. To navigate this situation, instructors should practice utmost transparency as to the motivations for screening *HGW*, clearly announce the intended learning benefits, and offer the opportunity for relevant groups to raise concerns beforehand. It is my hope that the thorough review of coursework alongside literature recommendations can help instructors introduce *HGW* into their classrooms. Instructors should also be prepared to offer an alternate assignment for those who are unwilling to attend the screening of *HGW*. Alternate assignments can still engage some of the key critical topics yet offer different materials for student analysis to build media literacy.

HGW certainly taps into many contemporary issues associated with online media and communication—sexualized social media culture, free online pornography, the exploitation of young women's sex labor, or the androcentric mediation of sexuality, pleasure, and intimacy, just to name a few. Digital media are changing dynamics in media consumption patterns and interpersonal interactions. The prevalence of online porn culture is hard to ignore. Within media and communication studies, instructors should concern themselves with these issues. *HGW* tackles online porn culture by interrogating common online behaviors, questioning labor conditions, and calling into question the meditations of gender and sexualiy. At the same time, the documentary does so in an accessible manner that engages audiences across age groups, ethnic identities, sexualities, or gender identifications. As a timely, interactive, and engaging intervention text, *HGW* is a valuable pedagogical tool to build critical feminist media literacy in the media and communication classroom.

NOTES

1. Covenant Eyes is the largest for-profit company that offers accountability software, aimed to control and monitor Internet access. Covenant Eyes currently has a consumer base of roughly 60,000 customers who pay monthly subscription fees to have their Internet access limited. The reason many parents sign up for this service is to monitor and control their children's access to indecent materials on the Internet and specifically, to prevent them from

viewing porn. In the past, Covenant Eyes has been critiqued for its religious agenda and for shaming the desire to view sexual content.

2. Hentai films are animated and the "actors" are manga-style animated characters.

3. "Professional amateur talent" refers to actors who are not established in the industry. The genre is characterized by quick turnover as productions should not appear "staged" or choreographed.

4. "Teen porn" is a generic term for porn that features women who are over 18 but look like they could be younger. Producers of this genre seek out petite women who are oftentimes asked to dress up to look like schoolgirls. Professional porn stars have commonly undergone breast augmentations, which make them unsuitable for this particular genre. Young, shorter women with small breasts and small body frames are particularly sought after as they can stimulate the fantasy of sexual intercourse with a minor.

ACKNOWLEDGMENTS

I dedicate this piece to the late Dr. Irwin Mallin, my first pedagogy professor.

REFERENCES

Aldridge Sanford, A., & Martin Emami, J. V. (2018). Addressing cultural intersections: Critical feminist communication pedagogy. In A. Atay & S. Toyosaki (Eds.), *Critical intercultural communication pedagogy* (pp. 195–216). Lanham, MD: Lexington Books.

Anderson, D. (Director/Producer). (2013). *Aroused*. [Documentary]. Sherman Oaks, CA: Ketchup Entertainment.

Attwood, F. (2005). What do people do with porn? Qualitative research into the consumption, use, and experience of pornography and other sexually explicit media. *Sexuality & Culture, 9*(2), 65–86. doi: 10.1007/s12119-005-1008-7

Bauer, J., Gradus, R., & Huckabee, B. (Director/Producer). (2012). *Sexy baby: A documentary about sexiness & the cyber age*. [Documentary]. Los Angeles, CA: Two to Tangle Productions.

Bauer, J. & Gradus, B. (Director/Producer). (2015). *Hot girls wanted*. [Documentary]. Los Angeles, CA: Two to Tangle Productions.

Bean, J. C. (2011). *Engaging ideas: The professor's guide to integrating writing, critical thinking, and active learning in the classroom*. San Francisco, CA: John Wiley & Sons.

Boyle, K. (2011). Producing abuse: Selling the harms of pornography. *Women's Studies International Forum, 34*(6), 593–602. doi: 10.1016/j.wsif.2011.09.002

Channel 4. (Producer). (2005). *The dark side of porn*. [Television series]. London, UK: Channel 4 Productions.

Clothier, P., & Glenn, I. (Director/Producer). (2003). *Operation landslide: Crash of an internet porn king*. [Documentary]. London, UK: British Broadcasting Corporation.

Covenant Eyes. (2016). Pornography statistics. Retrieved from https://www.covenanteyes.com/pornstats/.

Cooks, L. (2010). The (critical) pedagogy of communication and the (critical) communication of pedagogy. In D. Fassett & J. Warren (Eds.), *The SAGE handbook of communication and instruction* (pp. 293–314). Thousand Oaks, CA: Sage Publications.

David, C. (Director). (2014). *I'm a pornstar*. [Documentary]. Toronto, Canada: Border2Border Entertainment.

Dines, G., & Jhally, S. (2014). *Pornland: How the porn industry has hijacked our sexuality*. Northampton, MA: Media Education Foundation.

Elsaesser, T., & Buckland, W. (2002). *Studying contemporary American film: A guide to movie analysis*. New York: Arnold.

Fassett, D. L., & Warren, J. T. (2007). *Critical communication pedagogy*. Thousand Oaks, CA: Sage.

Fassett, D. L., & Warren, J. T. (2010). Critical communication pedagogy: Reframing the field. In D. L. Fassett and J. T. Warren (Eds.), *The SAGE handbook of communication and instruction* (pp. 283–292). Thousand Oaks, CA: Sage.

Foss, K. A. (1983). Celluloid rhetoric: The use of documentary film to teach rhetorical theory. *Communication Education, 32*(1), 51–61.

Fox, N. J., & Bale, C. (2018). Bodies, pornography and the circumscription of sexuality: A new materialist study of young people's sexual practices. *Sexualities, 21*(3), 393–409. doi: 10.1177/1363460717699769

Garlick, S. (2010). Taking control of sex?: Hegemonic masculinity, technology, and internet pornography. *Men and Masculinities,12*(5), 597–614. doi: 10.1177/1097184X09341360

Goldfarb, B. (2002). *Visual pedagogy: Media cultures in and beyond the classroom*. Durham, NC: Duke University Press.

Griffith, J. D., Mitchell S., Hart, C. L., Adams, L. T., & Gu, L. L. (2013). Pornography actresses: An assessment of the damaged goods hypothesis. *Journal of Sex Research, 50*(7), 621–632. doi: 10.1080/00224499.2012.719168

Hoffman, J. (Director). (2008). *9 to 5 days in porn*. [Documentary]. Munich, Germany: F24 Film.

hooks, b. (1992). *Black looks: Race and representation*. Boston, MA: South End Press.

Jacobs, S., & Klesse, C. (2014). Gender, sexuality and political economy. *International Journal of Politics, Culture, and Society, 27*(2), 129–152. doi: 10.1007/s10767-013-9151-x

Kamvar, M., & Baluja, S. (2007). Deciphering trends in mobile search. *Computer, 40*(8), 58–62. doi: 10.1109/MC.2007.270

Kellner, D., & Share, J. (2005). Toward critical media literacy: Core concepts, debates, organizations, and policy. *Discourse: Studies in the Cultural Politics of Education, 26*(3), 369–386. doi: 10.1080/01596300500200169

Lewis, J., & Jhally, S. (1998). The struggle over media literacy. *Journal of Communication, 48*(1), 109–120. doi: 10.1111/j.1460-2466.1998.tb02741.x

Luke, C., & Gore, J. (1992). *Feminisms and critical pedagogy*. New York: Routledge.

Marcus, A. S., & Stoddard, J. D. (2009). The inconvenient truth about teaching history with documentary film: Strategies for presenting multiple perspectives and teaching controversial issues. *The Social Studies,100*(6), 279–284.

McNair, B. (2009). Teaching porn. *Sexualities, 12*(5), 558–567. doi: 10.1177/1363460709340367

McRobbie, A. (2004). Post-feminism and popular culture. *Feminist Media Studies, 4*(3), 255–264. doi: 10.1080/1468077042000309937

Morse, N. E. (2015). Pornography in sex research: The construction of sex, gender, and sexual orientation. *Porn Studies, 2*(4), 314–328. doi: 10.1080/23268743.2015.1050060

Ogas, O., & Gaddam, S. (2011). *A billion wicked thoughts: What the internet tells us about sexual relationships*. New York, NY: Plume.

Parvez, F. (2006). The labor of pleasure: How perceptions of emotional labor impact women's enjoyment of pornography. *Gender and Society,20*(5), 605–631. doi: 10.1177/0891243206291109

Rich, B. R. (1983). Anti-porn: Soft issue, hard world. *Feminist Review, 13* (spring), 56–67.

Schweppe, J., & Rummer, R. (2014). Attention, working memory, and long-term memory in multimedia learning: An integrated perspective based on process models of working memory. *Educational Psychology Review, 26*(2), 285–306. doi: 10.1007/s10648-013-9242-2

Sherr Klein, B. (Director). (1981). *Not a love story*. [Documentary]. Montreal, Canada: National Film Board of Canada.

Silverblatt, A., Miller, D. C., Smith, J., & Brown, N. (2014). *Media literacy: Keys to interpreting media messages*. San Francisco, CA: ABC-CLIO.

Smith, N. J. (2011). The international political economy of commercial sex. *Review of International Political Economy, 18*(4), 530–520. doi: 10.1080/09692291003762498

Venner, E. (Director). (2007). *Teens hooked on porn*. [Documentary]. London, UK: BBC World Productions.

Wagoner, B. (Director). (2012). *After porn ends*. [Documentary]. West Hollywood, CA: Luck Media.

Chapter Eleven

Critical Communication Pedagogy and Film

Anthony Esposito and Ronald K. Raymond

The 1962 U.S. film *To Kill a Mockingbird* won three Academy Awards, including "Best Actor" for Gregory Peck, who portrayed Atticus Finch, a principled lawyer in a fictitious southern town, who attempted unsuccessfully to defend a Black man accused of raping a White woman (Awards, n.d.). Forty-one years later, the American Film Institute proclaimed Finch as the greatest movie hero of the twentieth century (AFI, 2003). Despite these accolades, movie critic Roger Ebert of the *Chicago Sun-Times* criticized the film (based on the Pulitzer Prize–winning Harper Lee novel of the same name) for focusing on the nobility of Finch and ignoring some troubling facts: "An innocent Black man was framed for a crime that never took place, he was convicted by a White jury in the face of overwhelming evidence, and he was shot dead in problematic circumstances" (Ebert, 2001). While this example is not meant as an indictment of the movie, it suggests the importance of evaluating films from a variety of different perspectives, a tactic particularly useful in today's classrooms.

Students in higher education who have lived their whole lives in a technologically advanced world have created new challenges and opportunities for communication instructors who teach courses in Interpersonal Communication, Argumentation and Debate, Rhetorical Criticism, Introduction to Communication, and Intercultural Communication. With various modes of didactic practices available, it is our hope to employ the medium of film as one tool to teach students the importance of critical communication pedagogy, especially a focus on teaching using critical, social justice–oriented approaches to the study of pedagogy. The aim of this chapter is to show how critical communication pedagogy can be supported through movies as representations of terms, concepts, and principles discussed in our respective communication courses. Lawless (2017) emphasized the importance of this process, stating that "critical communication pedagogy presents an opportunity for teachers to encourage students to contemplate the connection between individuals' everyday communication practices and larger social constructions of reality" (p. 25). In general, showing specifically selected films in a course which highlight topics such as race, socioeconomic class, and gender can increase students' interest, attention, and perception of abstract theories (Eaton & Uskul, 2004). According to Mallinger and Rossy (2003):

> Students today have become accustomed to learning through multimedia and are easily bored or distracted by traditional pedagogies. As a generation raised on television, film, and computers, they are more receptive to these new forms of information. Film is likely to improve retention by providing strong images and emotional content. (p. 609)

This quote provides a strong rationale for this chapter. In fact, films can expose students to class, racial, gender, and cultural issues beyond their experiences, enabling them to synthesize course materials for an increased understanding of others who come from different backgrounds. Cooper (1994) emphasized this importance, stating, "If we declare that we value different perspectives, perspectives of those new to a discipline or to academia, perspectives different from ours culturally, then we must develop practices that also value those differences" (p. 532).

Films as a form of communication have both national and international appeal, with some linking to communication theories discussed in our various courses. In fact, numerous communication scholars have recognized this potential and studied how film can be incorporated into various communication courses (Ott & Burgchardt, 2013). This reference list is not exhaustive, but indicative of the consensus for the implementation of film to teach various communication theories in a diverse set of courses. Over the last few decades, communication scholars have acknowledged the centrality of media and popular culture in the lives of students (hooks, 1996). According to Giroux (2001), "Not only does film travel more as a pedagogical form compared to other popular forms (such as television and popular music), but film carries a kind of pedagogical weight the other media do not" (p. 588). We concur with Giroux. In fact, it is this type of approach we will be enacting in this chapter.

Incorporating films into different communication courses helps instructors seeking to teach about gender, race, class, and other cultural topics. Critical pedagogy is an approach to teaching and learning that seeks to analyze and transform educational contexts by applying principles of critical theory (Giroux 1997). In courses that address critical issues, combining critical pedagogy with film can enable students to grasp differing voices from other cultural communities. In our situation, we teach at a state university located in a rural area of northwestern Pennsylvania. Many of our students come from similar regions across Pennsylvania, making it relevant to address the issue of rural poverty in our courses. In order to adequately assess movies as a form of critical mediated communication pedagogy, the following areas will be highlighted. First, we will discuss the learning practices of today's college student. Next, we will review in detail the lens of critical communication pedagogy, which will be employed in this essay. Third, we will discuss how films function as pedagogy, transformed into both class discussions and paper assignments. Special emphasis will be placed on how films are incorporated into our respective courses to teach issues such as race, class, gender, and sexuality.

LEARNING PRACTICES OF TODAY'S COLLEGE STUDENT

Today's students have often been referred to as "digital natives," a generation raised on technological advances far exceeding those of their predecessors. Cell phones, the Internet, Twitter, Facebook, YouTube, Instagram, and numerous other popular cultural artifacts have likely contributed to an overall increase in media literacy upon entering higher education. Some instructors, possibly raised on more of an oral tradition, may feel less knowledgeable than their students in these areas and may be hesitant to employ new methods as teaching tools in modern academic settings. Nonetheless, it is important to use different pedagogical techniques to reach a diverse student population. It is imperative to understand the role technology plays in the lives of students. According to Sellnow (2014), "Media popular culture can be defined as the everyday objects, actions, and events we experience through a media channel (e.g. movies, TV programs, songs, comic strips, advertisements) that may influence us to believe and behave in certain ways" (p. 3). We teach a variety of courses which employ popular culture as a pedagogical tool to discuss communication theories in relationship to cultural issues and identities. The visual and narrative impact of film seems particularly effective. Masters (2005) stated:

> Films can make dry and abstract content come alive and easy to remember and encourage a different type of learning by targeting the visual areas of the brain, in contrast to most educational content that focuses on the language areas. Commercial films also have advantages compared to educational films. They have an artistic richness to them that educational films usually do not have. They are in some ways more realistic in that the story is always unfinished. (p. 113)

At our university, most of our students are White, making it perhaps even more important to present student stories that share different perspectives and derive from varying environments. These may include narratives involving students of color, students from rural and urban backgrounds, gay, lesbian and transgender students, and students with disabilities. Such stories may be highlighted in class readings, discussions, paper assignments, and the implementation of popular culture artifacts, especially film, to generate discussion and foster understanding of cultural differences. According to Fassett and Warren (2007):

> If the classroom is a microcosm of worlds, a metonym of the cultures we'll encounter throughout our lives, then it is also a site of social change. It is a meaningful environment for engaging difference, for creating community, and for envisioning the kinds of social organization we want ourselves. We don't forget the ideological lessons we learn in school, and if we presume that, in the classroom, we cannot build a more just society, then we have already abdicated our agency; we have lost ourselves to a series of false worlds by never knowing how to make them real. (p. 63)

This type of meaningful environment is what we attempt to foster in all of our courses. It is our duty to implement artifacts that adhere to the above standard practices of didactic approaches, which could highlight themes that impact our students. Specifically, themes such as depression, interpersonal relationships, suicide, racial issues, and other concerns for students can be encountered through the medium of film. Sellnow (2014) wrote, "A mediated popular culture text is a subset of the broad range of popular culture texts limited to those conveyed through media channels (e.g. movies, music, TV programs, advertisements, comic strips)" (p. 6). Since the paradigm has changed dramatically over the last two decades, as professors we need to modify our pedagogical approaches to meet the learning needs of today's students.

It is significant to implement mediated popular culture texts into both class discussions and written assignments to meet the differences in our courses. Numerous films are employed to discuss the notion of "difference" in our classrooms, especially highlighting race, gender, socioeconomic class, and sexuality. Films that highlight issues of race include *Do the Right Thing, Fruitvale Station, Crash,* and *American History X*. Films that focus on culture or intercultural communication include examples such as *Beasts of No Nation, Slumdog Millionaire, In America,* and *Good Will Hunting*. Likewise, gender or sexuality issues can be examined by studying films such as *Girls Don't Cry, Far From Heaven, Brokeback Mountain,* and *The Danish Girl*. Documentaries such as *13th* and *Making a Murderer* can be particularly effective pedagogical tools. These documentaries consider the modern prison system from both race and class perspectives. The former concerns people of color, and the latter deals with a White man in a poverty stricken rural area in Wisconsin. The films highlighted here are a few examples among many that can engage students through popular culture texts.

The films alone may not overtly inform students of all of the messages embedded in the stories, but the instructor's role in the classroom should guide the lead-in to the viewing and direct the discussion and learning process afterwards. Kahl (2013) stressed the importance of using a lecture effectively in the classroom, stating, "However, lecture can be part of critical education, as long as instructors take their students' needs and interests into account. Lecture can be a useful way to transition into dialogue and knowledge construction" (p. 100). Films are implemented as effective pedagogical tools used to link course concepts into class discussions and written papers. Students' learning styles can be supported through mediated popular culture texts, especially those incorporating films that may connect with them from a cultural framework. Critical communication pedagogy presents a template to follow in teaching students to critically evaluate core differences and seek deeper understandings, or as Freire (1998) expressed, to experience a way of living in our educative practice.

Critical Communication Pedagogy

Critical pedagogy is a method of exploring what people know, what institutions contributed to this knowledge, and how this information is transformed into and by classroom environments (Fassett & Warren, 2007; Kahl, 2011; Rudick & Golsan, 2014). In a course that highlights rhetorical and intercultural communication issues, the task of understanding diverse student stories and their diverse cultural backgrounds, must be a central criterion. According to Fassett and Warren (2007), "Critical communication pedagogy takes as a central principle a commitment to questioning taken-for-granted, sedimented ways of thinking" (p. 100). It is this type of approach that benefits educators desiring to scrutinize some of the myths and realities of our diverse student populations.

One of the founding figures of critical pedagogy was Freire. In fact, Freire's germinal book, *Pedagogy of the Oppressed* (1970), was a catalyst bringing these teaching practices to classrooms around the world. Freire (1970) considered the current status quo of teaching as a "banking concept of education" (p. 72). Banking essentially required students to simply store and recall information provided to them by the instructor. From Freire's perspective, this approach prevented people from participating meaningfully in the process of knowledge construction (and, therefore, from becoming more fully human). It could never be empowering, as the student only received the knowledge or frame of the reference from the professor/teacher, without involving other voices in the classroom. This would effectively negate open communication about issues regarding to intercultural communication. Fassett and Warren's foundational publication, *Critical Communication Pedagogy* (2007), provides a clear teaching method on how to blend critical communication pedagogy with different student experiences, including race, gender, and disability, and how to link these topics into communication courses. Warren (2009) highlighted the importance of critical communication pedagogy, stating, "As such, critical communication pedagogy is hopeful in part because it builds on a long standing tradition of making education a site where one learns not only content, but ways of being critically reflexive citizens of the world" (p. 216). This definition aligns with our idea of a classroom that welcomes diverse voices from different cultures, supported through the implementation of critical communication pedagogy.

As instructors, we attempt to open up discussion through the medium of film. These open forums invite students from various backgrounds with different ethnicities, life experiences, world views, and personal challenges, the opportunity to share their cultures with a predominately White mainstream students. If classes are considered independent cultures (or villages), achieving accord among the various individuals and groups represented is one ultimate goal. It is our hope that students model our approach, incorporating language that is not sexist, racist, homophobic, or gender specific, and engage in discussions that could open them to hearing from other students whose experiences may differ significantly from their own. By employing various pedagogical techniques, such as examinations of movies, it is our hope that a person's racial or cultural identity can be expressed or analyzed through film, facilitating deeper relationships and increased understanding.

Film as Critical Communication Pedagogy

It is always a goal in our courses to implement unique teaching tools, especially incorporating films that deal with race and class issues, and highlight the significance of our diverse student populations—specifically in this study, experiences of students that come from poverty stricken areas, in either urban or rural cultures. Films can be very effective in courses dealing with culture and communication. In fact, scholars such as Bineham (2015), Cardon (2010), Ott and Burgchardt (2013), and Quinn (2013) have studied how film is utilized as an artifact to address diversity and cultural issues. Movies introduce ideas and produce content that allows for an examination of complex cultural issues that are pertinent and applied to numerous communication courses. This type of approach lends itself to providing texts that meet varied student experiences and serve as a teaching agent for White, Latino, African American, and Asian populations. Specifically, we want all of our students to consider how film can communicate different cultural components, highlighting concepts such as race and socioeconomic class in various ways. First, since films are powerful pedagogical tools, it is important to select texts that help engage students on concepts of race and class issues. Hooks (1996) provided a clear rationale for the implementation of film, writing:

> Whether we like it or not, cinema assumes pedagogical roles in the lives of many people. It may not be the intent of the filmmaker to teach audiences anything, but that does not mean the lessons are not learned . . . and my students learned more about race, sex, and class from movies than from all of the theoretical literature I was urging them to read. (p. 2)

The texts we employ in our classes meet the above requirements, especially in how race and class impact our diverse student populations. Movies allow the students to visually observe a part of the culture under study. Ott and Burgchardt (2013) provided a clear rationale for employing books and movies, suggesting:

> The development of critical consciousness depends, then, on creating and promoting opportunities for students to see themselves as active social agents, to engage and interpret texts in relation to their lived experiences, and to struggle meaningfully to connect and understand texts within larger social contexts. (p. 16)

We agree with the authors' sentiments in the above quote. Specifically, from a critical communication pedagogy framework, students should learn to think critically about societal issues. Kahl (2015) provided a basis for this approach, stating, "CCP approaches learning from the perspective that power is always present in the classroom and society. Thus, a goal of CCP is to examine the ways in which instructors and students can examine communicative practices to uncover marginalizing messages" (p. 2). In many instances, White students and students of color might have different life experiences; however, through critical inquiry and analysis, some parts of both communities can be expressed through research, personal experiences, and mediated texts, which may pertain to the frames of reference of our student populations. Warren (2009) highlighted a critical communication pedagogy approach when he said, "Regardless of the context of action, what counts is how one engages—the effort to see the self and other as complex beings, each striving for meaning and purpose, and to engage them with a kind of care that enables the ethics of a critically compassionate pedagogy" (p. 3). It is this type of engagement that we desire for our classes, and it is for this reason that our texts, if selected properly, can be valuable artifacts used to discuss cultural issues, primarily race and class in communication courses.

As an example, the Ava DuVernay documentary *13th*, which released in October 2016, highlights the prison system in the United States, and especially focuses on the situation for many African American men. The title of the film refers to the 13th Amendment of the Constitution, which reads, "Neither slavery nor involuntary servitude, except as a punishment for crime whereof the party shall have been duly convicted, shall exist within the United States." The film addresses themes such as poverty, police brutality, and racism, among others. In addition, it provides a thorough history of mass incarceration in the United States, and highlights how racism against African American men has been a catalyst in the high rate of people of color that reside in prisons in the U.S. This documentary emphasizes some of the perilous themes that continue to plague the Black community, including the themes of Black on Black crime and, far too often, schools that are inadequately prepared to meet the educational needs of their student populations. For example, some of these inner city schools are unable to provide books for every student, and if books are supplied, the content may already be outdated. In addition, statistics indicate that significant problems exist for this population. African American men comprise 1 million out of the total 2.3 million individuals (43.5%) incarcerated in the United States, with nearly half (49%) arrested before their twenty-third birthday (Brame, Bushway, Paternoster, & Turner, 2014).

Certainly some political topics can be discussed in films, especially documentaries. For example, this movie came out during the contentious 2016 Presidential election, and some of the themes, such as race and police brutality, are overtly present throughout the film. Films such as this can act as a pedagogical tool and as a form of critical communication pedagogy, which allows for honest discussions regarding issues of oppression. These include themes such as police brutality, unemployment, crime, violence, and drug abuse, obstacles faced by many African American students residing in degraded conditions in urban areas throughout the United States. In addition, the movie depicts the reality of life for some people of color, focusing especially on African American men in relation to issues of police brutality. Viewing the film together offers African American students the opportunity to share various parts of their culture in the classroom setting, highlighting the pluralistic voices that are often times muted in college classrooms. Sfeir (2014) provides a strong rationale for inclusion of this approach:

> The process of becoming a critical teacher of popular culture is a demanding task that requires subtle observation, deep, self-reflection, cultural and societal sensitivity, heightened awareness of interactions between the behavior of the students and their environment, as well as courage to challenge the traditional political status quo imposed on schooling. The educational benefits, as outlined above, are worth the effort. (p. 23)

The above quote highlights the approach we enact in all of our courses. In fact, the film as a form lends itself to critical communication pedagogy, connecting the educational environment with societal issues ripe for discussion and analysis. Alexander and Warren (2002) supported the importance of discursive perspectives when they stated, "It asks the readers to reflect upon their own experiences within the educational context and how issues of race, culture, ethnicity, sex and gender rubbed against the always and already fragile construction of their own identities" (p. 330). Utilizing this movie as a form of critical communication pedagogy allows for honest discussions regarding themes of oppression, including historical issues such as police brutality, unemployment, crime, violence, and drug abuse, obstacles faced by many African American students growing up in challenging environments. These discussions are informative and often eye-opening for many White students whose experiences in their own cultural communities are quite dissimilar.

After viewing the movie with our students, it is important to collectively consider why segments of the population responded with such outrage, particularly in instances addressing police brutality and the historical incarceration of African American men in American prisons. A spirited yet collegial discussion is typical, with different views presented on accusations of police brutality and the relevance of the subsequent Black Lives Matter Movement. It is evident through these discussions that our African American students usually have different perceptions than White students regarding the incidents. It is also common for African American students to share their own experiences in dealing with police officers, encounters which, for the most part, are negative. Many African American students express feelings that they have been stereotyped by media portrayals, and specifically African American men who are often presented as both scary and dangerous (Glassner, 2001).

Discussing these realities allows White students to better understand how pressing the issues of police brutality and incarceration are to students of color, especially African American men. It becomes clear to students in our various communication courses that this is not simply a racial problem as some suggest, but an American blight that is becoming an exigent issue that needs to be discussed and addressed as a pandemic that affects all communities. Racism is not just a problem for people of color, and individuals from every background and ethnicity need to be aware of the perspectives and concerns of others and how they may contribute to the problem or work to negate issues. Later in this chapter, the documentary, *Making a Murder,* will explore important issues from a different racial position. However, the movie, *13th,* specifically addresses the issue of African American men being incarcerated at higher rates than other races. This is a paramount issue that should be discussed in college classrooms as students from various backgrounds are made aware of the realities facing people of color. This is evidenced by Martin, Trego, and Nakayama (2010) who stated, "As intercultural communication scholars and practitioners, however, our ultimate goal is to work to improve conversations about race and race relations. In order to facilitate more meaningful racial dialogue, we need to better understand how Americans, particularly young people, currently conceptualize race and racial categories" (p. 98).

Instructors employing this pedagogical approach can make use of unique racial narratives from different communities. Preparing our classes from this perspective allows the lived experiences, especially narratives taken from our African American students, to be shared in a mixed classroom that supports and embraces differences within and between the varied student populations. After viewing the movie and discussing its relationship to historical implications of race and culture, these thought provoking conversations in the classroom are transformed into individual insight papers in which students compare and contrast the racial and class differences of diverse cultural communities. The assignment requires students to compare their own racial and cultural differences in relation to the characters and stories in the documentary by applying terms and concepts from class and adding them to their respective papers. This type of critical approach should be part of all communication courses that seek to hear voices of diversity, especially ones that differ from White mainstream ideologies. Warren (2009) stressed the importance of critical communication pedagogy when he said:

> Regardless of the context of action, what counts is how one engages—the effort to see the self and other as complex beings, each striving for meaning and purpose, is to engage them with a kind of care that embraces the ethics of a critically compassionate communication pedagogy. (p. 215)

Various questions can be posed to the students. The instructor may ask the overall group, "Do you think that a White person can truly understand the oppression faced by African American males in both society and within American prison systems?" African American students may be asked, "Does anything presented in the movie resonate with your experiences in our culture today?" It is even appropriate to ask students for suggested texts that they feel may be relevant to further discussions and understanding. Mora (2016) expounded upon the employment of critical communication pedagogy by stating:

> A final use of readings for the course was in how they link the student's realities with the topic through their prior experience or as a result of the experiences that occur within the class. Because critical pedagogues are concerned with the margins of society, they seek out individual voices, texts, and perspectives that have been previously excluded in order to bring them into the conversation, resonate with the students, and provide examples of the many different voices struggling to be heard. (p. 87)

A movie such as *13th* may be discussed from a myriad of positions. Overall, the student reactions to the texts generally provide insightful discussions, with students empowered to discuss difficult issues in a collegial environment. By giving a forum to talk in class, the space becomes more inclusive for students to describe their experiences as people of color in the U.S. The issue of stereotyping seems to be one that most resonates with African American men. A former student, for example, said that the media tends to portray African American men as either thugs or criminals. It is not difficult to find examples in several movies that back up his observations. However, in opposition, he said he fit neither of those stereotypes, nor that of the extraordinary Black athlete. He described himself as a scholar and someone that was ineffectual in any platform of athletics. These types of extended narratives represent instances that provide White students in particular an insider's view of someone from another race. In these occurrences, our White students can gain an appreciation of a view from a culture that may differ from their own experiences.

These types of learning experiences, with the implementation of critical communication pedagogy, enable the creation of a classroom environment that is open to views often not discussed due to discomfort levels. In fact, Ott and Burgchardt (2013) argued for this approach stating:

> It urges teachers-scholars to see criticism not as an isolated act aimed at imposing a final signified on the text, but as part and parcel of pedagogical practice designed to engage the lived experiences of individuals and promote agentive citizenship in an increasingly globalized world. (p. 29)

This approach to critical communication pedagogy helps us understand the nuanced voices of our diverse classrooms, especially with an emphasis on the racial voices of our African American students.

Several documentaries also highlight rural White culture, addressing the impact of poverty as a catalyst for escalating crime and drug abuse, and how some poor White Americans are treated improperly by the U.S. justice system. White poverty and unemployment became important topics during the recent election process. According to Gurley (2015), "As a result there is an implicit belief that Whites, who have benefited from all of the advantages that come with being White, don't have a good reason to be poor. In other words, that when Whites live in poverty, it is their fault, or even their choice" (p. 2). One of the texts we incorporate is the documentary, *Making a Murderer,* released in 2015 to critical acclaim. The documentary presents the story of Steven Avery, a White man from Wisconsin, who was accused of a murder and sent unjustly to prison for 18 years. Browne (2016) provided a synopsis of the series:

> Produced and directed by Laura Ricciardi and Moria Demos—two filmmakers with backgrounds in the law and film editing, respectively, *Making a Murderer* devotes its first hour to Avery's initial arrest and trial in the Eighties. The next nine episodes follow Avery's arrest in the Halbach murder and the subsequent trial. From the crime itself to the suggestions of tampered evidence and repeated shots of bleak Wisconsin winters, *Making a Murderer* is unrelenting, intense, and sometimes infuriating. (p. 2)

The documentary spotlights the shortcomings of this rural White community, illustrating the struggles and challenges of people growing up in rural poverty. We have used it in our courses, especially those dealing with cultural issues, to facilitate discussion. Many of our students from rural Pennsylvania areas suggest they sometimes feel their voices are not heard in mainstream readings, unless labeled in a very negative way, such as rednecks or country bumpkins. They feel disconnected and viewed differently than other White students coming from city or suburban environments.

Probing questions can be explored on the concepts of power and hegemony, and specifically issues of wealth and class distinction in the United States. The documentary allows for the implementation of critical communication pedagogy and a deep discussion on poverty and White privilege in America. Some African American students revealed they had not considered rural poverty in relation to White culture before, a situation that is endemic to certain parts of the rural Pennsylvania area. According to Sfeir (2014):

> Many educators and researchers have explored the relationship between critical pedagogy and popular culture to promote learning that fosters values, social empowerment and social justice, among others, while serving the broad interests of the diverse classroom in our highly mediated-saturated society. (p. 15)

This relationship certainly generates significant and thoughtful discussions and stimulates deep considerations.

Documentaries such as *Making a Murderer* can be incorporated as valuable tool to teach about rural culture and race. One White male student in a previous course said he identified with the topic based on his personal experiences residing in a poverty-stricken and drug-infested area in northwestern Pennsylvania. He appreciated that the documentary was employed for the course, and felt it enabled his voice and culture to be included in the pedagogical experience. For some, this documentary acted as a form of instruction that told a narrative not often displayed in mainstream college classrooms. However, it must be emphasized that students have differing experiences, so wide generalizations about White rural America must be avoided. In fact, many of our rural students pointed out ways in which their personal experiences differed significantly. This was beneficial, allowing the class as a whole to become more aware of the divergent perspectives of the rural experience in Pennsylvania. These discussions provided pluralistic voices from different racial and class perceptions, allowing students the opportunity to apply class principles to the issues presented in the film. Our hope is that knowledge gained in the course will empower students to bridge gaps between race and class, and use their communication skills to mollify some of the classism embedded into mainstream society. Embracing issues of cultural diversity in the classroom allows students of different ethnic backgrounds to dialogue in an open and honest fashion and to acquire a better understanding of each other. This is a constant focus in our classes, and an emphasis of critical communication pedagogy.

CONCLUSION

In our didactic approaches, it is significant for us to celebrate the richness of each student's experiences, and both the different racial and class communities from which they come. In sum, it is important to implement film, especially documentaries, which show the uniqueness and diversity of our student populations. Mallinger and Rossy (2003) stated, "One of the strongest arguments for using film for intercultural learning is they can stimulate the natural observation process that takes place when encountering other cultures" (p. 151). In regard to this essay, the focus is on the nuanced voices of African American and White students from both urban and rural environments, and the sharing of their diverse experiences as instigated through related movies and class readings. The inclusion of mediated communication and critical communication pedagogy enhances the classroom climate and should be a primary goal for any professor, in part because it welcomes the voices of people of color and student representatives of rural White communities. We hope to make all of our students feel comfortable enough to share their unique narratives and cultural experiences. In doing so, we increase understanding of others and are more likely to view each other with respect and empathy. Sfeir (2014) supported the significance of the implementation of movies in courses by stating:

> I argue that these participants having admitted that the media helped them understand the difficulties of marginalized groups means they actually become more open for further exploration of such issues and for the reflections on their attitudes towards marginalized groups. (p. 17)

Instructors can informally and formally assess student learning both from comments during class discussions and structured student research papers. Both elements allow students an opportunity to provide critical analysis and reflection and relate course principles to the topics at hand.

While there is considerable benefit to using film as a form of critical communication pedagogy, some disadvantages in the implementation of the texts must also be acknowledged. Selecting popular cultural texts, such as film, as a form of critical pedagogy can be an arduous experience for professors in communication studies. Some professors may lack the expertise necessary for selecting texts that are both thought-provoking and germane to the culture under study or investigation (Callahan & Low, 2004). Plot summaries or quick scans are not sufficient when selecting films for pedagogical purposes. Movie texts deserve close scrutiny before selection with the instructor fully aware and knowledgeable about the characters, story details, and pertinent themes relevant for class discussion. Films that are not carefully considered before implementation could perpetuate negative attitudes of racism, sexism, and gender inequality, increase confusion, and mute the voices of students the movie is supposed to represent. Likewise, if we only show films produced from a White middle class perspective, we effectively negate voices from either students of color or White students that do not have access to mainstream institutions. From a critical pedagogy framework the professor must take risks to the traditional assumptions of just showing movies that perpetuate injustices from both racial and class inequalities. If we employ films that do not take into account students' cultural backgrounds, we fail to recognize how these factors are inherently influenced by the cultural upbringings of our students. If we do not incorporate divergent texts, especially movies, as a form of critical communication pedagogy, we would fail to open up opportunities to better understand each other. Doing so, however, can present transformative experiences for students of color and others who feel the narratives of mainstream society are often too stereotyped and narrow, and are not an accurate description of the experiences of our students of color and their cultural communities.

The inclusion of film as a critical pedagogy may offer many educational benefits for providing different, and frequently alternative, voices in class discussions. This helps students understand each other better and provides a dynamic class environment. Sfeir (2014) suggested that students receive significant benefits:

> (They) become more engaged and interested in evaluating and negotiating their own perspectives on the connection between learning, personal experiences, and social values. They become effective agents of change of their lives, the lives of people around them and society as a whole. (p. 24)

By welcoming differing cultures and student experiences through film, scholars of different races and backgrounds have the opportunity to hear narratives that are not often presented within their own cultures and academia. In addition, all educators can use popular culture texts, such as music, blogs, and comic books, to highlight different cultural issues by focusing on issues of gender, race, socioeconomic class, and sexual orientation. In this way, diversity in the classroom is valued and clearly linked with critical communication pedagogy and popular culture texts.

REFERENCES

AFI's 100 years . . . 100 heroes & villains. (2003). Retrieved from http://www.afi.com/100years/handv.aspx
Alexander, B. K., & Warren J. T. (2002). The materiality of bodies: Critical reflections on pedagogy, politics, and positionality. *Communication Quarterly, 50*(3–4), 328-343.
Awards. (n.d.). Retrieved from https://www.imdb.com/title/tt0056592/awards.
Bineham, J. L. (2015). How the *Blind Side* blinds us: Post racism and the American dream. *Southern Communication Journal, 80*(3), 230–45.
Brame, R., Bushway, S. D., Paternoster, R., & Turner, M. G. (2014). Demographic patterns of cumulative arrest prevalence by ages 18 and 23. *Crime & Delinquency, 60*(3), 471–86.
Callahan, M., & Low, B. (2004). At the crossroads of expertise: The risky business of teaching popular culture. *The English Journal, 93*(3). 52–57.
Cardon, P. W. (2010). Using films to learn about the nature of cross cultural stereotypes in intercultural business communication courses. *Business Communication Quarterly, 73*(7), 150–65.
Cooper, M. M. (1994). Dialogic learning across disciplines. *Journal of Advanced Composition, 14*(2), 531–546.
Eaton, J. J., & Uskul, A. K. (2004). Using the Simpsons to teach social psychology. *Teaching of Psychology, 31*(4), 277–78.
Ebert, R. (2001, November 11). To Kill a Mockingbird movie review (2001). Roger Ebert. Retrieved from https://www.rogerebert.com/reviews/to-kill-a-mockingbird-2001.
Fassett, D. L. & Warren, J. T. (2007). *Critical communication pedagogy*. Thousand Oaks, CA: Sage.
Freire, P. (1998). *Pedagogy of freedom: Ethics, democracy, and civic courage*. Baltimore, Maryland: Rowman & Littlefield.
Freire, P. (1970). *Pedagogy of the oppressed*. New York, NY: Continuum.
Giroux, H. A. (2001). Breaking into the movies: Pedagogy and politics of film. *JAC, 21*(3), 583–98.
Glassner, B. (2001). *The culture of fear: Why Americans are afraid of the wrong things*. New York: Basic Books.
Gurley, L. K. (2015, October 29). Why the left isn't talking about rural American poverty. *Rural America: In these times* (p. 2).
hooks, b. (1996). *Reel to real: Race, sex, and class at the movies*. New York: Routledge.
Isenberg, N. (2016). *White trash: The 400-year untold history of class in America*. New York: Viking.
Kahl, D. H. (2015). The classroom as a space of resistance: Disrupting neoliberal politics through critical communication pedagogy. *Cinema Journal: The Journal of the Society for Cinema & Media Studies, 3*(2), 1–7.
Kahl, D. H. (2013). Viewing critical communication through a cinematic lens. *Communication Teacher, 27*(2), 99–103.
Kahl, D. H. (2011). Autoethnography as pragmatic scholarship: Moving critical communication pedagogy from ideology to praxis. *International Journal of Communication, 5*, 1927–46.
Lawless, B. (2017). Making the "minority" voice heard: Critical communication pedagogy and dissent. *Communication Teacher, 32*(1), 25–29.
Mallinger, M., & Rossy, G. (2003). Film as lens for teaching culture: Balancing concepts, ambiguity, and paradox. *Journal of Management Education, 27*, 608–24.

Martin, J. N., Trego, A. B., & Nakayma, T. K. (2010). College students' racial attitudes and friendship diversity. *The Howard Journal of Communications, 21*, 97–118.
Masters, J. C., (2005). Hollywood in the classroom: Using feature films to teach. *Nurse Educator, 30*(3) 113–16.
Mora, J. (2016). Socially constructing learning space: Communication theory and pedagogy for social justice. *Review of Communication, 16*(2–3), 176–91.
Ott, B. L, & Burgchardt, C. R. (2013). On critical-rhetorical pedagogy: Dialoging with *Schindler's List*. *Western Journal of Communication, 77*(1), 14–33.
Quinn, E. (2013). Black talent and conglomerate Hollywood: Will Smith, Tyler Perry, and the continuing significance of race. *Popular Communication: The International Journal of Media and Culture, 11*(3), 196–210.
Rudick, C. K., & Golsan, K. B. (2014). Revisiting the relational communication perspective: Drawing upon relational dialectics theory to map an expanded research agenda for communication and instruction scholarship. *Western Journal of Communication, 78*(3), 255–73.
Sellnow, D. (2014). *The rhetorical power of popular culture: Considering mediated texts.* (2nd edition). Los Angeles: Sage.
Sfeir, G. (2014). Critical pedagogy through popular culture. *Education Matters, 2*(2), 15–25.
Vance, J. D. (2016). *Hillbilly elegy: A memoir of family and culture in crisis.* New York: Harper Collins.
Warren, J. (2009). Critical communication pedagogy. In S. W. Littlejohn, & K. A. Foss (Eds.), *Encyclopedia of Communication Theory* (pp. 213–16). Thousand Oaks, CA: Sage.

Index

#MeToo, 103, 108

audience, 77, 79, 82, 89, 102–103, 130, 131, 133, 133–134, 134, 135, 136, 138, 147, 152, 157, 163, 164, 167, 169, 175

The Big Bang Theory, 79, 81–83, 89–90, 91n1
Black Lives Matter, 103, 187
Burbules, Nicholas C., 19

community building, 70, 138
context, 1, 4, 5, 15, 17, 18, 26, 27, 47–48, 49, 50, 51, 52, 52–53, 55, 56–57, 57, 62, 64, 68–69, 72, 77, 78, 80, 82, 85, 86, 87, 90, 97, 98, 103, 104, 132, 136, 141, 164, 167, 171, 172, 174, 180, 185, 186, 188
critical assessment, 16, 34, 40, 41, 43, 44
critical feminist media literacy, 9, 165, 166, 167, 170, 171, 172, 173–174, 174, 175, 176
critical media analysis, 8, 80, 83, 87, 89, 90
critical media theory, 36–37, 37, 39, 44

dialogue, 1, 5, 6, 7, 7–8, 13, 14, 15, 16–17, 17–18, 18–20, 21, 22, 23–24, 25, 28, 29n3, 29n6, 41, 42–43, 43, 44, 50, 57n1, 62, 71–73, 78, 100, 114, 119–120, 121, 122, 123, 124–126, 129, 130, 131, 132, 133, 135, 136, 137–138, 138, 140, 141–142, 150, 151, 151–152, 167, 183, 187, 190
digital, 1, 2, 3, 3–4, 4, 7, 8, 14, 21, 22, 25, 28, 47–48, 49, 50, 51, 52, 54, 57n2, 61–62, 63, 65, 66, 67, 71, 73, 108, 129, 132, 133, 136, 150, 163, 164–165, 170, 173, 175, 176, 181
disability, 64, 145, 146, 147, 149, 149–150, 150, 151, 152, 154, 156, 157, 158–159, 183
dissemination, 7, 14, 18, 21, 24, 25, 28
diversity, 5, 8, 9, 23, 24, 29n7, 62, 63–65, 67, 68, 69, 70, 71, 73, 89, 96, 145, 165, 167, 170, 172, 173, 175, 184, 188, 190, 191, 192
documentary film, 165, 168
doubt, 7, 13–14, 15, 17, 19, 20, 24, 25–26, 26, 27, 28, 71, 96, 150

Ellsworth, Elizabeth, 14–20, 29n3, 132–133
ethics, 8, 91n1, 96, 97–98, 100, 185, 189

Facebook, 3, 96, 103, 108, 109, 181
Fassett, Deanna L., 1–2, 5, 5–6, 7, 14, 20, 27, 29n1, 40, 41, 50, 51, 54, 65, 78, 80, 96, 98, 99, 104, 105, 107, 115, 119, 121, 123, 124, 126, 129, 132, 136, 138, 141, 142, 146, 149, 166, 182, 183
feedback, 96, 116, 117, 130, 133–134, 135, 136–137, 138, 152

feminism, 118–119, 166–168
First Amendment, 98–101
free speech, 22, 100
Freire, Paulo, 13, 14–16, 19, 19–20, 29n1, 34, 39, 41, 42, 43–44, 45, 49, 65, 85, 86, 96, 135, 141, 167, 183

gender, 9, 17, 38, 39, 64, 67, 75, 76, 82, 83, 84, 91n2, 101, 103, 118, 122, 131, 134, 136, 139, 163, 164, 165, 166, 167, 168, 170, 171, 172, 173, 174, 175, 176, 179, 180, 182, 183, 184, 186, 192
Generation Z, 2, 65–67

Hall, Stuart, 77, 89
hegemony, 8, 33, 35, 36, 37, 39, 40, 41, 42, 43, 44, 77, 79, 80, 83, 88, 91n1, 166, 175, 190
hooks, bell, 18, 89, 171, 180, 184
How I Met Your Mother, 79, 82, 83, 84, 88, 90, 91n1
hybrid courses, 49

identity, 5, 21, 22, 23, 29n5, 38, 41, 64, 65, 67, 70, 76, 76–78, 82, 89, 91n1, 104, 132, 133, 134, 136, 141, 145, 166, 167, 184
intersectionality, 17, 37, 38–39, 40, 44–45, 167

Let's Plays, 9, 129, 134, 135, 136

marginalized groups, 4, 36, 38, 64, 121, 191
media literacy, 1, 7, 8, 9, 14, 26, 64, 85, 165, 165–166, 167, 167–168, 170, 171, 172, 173–174, 174, 175, 176, 181
millennial, 2, 65–66, 66, 67, 102

narrative, 3, 16, 69, 78, 80, 82, 86, 87, 88, 89, 135, 136, 181, 182, 188, 189, 190, 191, 192
neoliberalism, 5, 36
Netflix, 66, 168
new media, 1, 2, 3–4, 6, 7, 8, 9, 28, 62, 63, 64–65, 65, 67–68, 70–73, 73, 105

Peters, John D., 14, 24, 29n8
pornography, 9, 163, 164, 171, 176

Praxis, 2, 5, 6, 13, 41, 43–44, 44, 48, 51, 52, 57, 80, 91n1
Privilege, 5, 6, 9, 15, 17, 33, 36, 38, 40, 48, 57n2, 67, 70, 81, 82, 100, 141, 154, 166, 190
public pedagogy, 9, 129, 130, 131, 132, 134, 140
popular culture, 8, 76–77, 82–83, 84, 87, 89, 90, 180, 181, 182, 182–183, 186, 190, 192

online discussions, 9, 116, 117, 123, 124, 125–126
online learning, 40, 49, 55
online platforms, 3–4, 8, 133
online porn, 168, 173, 176. See also pornography

reflection, 13, 57, 78, 80, 90, 114, 119, 124, 140, 167, 186, 191
reflexivity, 7, 9, 41–42, 42, 43, 44, 78, 124, 129, 130, 132, 133, 134, 137, 139, 141, 142, 167

setting, 5, 9, 54, 57n2, 71, 73, 86, 129, 133, 146, 147, 156, 181, 186
sexuality, 9, 64, 76, 82, 83, 84, 102, 120, 121, 139, 164, 165, 167, 168, 171, 173, 174, 175, 176, 180, 182
social media, 1, 4, 7, 8, 26–27, 35, 66, 76, 83, 91n1, 95–99, 100, 101–102, 103, 104, 105–106, 107–108, 109n1, 131, 138, 165, 168, 174, 175, 176
special populations, 8, 33, 34, 35, 36, 37, 38, 39, 41, 42, 44, 44–45
stereotypes, 9, 77, 78, 83, 89, 113–114, 115, 117, 118, 119–120, 121, 122, 123, 124, 167, 175, 187, 189, 192

TAMS, 117
teaching, 2, 3, 4, 5, 8, 9, 13, 14–15, 16, 18, 23, 28, 33, 47, 48, 49, 50, 53–54, 55, 57, 61, 63, 69, 72, 76, 77, 78, 85, 86, 90, 91n1, 97, 103, 105–106, 108, 109n1, 115, 117, 125–126, 126, 129–130, 131, 132, 133, 134, 140, 141–142, 151, 157, 166, 167, 171, 172, 175, 179, 180, 181, 183, 184

technology, 4, 6, 8, 34, 36, 38, 42, 44, 52, 57n2, 62, 65, 73, 95, 105, 106, 107, 108, 109n1, 125–126, 126, 146, 149–150, 150–151, 152, 154, 156, 157, 163, 181

Twitter, 21, 26, 29n9, 35, 101, 102, 103, 106, 108, 139, 181

vlogs, 71, 138

The Walking Dead, 79, 87, 88, 90, 91n1

Warren, John T., 1–2, 5, 5–6, 7, 14, 20, 27, 29n1, 40, 41, 50, 51, 54, 65, 78, 80, 96, 98, 99, 104, 105, 107, 115, 119, 123, 124, 129, 132, 136, 138, 141–142, 166, 182, 183, 185, 186, 188

Yammer, 103

YouTube, 3, 4, 21, 35, 130, 135, 155, 181

About the Editors

Ahmet Atay (Ph.D. Southern Illinois University, Carbondale) is Associate Professor of Communication at the College of Wooster. His research revolves around cultural studies, media studies, and critical intercultural communication. In particular, he focuses on diasporic experiences and cultural identity formations of diasporic individuals; political and social complexities of city life, such as immigrant and queer experiences; the usage of new media technologies in different settings; and the notion of home. He is the author of *Globalization's Impact on Identity Formation: Queer Diasporic Males in Cyberspace* (2015) and the co-editor of 9 books. His scholarship has appeared in number of journals and edited books.

Deanna L. Fassett (Ph.D., Southern Illinois University, Carbondale) is Director of the Center for Faculty Development at San José State University. She was most recently Professor of Communication Pedagogy and coordinator of her department's graduate teaching associate program. She is the author (along with the late John T. Warren of Southern Illinois University) of *Critical Communication Pedagogy, Communication: A Critical/Cultural Introduction*, and *Coordinating the Communication Course: A Guidebook*. Her scholarship seeks to create spaces for educators to explore and engage in communication and/in instruction as inclusive, intentional and attentive to power, privilege and justice.

About the Contributors

Allison D. Brenneise (Ph.D. Southern Illinois University, Carbondale) is Lecturer of Communication at the University of Minnesota. She researches communication and disability from the perspectives of critical communication pedagogy, intercultural communication, and rhetorical study. Specifically, she focuses on researching with her participants to destigmatize disability, disrupt the notion of normative communication expectations, create truly inclusive institutions of society, and to increase the disability literacies of those she encounters. She is the author of *Social Experiences of Young Adults with Autism Spectrum Disorders: Toward an Understanding of Communication* (2018) and advocates for people with disabilities, their families, and their key support people across the United States.

Marcy R. Chvasta (Ph.D., Southern Illinois University, Carbondale) is Assistant Professor of Media Studies in the Department of Communication Studies at the California State University, Stanislaus. She has published essays on the ontologies of live and mediated performance, the efficacy of anger and irony in activism, the onto-epistemological complexities of reality television, and "political rock" controversy as "the collision of bodies." She is the co-founder of *Liminalities: A Journal of Performance Studies*.

Anthony Esposito (Ph.D., Bowling Green State University) is Professor of interpersonal communication and rhetoric in the Department of Communication, Journalism and Media at Edinboro University of Pennsylvania. His publications and book chapters have highlighted his interests in community and memory, working class communication, music, and sports. In addition, his research analyzes the intersections between race, class, and critical communication pedagogy. He teaches such subjects as Public Speaking, Rhetoric and Popular Culture, Argumentation and Debate, Introduction to Communication Studies, and Interpersonal Communication.

Tabitha Hart (Ph.D., University of Washington) is Associate Professor of Communication Studies at San José State University, where she teaches courses on communication theory, ethnography, social justice, and business and professional communication. As a researcher she uses the ethnography of communication, speech codes theory, and discourse analysis to study inter/cultural communication and technology-mediated communication.

David H. Kahl, Jr. (Ph.D., North Dakota State University) is Associate Professor of Communication at Penn State Erie, The Behrend College. He conducts research in critical communication pedagogy (CCP). He is particularly interested in investigating ways in which pedagogy can be used to respond to cultural and economic hegemony inside and outside of the classroom. Kahl has published numerous articles in state, regional, national, and international communication journals. He has also authored a variety of book chapters in edited books published by reputable presses. Kahl has made over 60 presentations at a variety of academic conferences and has received awards for his work at both the regional and national levels. He currently serves on various editorial boards, including Communication Education and *Journal of Communication Pedagogy*, and is Editor-Elect of *Communication Teacher*.

Yannick Kluch (Ph.D., Bowling Green State University) is an assistant professor of sports communication and media at Rowan University, where he also serves as an affiliate faculty member for the university's Center for Sports Communication and Social Impact. His research focuses on cultural studies of sport, critical pedagogy, athlete activism, gender, diversity and inclusion in intercollegiate athletics, and identity construction in sport. He is particularly interested in examining the potential of sport to be used as a vehicle for social change. His research has been published in *Interactions: Studies in Communication & Culture*, *The Journal of Popular Culture*, *International Review of Qualitative Research*, and *Learning Landscapes*. He has presented his research at various national and international conferences, including the annual conventions of the North American Society for the Sociology of Sport, the National Communication Association, the Global Communication Association, the Central States Communication Association, and the International Association for Communication & Sport. Kluch is the founder and executive director of We Are One Team (WA1T), an award-winning initiative that uses sport to promote diversity, inclusion, and social justice on U.S. college campuses. For more information, visit his website at www.yannickkluch.com.

Lara Martin Lengel (Ph.D., Ohio University) began researching transnational communication and technology when she was a Fulbright Research Scholar and American Institute of Maghreb Studies Fellow in Tunisia (1993-1994). As Professor, School of Media and Communication, Bowling Green State University, she teaches Ph.D., M.A., and undergraduate courses in International and Intercultural Communication, Technology for Transnational Communication, Environmental Communication, Gender and Communication, Communication and Conflict, and Research Methods. She is published in, among others, *Journal of International and Intercultural Communication, Text and Performance Quarterly, Journal of Communication Inquiry, Communication Studies, International Journal of Communication, Journal of International Women's Studies, Feminist Media Studies, Global Media Journal, International and Intercultural Communication Annual, Studies in Symbolic Interaction, Convergence: Journal of Research into New Technologies,* and *Information Technology, Education and Society.* Her books include *Computer Mediated Communication*, a textbook authored with Crispin Thurlow and Alice Tomic, and edited volumes, *Culture and Technology in the New Europe*; *Intercultural Communication and Creative Practice*; and *Casting Gender: Women and Performance in Global Contexts*, with John T. Warren. She was a presenting delegate at the UN World Summit on the Information Society (UN WSIS) on gender, technology, and sustainable development in the Middle East and North Africa.

Jeremy M. Omori (MA. Arizona State University) is an independent scholar and an Instructional Specialist Senior for Arizona State University Online. His research revolves around critical intercultural communication pedagogy, public pedagogy, and critical autoethnography. Specifically, he focuses on how teachers and learners grow through dialogue, self-reflexivity, and failure in an intercultural communication context; how one performs one's identities at the intersection in a teaching/learning context; and community and alliance building among marginalized identities.

E. Michele Ramsey (Ph.D. University of Georgia) is Associate Professor of communication arts and sciences and women's studies at Penn State, Berks College. Her research interests include: feminist media and rhetorical criticism; political communication, with a focus on women's rights rhetoric; social movements; and the rhetoric of American horror film. She's the co-author of *Major Decisions: College, Career, and the Case for the Humanities* (forthcoming from the University of Pennsylvania Press). Her scholarship has appeared in *Critical Studies in Media Communication, Western Journal of Communication, Feminist Media Studies, Women's Studies in Communication, Women and Language, Journal for the Association of Com-*

munication Administration, *Journal of Media Literacy Education*, *Journal of Religion and Business Ethics*, *Communication Teacher*, *Teaching Ideas for the Basic Course*, and the *Encyclopedia of Health and Risk Management Design and Processing* (Oxford University Press).

Ronald K. Raymond (Ph.D.. Indiana University of Pennsylvania) is Associate Professor of Communication, Journalism and Media at Edinboro University of Pennsylvania. He is the faculty advisor for the campus radio station and newspaper, business manager for all of the university's campus media organizations, and also serves as the department's internship director and journalism program coordinator. His research interests include journalism and mass media, intercultural studies, management and leadership, pedagogy, and popular culture.

Giuliana Sorce (Ph.D. Penn State University) is a postdoctoral scholar in the Institute of Media Studies at the University of Tübingen, Germany. Her research centers global media, critical/cultural studies, and feminist theory. Broadly focusing on media's relationship to social change, she is particularly interested in (digital) media activism, media participation and protest, global media cultures, and issues of gender. An award-winning scholar, she has published in journals such as International Journal of Communication, *Global Media Studies* (German Edition), and *Feminist Media Studies*.

Julie L. G. Walker (M.A. in Communication Studies and M.F.A. in Forensics in Communication from Minnesota State University, Mankato) is an Assistant Professor of Communication Studies and the Assistant Director of Forensics at Southwest Minnesota State University. Julie studies identity through the frameworks of performance and materiality. She hopes her work elevates voices whose stories are otherwise unheard within structures and throughout research. Her scholarship has appeared in several journals, edited books, and conference proceedings.